CAMBRIDGE LATIN AMERICAN STUDIES

EDITORS
MALCOLM DEAS   CLIFFORD T. SMITH
JOHN STREET

28

CORONELISMO:
THE MUNICIPALITY AND REPRESENTATIVE
GOVERNMENT IN BRAZIL

THE SERIES

Coronelismo: the municipality and representative government in Brazil

VICTOR NUNES LEAL

Translated by June Henfrey
with an introduction by Alberto Venancio Filho

CAMBRIDGE UNIVERSITY PRESS
Cambridge
London   New York   Melbourne

Published by the Syndics of the Cambridge University Press
The Pitt Building, Trumpington Street, Cambridge CB2 1RP
Bentley House, 200 Euston Road, London NW1 2DB
32 East 57th Street, New York, NY 10022, USA
296 Beaconsfield Parade, Middle Park, Melbourne 3206, Australia

Coronelismo, enxada e voto. O municipio e o regime representativo no Brasil
first published by Revista Forense, Rio de Janeiro, 1949. © Victor Nunes Leal.

English translation © Cambridge University Press 1977

First published 1977

Printed in Great Britain
at the Alden Press, Oxford

Library of Congress Cataloguing in Publication Data
Leal, Victor Nunes.
Coronelismo.
(Cambridge Latin American studies; 28)
Translation of Coronelismo, enxada e voto.
Bibliography: p.
1. Municipal government – Brazil. 2. Elections – Brazil.
I. Title. II. Series.
JS2405.L413   320.9'81   76-46044
ISBN 0 521 21488 2

Contents

Editor's note

Since its first appearance in Brazil in 1949, Victor Nunes Leal's *Coronelismo, Enxada e Voto*, here entitled *Coronelismo: The municipality and representative government in Brazil*, has come to be recognised as a classic analysis of the system that emerges from 'the superimposition of structural forms evolved through the representative process on an inadequate social and economic structure'.

The text is here published without any substantial change or addition, according to the author's wish. His insights and approach remain as suggestive as when they first appeared; as Barbosa Lima Sobrinho pointed out in the preface to the second Brazilian edition, the work is not only the analysis of a structure, but the record of that structure and of the arguments about it at a certain time, a record important in itself.

Its place in the development of political analysis in Brazil is set out in Alberto Venancio Filho's introduction: 'a divide in the history of political science in Brazil . . . the first landmark of the study of politics in our universities'. The work is everywhere recognised as an essential text for the student of that country.

It is also an essential text for the student of *caciquismo* in the hispanic and mediterranean world. Dr Nunes Leal's material is the history of Brazil, the laws of Brazil and the Brazil of 1949, but his model investigation provides guidance and stimulus to all those interested in that area where conventional political science and the study of the local community by sociologist or anthropologist so often fail: the nexus between superior government and locality, the boundaries of private and public power and their interdependence, the imperfections and constraints of democracy at its not-very-fertile root, whether in Brazil or elsewhere.

M.D.

Introduction

It is a happy initiative to produce an English version of Victor Nunes Leal's book. It appeared in 1948 as a thesis presented in the competition for the chair in politics in the National Faculty of Philosophy in the University of Brazil, under the title of *The Municipality and the Representative Regime in Brazil – A Contribution to the Study of Coronelismo*, and was made known to the public under the title of *Coronelismo, Enxada e Voto*. In Brazil, the edition rapidly went out of print, and today it is a bibliographical rarity avidly sought after in the second-hand bookshops. Perhaps its publication in English will also make it easier for Brazilian students to get to know this fundamental work on the political institutions of their country, one that marks a divide in the history of political science in Brazil, being the first landmark in the study of politics in our universities.

These remarks are not lightly made, but correspond to the strictest truth. Before that date, studies in political science in Brazil were carried out by the self-taught amateur. Some had genius, as did Tavares Bastos, Alberto Torres and Oliveira Viana, but all suffered nonetheless from a lack of systematic culture in this field and from little contact in the university with foreign literature and the foreign masters. And coming as nearly all of them did from the faculties of law, their works ran parallel to those in public law, such as Pedro Lessa's *O Poder Judiciário*, or Anibal Freire's *O Poder Executivo na República Brasileira*.

The decade of the thirties saw the first university beginnings in the social sciences in Brazil, and the first signs of political science. The law faculties, timid, casual, wedded to the old Coimbra tradition, were in no condition to maintain their hegemony in these new fields, and they unconsciously let them pass, the study of politics included, to other departments of higher learning. In São Paulo, under the inspiration of Julia Mesquita Filho and of Fernando de Azevedo, Armando Sales de Oliveira created the Faculty of Philosophy, Sciences and Letters, *Filosofía, Ciencias e Letras* in the University. In the *Distrito Federal* Anisio Teixera called Afranio Peixoto to the Rectorship of the University, and he placed two great lawyers in charge, respectively, of the schools of Philosophy and Letters and of Law and Economics, the much-regretted Professor Edgardo de Castro Rebello and Professor Hermes Lima. The poverty in which we found ourselves in the social sciences was so great that the directors of these new universities had the prudence and honesty to seek a way out by contracting teachers abroad, the only serious way of laying the foundations for this novel teaching in Brazil. Professors of the calibre of Henri Hauser, Emile Brehier and Eugene Albertini came to the University of the Federal District, and they left an indelible impression, some of them even staying on after the extinction of the University and the incorporation of these original two schools into the National Faculty of Philosophy.

Professor André Gros was contracted to teach politics at the University of the Federal District, and some time afterwards it was his post that came to be occupied by the author of this monograph of 1948. Of modest origins, born in a small community in the state of Minas Gerais, Victor Nunes Leal made his university studies in the National Faculty of Law, engaged in journalism, and began his career as a lawyer in the offices of Pedro Batista Martins. He formed part of the editorial staff of the *Revista Forense*, under the aegis of Carlos Medeiros, of whom he was later to write with emotion and respect. He at length joined the group of young intellectuals with which Gustavo Campanema surrounded himself while he was Minister of Education and Health.

With the gradual return of the foreign professors to their homelands there arose occasions for competitions, the traditional *concurso* for filling a post, and it was precisely for the *concurso* for the chair of politics that Victor Nunes Leal prepared the thesis that is here published for English and American readers. It is a model monograph, which shows the most acute vision of the problems of municipal organisation in Brazil, and the fullest mastery of the historical sources. These are sifted and analysed by a privileged intelligence, which brings together with rare precision the points of view of the political scientist and the lawyer. That carelessness of the law faculties in the thirties, by which they were cut off from political science, appears to have something to do with the precarious subsequent evolution of the study of politics, and to account in part for the deficiencies of the works that were produced, until recently, even by the most important centres such as the Faculty of Philosophy at the University of São Paulo. The present study is one of the honourable exceptions.

After his brilliant contribution to the *concurso*, the author continued to write studies on politics, which were published by the Institute of Public Law and Political Science of the Getúlio Vargas Foundation, and in the *Revista Brasileira de Estudos Políticos*. But university life in Brazil, with its struggle between 'the authentic and the false, between science and mystification, between indifference and politics, between merit and faction', did not manage to hold the talents of this academic. His law business prospered and expanded. He was called to new tasks as *Procurador Geral de Justiça* of the Federal District, where he threw himself into various schemes of reorganisation. From there he went to be head of staff to President

Juscelino Kubitschek, and finally to membership of the High Court, the
Supremo Tribunal Federal.

Here too his passage left its mark, both in the rationalisation of the
Court's work, where he showed his great organising ability once again, and
in his strictly judicial activities, where he gave proof of his great legal culture, his rapid grasp of every sort of problem and ability to match social
reality with juridical norms. His achievement there puts him on a level
with the great figures of the Supreme Court, such as Amaro Cavalcanti,
Pedro Lessa, Castro Nunes, Anibal Freire and Philadelpho Azevedo. His
likeness to the last named is more than just a legal one, for the two share a
physical similarity: low of stature, the discreet smile, affability and ease of
manner, dynamism and enthusiasm. Both great organisers, and very open
to the young, their careers followed a similar course: both came from the
university, one from philosophy and the other from political science, and
both had been *Procurador Geral*.

The day after his mistaken removal from the High Court, Victor Nunes
Leal reopened his law office with all the enthusiasm of the most recently
graduated lawyer, and collected around him in Brasilia a brilliant group of
young lawyers, a real community of lawyers, linked with his other offices
in Rio and São Paulo by every modern means of communication, computer
included.

Today, ten years later, with the publication of his old thesis in English,
he does not wish to add a line to a work that is already twenty-nine years
old. In part this is the instinct of a man who does not return to the past,
but who still looks to the future.

The author's attitude has a further significance, because in truth there is
little to add to this monograph. It is still valid in its penetrating analysis of
one of the most important phenomena of Brazilian political life, which
those twenty-nine years have done little to alter. This 'simple contribution'
is the basic work for the study of municipal organisation in Brazil, and the
most substantial individual contribution made in Brazil to the field of
political science. It can only be compared to the collection of the *Revista
Brasileira de Estudos Políticos* and its monograph supplements, which owe
so much to the guidance of Orlando Magalhães Carvalho. Those other
writers 'better equipped' for these studies never appeared, and now when
there is so much presumptuous talk of a 'Brazilian political model', in
which the district vote is seen as the panacea for all national political life,
a reading of Victor Nunes Leal's book offers us a dose of modesty and
humility in our attempt to understand a little about four centuries of
Brazilian political life. The scientific treatment he gives to the singularities
of the Brazilian case enable it to be compared with other ideal types of

Latin American society, and indeed of many societies elsewhere in the Third World, and this justifies the publication of the work in English, so it can be known through the *lingua franca* of the international academic community.

England has given Brazil acute analysts of her political and social reality, writers like Armitage, Southey and, among the living, Charles Boxer. Today Brazil is returning some of that interest in the English publication of this monograph of Victor Nunes Leal.

Alberto Venancio Filho

A note on the term coronelismo

It seems best to retain the Brazilian term *coronelismo* as there is no exact or even approximate English equivalent. By the same token, the form *coronel* (pl. *coronéis*) in the political, not the military, sense will be preferred.

The eminent historian and philologist, Professor Basílio de Magalhães was kind enough to write for this work, at our request, the following note on the origin of the term *coronelismo*: 'The term *coronelismo* has, for some time, existed in our language with a specific meaning. Consequently, it is listed as a "Brazilianism" in dictionaries which appear on the other side of the Atlantic. Its relatively remote origin in this transposed sense, must unquestionably derive from the colonels, authentic or otherwise, of the now extinct National Guard. What emerged was that, apart from those who had actually held this rank, the style of address, *coronel*, began to be used by the rural population with respect to any and every political leader, any and every person of influence. Even today, in the interior of our country, the man of authority who has passed through an establishment of higher education (for these the style *doutor* (doctor), which strictly speaking should be applied only to physicians, is reserved) will inevitably, in the speech of the people, be accorded the title of *coronel*. Moreover, at the end of the eighteenth century there was the strange occurrence when one of the most distinguished figures in our political and literary history became better known by the military title which he accepted, than by his original academic qualifications, even though it was through the latter that he became judge in the district of Rio-das-Mortes: Dr Inácio José de Alvarenga Peixoto became simply: Colonel Alvarenga.

'The National Guard came into being on 18 August 1831, with Father Diogo Antônio Feijó as its spiritual leader. By law, it came under the authority of the Minister of Justice (this office was then held by the immortal *Paulista* [Diogo Antônio Feijó, a native of the state of São Paulo]. At the same time those bodies of militia and special forces (like, for example, the more recent municipal guards) which came under the authority of the Ministry of War, were abolished. In his work, *Efemérides* (p. 465, 2nd ed. of the Instituto Historico), the Baron of Rio-Branco has this to say about the National Guard: "The Brazilian National Guard which was created by the Liberals in 1831, performed valuable service in the interest of public order, and was of great assistance to the regular army in our foreign wars, 1851–2 and 1864–70." Since this last date it has become purely decorative.

For nearly a century, a body of the National Guard existed in each of our municipalities. The rank of *coronel* was generally accorded to the political boss of the community. He and other officers, once they were established in their various ranks, immediately set about obtaining the patents, paying the emoluments and dues, so that the ranks became legally effective. One advantage, in legal terms, was important: officers of the National Guard, if arrested and subjected to criminal proceedings, or if convicted, could not be detained in ordinary cells, but had to be held in custody in the so-called "open room" of the public gaol of the locality to which they belonged. Every officer possessed the uniform and the insignia of the rank to which he had been assigned. In this military dress they took part in wars and also in religious and secular ceremonies in their home towns or districts.

It was usually the wealthiest landowners or the richest members of the commercial and industrial community, who exercised, in each municipality, the high command of the National Guard, and at the same time the patriarchal — all but dictatorial — political control invested in them by the provincial government. This state of affairs existed under the Republic as well as under the monarchy until Feijó's creation was abolished. But the system was so engrained in the mentality of the rural population that even today the style of *coronel* is still accorded to those who hold in their hands the political staff of office, or the leaders of the parties which have greatest influence in the community, that is to say the despots of village conventicles. To the same group belong those whom Orlando M. Carvalho, on page 26 of his interesting study *Politica do Municipio* (*Ensaio histórico*) (Rio, 1946), describes as "traditional *coronéis*", that is, "the Duke of Carinhanha, *Coronel* Franklin de Pilão-Arcado and *Coronel* Janjão de Sento-Sé".

Rich men haughtily displaying their wealth, squandering their money in licit and illicit pleasures — such were the *coronéis*, whose behaviour provided the occasion whereby this elevated military rank assumed a special meaning, implying, in socio-psychological terms, "the person who foots the bill". And so the term *coronelismo* became part of the social and political activity in the rural municipalities.'

1. Notes on the structure and functioning of coronelismo

I. Introductory remarks

Anyone who wishes to understand the nature of political life in rural Brazil must, first of all, take into account the notorious phenomenon of *coronelismo*. It is not a simple phenomenon, involving, as it does, a number of complicated factors relating to politics at the local government level. It will be the object of this work to examine these characteristics. Given the regional peculiarities of *coronelismo* and its variations over periods of time, the present study could only have been totally satisfactory if it had been based on detailed regional analyses of a kind which we were unable to undertake. Nevertheless, the most accessible documentation, and that relating to different regions, revealed such similarities in essential aspects, that we can undertake an over-all examination with the available material.

As a preliminary observation, we must stress that we conceive of *coronelismo* as the result of the superimposition of structural forms, evolved through the representative process, on an inadequate social and economic structure. It is not, therefore, a mere survival of private power whose hypertrophy constituted the typical phenomenon of our colonial history. It is, rather, a specific manifestation of private power or, to put it another way, an adaptation whereby the residual elements of a previously extravagant private power have been able to coexist with a political regime which accepts the principle of broadly based representative government.

Because of this, *coronelismo* is above all a compromise, a trading of interests between the public authority, itself continually being strengthened, and the declining social influence of the local bosses — notably the big landowners. It is therefore not possible to understand this phenomenon without reference to our agrarian structure, the basis on which are maintained those manifestations of private power still so much in evidence in rural Brazil.

Yet, paradoxically, these remnants of private power are sustained by the public authority. This can be explained precisely in terms of a representative regime based on a wide franchise: the government cannot proscribe the rural electorate, which nevertheless still exists in a situation of absolute dependence.

1

From this fundamental compromise spring the secondary characteristics of the system of *coronelismo*, for example, authoritarianism, nepotism, rigging of ballots, the disorganisation of local public services.

With these preliminary explanations, we now go on to examine the principal features of political life in our rural municipalities.

II. Land ownership as a factor in local political leadership

The most striking aspect is that of leadership with the figure of the *coronel* occupying the most prominent position. The political bosses of our municipalities are not always real *coronéis*. The wider diffusion of higher education in Brazil created everywhere a class of doctors and lawyers whose relative distinction, combined with qualities of leadership and dedication, accustomed them to taking political charge.[1] But these same 'doctors' are either relations or kinsmen[2] or political allies of the *coronéis*.[3]

In other cases, the leader of the municipality, once he has built up, inherited or consolidated his position, becomes an absentee. He only returns to his political fief periodically, on holiday, to visit members of his family, or, more usually, for party-political reasons. Political fortune will already have raised him to the rank of state or federal deputy, to a portfolio in a ministry, a high administrative post, or even a lucrative position in the state or federal capital. Success in business or his profession can also be a reason for his absence from the municipality while retaining the political leadership of it. The lieutenants who remain on the spot themselves become the real local bosses, dependants of the higher chief who is an absentee. Absenteeism is a situation which is full of risks: when the absent boss falls out with the government, defections among his subordinates are by no means rare. At other times, it is he himself who advises this course of action when he wants to beat a tactical retreat.

Whatever or whoever this municipal leader may be, the typical example of him is the *coronel* who arbitrarily commands a considerable number of 'block votes'. [The Brazilian term is stronger and more pejorative than the English 'block votes': *votos de cabresto*, *cabresto* meaning a 'halter' — *Translator*.] Electoral strength lends him political prestige, the natural culmination of his social and economic position as a landowner. Within his own sphere of influence, the *coronel* himself unites important social institutions without replacing them. For example, he exercises considerable juridical power over his dependants, settling quarrels and disagreements, and sometimes handing down actual judgements which are respected by the interested parties. He also accumulates, officially or unofficially, numerous police functions which he often discharges simply by force of his social ascendancy, but which he can, ultimately, render more effective with the help of employees, household servants or hired assassins.[4]

This ascendancy results quite naturally from his position as a rural property-owner. The masses who eke out an existence on his land live in the most appalling state of poverty, ignorance and neglect.[5] Compared with them, the *coronel* is rich. There are, certainly, many solid and prosperous landowners, but the general rule today is the landowner who is simply 'well-off', a man who has property and businesses but who does not possess ready cash; whose livestock may be in pawn and his land mortgaged; who haggles over rates and taxes, pleading for fiscal consideration; who courts the banks and other creditors in order to be able to pursue remunerative activities. Anyone who has travelled in rural areas will have observed the lack of comfort in which most of our landowners live. They tend to eat well, or at least abundantly — drinking milk and eating eggs, chicken, pork and desserts — and their houses do offer a minimum of comfort of the sort unavailable to the agricultural worker — sometimes running water, modern bathrooms, and even electric light and radios. The worker, therefore, always sees the landowner as a rich man even when he is not rich in absolute terms but only in comparison to the worker's own unmitigated poverty.[6] Furthermore, in rural society, it is the owner of land or of livestock who has the means to secure financial backing. From this arises most of his political prestige, through 'understandings' with the banks. It is therefore to the *coronel* himself that the worker appeals in times of hardship, buying on credit in his shop in the hope of paying with the harvest, or asking for cash loans on the same terms for other necessities.

If the middle class is small in the towns of the interior, the numbers are even more restricted in the countryside where the owners of smallholdings, tenant-farmers or sharecroppers and even independent small farmers are very little above the wage-earner since many of them often work under a wage system as well. There the two terms are still generally represented by the big landowner and his dependants.[7] Completely illiterate, or almost so, without medical help, without newspapers or magazines in which he could do no more than look at the pictures, the rural worker, except in isolated cases, sees his employer in the guise of benefactor. And it is, in fact, from his employer that the worker receives the only favours which his dreary existence knows.[8] In such a situation it would be illusory to pretend that this new pariah has any awareness of his right to a better life or struggles for this right with the independence of a citizen. The logic of the situation is what we observe: on the political level he fights with the *coronel* and for the *coronel*. Hence the 'block' votes which, for the most part, are the result of the form of economic organisation which exists in the countryside.[9]

III. Concentration of rural agricultural property

For a better understanding of the political influence of the big landowners, such an important factor in the mechanism of local leadership, we must examine some aspects of the distribution of property and the composition of classes in Brazilian rural society. The census of 1940, the partial analyses of its results, elaborated by a competent system of subdivision, and the interpretations by other scholars using criteria not necessarily based on the census, provide very instructive data.

When the problem is considered in broad terms, it emerges that the concentration of property is still, at the present time, the dominant fact of rural life. The higher incidence of small and middle-sized properties in some places can be explained by several factors. In the case of São Paulo, Caio Prado Júnior set out to enumerate them in a study published more than ten years ago. The factors which he indicated (in the sequence adopted by him and which is not in order of importance) were the following: (1) Official settlement, the main purpose of which, according to a number of authoritative declarations, was to form a reserve of manpower for the landowners. (2) Private settlement, less significant than the first, but both seeking to create conditions capable of attracting immigrant groups. (3) Proximity of the large estates on whose outskirts the smaller property developed as a sort of storehouse of labour for the larger venture. (4) Disintegration of the large estate by the impoverishment of the soil, by erosion, by misfortune, by economic crisis, etc. (5) Influence of the large urban centres whose needs demand the production of types of food-crops incompatible with large-scale agriculture. In dealing with the decline of the large estates the author further noted, a little out of place perhaps, the presence of the small property in areas in which 'the management of the estate, when it came across land of inferior quality, simply bypassed it, leaving room for the establishment of small properties'.[10]

This work, as has been stated, refers especially to São Paulo. In a more recent work, dealing with the whole country, the same writer gives primary importance to immigration in the creation of the small estate, a fact which is borne out chiefly in the extreme South: Rio Grande, Santa Catarina and Paraná. In São Paulo, this factor played a far less important role because of competition from the large coffee plantations which absorbed most of the immigrant labour. The production of vegetables, fruit, poultry and eggs, flowers etc., to supply the larger urban and industrial centres was of great importance for the development of the smallholding not only in São Paulo but also, in a general way, although with variations, in other states. The decline of the large estates, chiefly because of economic crises and the predatory type of agriculture which we practise, is also a factor which is not limited to São Paulo but is generalised at least throughout the whole of the coffee-growing region: 'In its constant moving from one place to another, coffee-growing leaves behind impoverished land rendered unsuitable for large-scale cultivation; this devalued land was often taken up by the less wealthy sections of the rural population, which set themselves up as small landowners.'[11] This fact can be easily observed in Espírito Santo, the states of Rio de Janeiro and Minas Gerais, and especially in the Valley of Paraíba. In other regions other causes, the particular physical characteristics of the area, have also played a part.

Yet, in spite of the increase in the number of small estates in Brazil, the percentage of concentration of rural property has not fallen. This has already been observed by Professor Jorge Kingston in his analysis of the agricultural and zootechnical census of the state of São Paulo in 1934, where, 'rather than a more rational distribution of land holdings . . . a worsening of agrarian concentration' could be observed.[12] The reasons for this contradiction must lie in the greater fragmentation of middle-sized properties;[13] in the re-establishment of large estates[14] compensating for those which are broken up; or again, in the survival of large estates, even in conditions of decline, by the substitution of cattle-rearing,[15] for example, for cultivation. The easy accessibility of fertile, virgin lands, especially in the case of coffee, was the basic reason for the formation of large estates which could show a high level of productivity albeit under a system of extensive and predatory exploitation. This process, however, is approaching its final stages, at least in São Paulo, where the phenomenon assumed enormous proportions. The cultivation of coffee, starting in the river basin, has now spread across and despoiled a large part of the states of Rio and Minas Gerais. New factors may emerge favourable to the re-establishment of large estates (as happened in the case of cotton) or which prevent existing latifundia from disintegrating (as possibly the development of cattle-rearing, or the introduction of some large-scale operation of a typicallly capitalist type, using advanced technology). But, in the absence of these new factors, conditions are becoming more and more unfavourable to the survival of latifundia, as is evidenced by the present precarious state of the major agricultural industries of the country: sugarcane, coffee and cotton.[16]

In spite of these perspectives, the dominance of the large estate is still obvious at the present time, as was proved by the agricultural census of 1940, whose data were interpreted by Professor Costa Pinto in a recent work.[17] Classifying rural properties by area, he obtained results which we have summarised as follows:[18]

Table 1

Area	% of the total number	% of the total area
Super estates and latifundia (1000 hectares and more)	1.46	48.31
Large estates (200–1000 hectares, exclusive)	6.34	24.79
Middle-sized estates (50–200 hectares, exclusive)	17.21	15.90
Small estates (5–50 hectares, exclusive)	53.07	10.45
Micro-properties (less than 5 hectares)	21.76	0.55

Not every rural landowner has a single property only, but even if we ignore this for the moment, it is evident that the small landowners (up to 50 hectares), who represent about three-quarters of all landowners (74.83%), possess only 11% of the total area of agricultural establishments in the country. Of the remaining area (89%), only a small part (15.90%) belongs to owners in the middle category, leaving not less than 73.10% of the total area to the big landowners (200 hectares and more), who represent only 7.80% of the total number of owners. Together the big and middle-sized properties belong to just over a quarter of the landowning population, but this property covers almost nine-tenths of the total area of agricultural establishments.[19]

The situation of the small landowner is characteristically a difficult one in our country, especially when in contact with a large and expanding property. This precariousness is aggravated by the low productivity of the soil in those cases where the division of the land was caused by the decline of a large estate. There are also difficulties of running costs. All these problems weigh much more heavily on the very small holdings – those of less than 5 hectares – which in 1940 constituted 21.76% of the total number of agricultural establishments. The prosperous smallholding is an exception, save in those regions in which it is not subject to competition from the large estate and where it does not owe its very existence to the ruin of the latter.

This is the picture presented by the sector of rural landowners, a derisive minority of the population. It is a picture which reflects the immense poverty of the people who live in rural society, given that the number of those owners possessing more than 200 hectares was, according to the 1940 census, no more than 148,622, this figure being based on the assumption of one owner to each property. As owners in the middle category — following the same criterion — totalled 327,713, we have the situation where, out of a rural population of 28,353,866,[20] only 476,335 are owners of agricultural establishments capable of remunerative production. It will be clear that such figures do not represent the exact state of our agrarian economy, since there are also prosperous smallholdings and ruinous latifundia; they are, however, sufficiently indicative to give us a very clear idea of the mean existence which is the lot of millions of people who live in Brazil's rural areas.[21]

IV. Some aspects of class composition in rural society

The situation we have just described becomes clearer when we look at the principal aspects of class composition in rural society. Here again, we shall follow Professor Costa Pinto's elaboration set out in the work referred to above, although this entails modifying his results and sometimes doubling his figures.

The agricultural census of 1940 provided him with the following breakdown of the active population, grouped according to the position occupied by the various categories whose members work chiefly in cultivation, cattle-rearing and forestry:[22]

Table 2

Categories	Number (men and women)	%
Employers	252,047	2.67
Employees	3,164,203	33.47
Self-employed	3,309,701	35.01
Members of family	2,665,509	28.19
Position unknown	62,052	0.66
Total	9,453,512	100.00

Calling table 2 a 'census pyramid' of rural society, the author attempted to regroup the data following criteria that would make for a better understanding of the class position of the various groups in order to set up what he called a 'social pyramid' of Brazilian rural society. Two of the groups indicated above, 'employers' and 'employees', are self-explanatory, and the fifth — 'position unknown' — can be ignored because it comprises only 0.66% of the total number. The difficulty lies therefore in the interpretation of the two categories which the census labelled 'self-employed' and 'members of family'. The definitions adopted by the census administrators themselves provide valid interpretations.

The category of self-employed, represented by 'those who work for themselves either alone or with the help, not directly paid for, of members of their own family', includes, apart from the owners of small tracts of land, those 'tenants' or 'leaseholders' who work on a sharecropping basis. Everything leads us to believe that the sub-category of sharecroppers is much larger than that of smallholders and Costa Pinto sought to demonstrate this numerically. Admitting, as a rule, that the smallholder has only one property and considering that for 3,309,701 'self-employed' there were only, in 1940, 1,425,291 properties of less than 50 hectares, he concluded that there were 1,425,291 'self-employed'/owners, as against 1,884,410 'self-employed'/non-owners; or 43.07% for the first and 56.93% for the second.[23]

As for the other category not easily interpreted – 'members of family' – the census defines them as follows: those 'who work for the benefit of another without receiving a fixed wage, or by the job', and it goes on to explain that the 'great majority' are members of the families and helpers of the 'self-employed'.[24]

If we take all the members of this category as being associated with the group of 'self-employed'[25] we can divide it, too, in roughly the same proportions, into the two sub-categories of 'self-employed'/owners and 'self-employed'/non-owners. Thus the 2,665,509 labelled 'members of family' will add 1,517,474 of their number to the sub-category, 'self-employed'/non-owners (which then rises to a total of 3,401,884), and 1,148,035 to the 'self-employed'/owners (which then rises to a total of 2,573,326).

If, however, we do not take the 'members of family' as being exclusively tied to the category of 'self-employed',[26] this calculation becomes more faulty, but in either case it is still very significant because the greater margin of error is unfavourable to the conclusions which we must draw. We might adopt the following criteria:

In the first place, let us admit that the 'members of family' of the group 'position unknown' and of the group 'employers' collaborate with them, in agricultural activities, in the same proportion as the 'members of family' of the 'self-employed'. There we have the first margin of error, unfavourable to our conclusions, because it is clear that in the class of the 'employers' the number of members of the family who work with them is proportionately smaller.

In the second place, one observes a perceptible difference between the number of 'employers' (252,047) and the number of large and middle-sized estates (476,335). This can be explained, quite naturally, by the existence of middle-sized owners who do not employ salaried workers, or by the existence of large landowners who own more than one property, or, as is probably the case, by both reasons at the same time. Nevertheless, we shall take this difference (224,288) as representing only the middle-sized land-owner who does not employ paid labour and, for this reason, should be included in the category of the 'self-employed'. Here we have a second margin of error unfavourable to our conclusions, because we are not taking into account those cases in which more than one large property belongs to a single person. And everything indicates that such cases are more numerous than those of middle-sized owners who do not use 'employees'.

When the calculations are based on the premise we have described, the category 'members of family' has a pattern of distribution as follows: for the 'employers', 185,519; for the 'self-employed'/middle-sized owners, 164,995; for the 'self-employed'/small landowners, 1,048,345; for 'self-employed'/non-owners, 1,221,070; for those of 'unknown position', 45,580. The category of 'employees' is excluded from this distribution, since they, by definition, are counted *per caput*.

Putting together the data obtained and basing our calculations on two different premises, we arrive at the results shown in Schemes 'A' and 'B'.

The two schemes represent a doubling of the figures given by Professor Costa Pinto and based on the official census. We have subdivided the census categories of 'self-employed' and 'members of family' according to the criteria already described, and have arrived, in the hypothetical situation most unfavourable to our conclusions, at the following result: at the time of the census, 63.95% of the working population employed in agriculture, cattle-rearing and forestry, belonged to the categories of employees and sharecroppers (non-owners); if we add to these the smallholders (up to 50 hectares) whose position in many places is most precarious, the proportion rises to 90.12%.

In spite of the obvious deficiencies of the approximate criteria which we have adopted, it will not be difficult in the face of such significant data, which moreover refer to the working population only, to appreciate the dependent status of the people who work in the countryside, especially as there is so little difference between the misery of the rural wage-earner and that of the sharecropper or smallholder. There is, consequently, no obvious way of alienating the 'block' votes.

Scheme 'A'

Division of the 'members of family' only among the 'self-employed', taking as belonging to this category small landowners (up to 50 hectares) and non-owners (shareholders):

Category	No.	Members of family	%	Total	%
I Employers	252,047	–	–	252,047	2.67
II Self-employed					
a) Smallholders	1,425,291	1,148,035	43.07	2,573,326	27.22
b) Non-owners	1,884,410	1,517,474	56.93	3,401,884	35.98
III Employees	3,164,203	–	–	3,164,203	33.47
IV Of unknown position	62,052	–	–	62,052	0.66
TOTAL	6,788,003	2,665,509	100.00	9,453,512	100.00

Scheme 'B'

Division of the 'members of family' by all categories (except that of 'employed'), including among the 'self-employed', as middle-sized owners, the difference between the number of 'employers' and the number of large and middle-sized properties:

Category	No.	Members of family	%	Total	%
I Employers	252,047	185,519	6.96	437,566	4.63
II Self-employed					
a) Middle-sized owners	224,288	164,995	6.19	389,283	4.11
b) Smallholders	1,425,291	1,048,345	39.33	2,473,636	26.17
c) Non-owners	1,660,122	1,221,070	45.81	2,881,192	30.48
III Employees	3,164,203	–	–	3,164,203	33.47
IV Of unknown position	62,052	45,580	1.71	107,632	1.14
TOTAL	6,788,003	2,665,509	100.00	9,453,512	100.00

V. Electoral expenses. Local improvements

There is also the question of electoral expenses. The majority of the Brazilian electorate lives and votes in the municipalities of the interior.[27] And in the interior the rural element predominates over the urban.[28] This rural element, as we have already observed, is poverty-stricken. It is therefore the big landowners and local 'bosses' who meet the expenses of registration and of the election itself. With no money and no direct interest, the labourer could not be expected to make the least sacrifice in this cause. Documents, transport, lodging, refreshments, working days lost, and even clothes, shoes and hat for election day, all are paid for by the political mentors concerned that the rural worker should be qualified to vote and also exercise his right.[29] As the local bosses themselves are, for the most part, only 'well off' financially, subsidising these expenses presents certain interesting details, which, in the interest of clarity, will be explained later. The old procedure of the stroke-of-the-pen-system (*bico de pena*) reduced electoral expenses considerably. The new regulations, increasing the electorate[30] and requiring the actual presence of the voters, raise the costs. Because of this it is perfectly understandable that the field-hand, when he casts his vote, does so in compliance with the wishes of the man who pays all his expenses and who insists that the field-hand should perform an act in which the latter is himself completely uninterested.

This picture, however, is already being modified according to observations made in the elections of 1945 and 1947. In the heart of the rural electorate there were examples of *betrayals* of big landlords by their employees. This fact deserves to be closely studied and has not yet been so. Local observers tend to attribute it, in large measure, to radio propaganda. In towns in the interior the number of radios is already large and rural workers now have greater possibility of contact with the urban centres because of the widespread use of road transport. Radios are also being introduced on the large estates themselves, the use of batteries partially solving the problem of electricity. In addition, it must not be forgotten that, during the war, there was a marked increase in the migration of workers from the countryside to employment in the towns – in factories, public works, military bases. There was also a movement away from agriculture to other activities like rubber extraction, and mineral prospecting, more particularly for rock crystal and mica. Greater ease in arranging work in the large cities and the information on these matters which is relayed to relations and friends, activates nomadism in the rural population – already accustomed to moving from declining areas to more prosperous ones[31] – reducing the degree of its dependence in relation to the landowner. But it is still too early to draw any more positive conclusion from this phenomenon, because the elections of 1945 and 1947 present certain peculiarities which disrupted the traditional electoral alternatives of government and opposition[32] which had long been present in Brazil.

A lack of public spirit so often imputed to the local political boss is frequently belied by his zeal for the progress of his district or municipality. It is to the interest which he shows, and to his insistence, that the main improvements in the locality are due. The school, paved road, post office, telegraph office, railway, church, medical post, hospital, club, football field, shooting range, electricity, main drainage, running water — everything demands effort on his part, sometimes painful effort, not far short of heroism. It is on these successes in the field of public utilities — some of which depend solely on his own concern and his own political prestige, while others require his own personal contribution as well as the help of his friends — that the boss builds and maintains his position of leadership.[33]

In spite of this the *coronel* has not been spared in our political literature, especially in that with a party-political bias. Responsible, in large measure, for the electoral victories of the candidates drawn from the bureaucracy, he is frequently accused of having no political ideals. His restricted vision, confined to his municipality where the interests of his faction are superimposed on national ones, his disregard for the qualities or defects of candidates in state or federal elections, all this instils in the minds of defeated candidates a bitter scepticism as regards the future of democratic government in our country. And, habitually, this scepticism persists until the moment when the interested party, taking part in a new election on the government side, finds himself the beneficiary of the *coronel*'s 'block' • votes.

It is undoubtedly the case that it is the mentality of the small municipality which has tended to be the dominant one in our elections. But it is erroneous to suppose that the local boss acts on mere caprice or that his sense of public service is blunted or perverted. It is sufficient to remember that the will to govern is the distinguishing mark of this mentality in order to see that some reason more powerful than mere personal whim is involved. Speaking in general terms, and taking into account the 'highs' and 'lows' of his behaviour, the *coronel*, who functions in the small political arena of the municipality, is no better and no worse than those who operate in wider spheres. State and federal politicians — with exceptions, naturally — started out in the municipalities, where they displayed the same lack of idealism which later on, when they find themselves in opposition, they are wont to impute to the local bosses. The problem is not, therefore, related to the individual, although factors deriving from the per-

sonality of each one can present, in one case or another, more or less
marked characteristics. The problem is intricately bound up with our economic and social structure.

VI. Favours and persecution. Lack of organisation in local public services

Political leadership in the municipalities is not totally explicable in terms
of the factors already shown. We still have to consider personal favours of
every description, from arranging jobs in the public service to the smallest
acts of homage.[34] It is under this heading that paternalism occurs, as well
as its opposite: withholding bread and water from one's opponents. In
order to perform services for his friends the local boss can often be found
groping in the twilight zone between legality and illegality, or his actions
may fall indisputably outside the law, but party-political solidarity passes
over his 'crimes' and wipes the slate clean. His final rehabilitation comes
with political victory, because, in politics, according to his own criterion:
'the only crime is to lose'. Because of this, patronage plays a large part in
the lack of organisation which is so marked in the administration in the
municipalities.

One of the chief causes of maladministration is the low level of education which exists in rural Brazil, a reflection, in aggravated form, of the
low level of education which exists in the country as a whole. If the state
and federal governments themselves have difficulty in finding competent
civil servants, even having to create makeshift 'experts' overnight, one can
imagine the extent of the problem in the more backward municipalities.
Inquiries carried out on this subject in various states after the revolution of
1930 revealed a number of surprising facts. This led to the creation of
special departments for the municipalities, which, besides giving technical
assistance, were not slow to assume specifically political functions. But the
unpreparedness of the municipalities only partly explains the administrative anarchy which exists in them. The rest can be explained, on the one
hand, by patronage, which encourages many of the leader's protégés to
'drink from the public drinking trough', and, on the other, by the fact that
the municipal government's money and resources are used in election campaigns.

The other face of patronage is the arbitrary use of personal power,
employed in the persecution of political opponents: 'bread for his friends,
a stick for his enemies'. [The saying is more forceful in the original, play
being made with the closeness of the words *pao* (bread) and *pau* (a stick)
– *Translator*.][35] The relations between the local chief and his opponents
are rarely cordial, and the normal state is one of open hostility.[36] Aside
from this, there is obviously the systematic refusal to grant any favours to

political opponents who, for the most part, would consider it humiliating to ask for them.

It is in the periods just preceding elections that the atmosphere of oppression is at its most acute.[37] In the intervals between election campaigns, relations between the factions improve considerably, eventually becoming courteous and respectful. It is during this phase that certain understandings are reached, allowing the faction which is in power or which is supported by the state government, to swell its ranks by attracting election agents from the towns or from among the *coronel*'s followers. [*Cabo eleitoral*, agent, refers to an individual who for certain favours pledges a number of neighbourhood, class, or professional votes, from urban areas to a candidate with whom he has an understanding — *Translator*.] A favourable climate for political deals also reaches its optimal state as the elections approach, but before the assumption of specific electoral pledges. Once positions have been clearly defined, we enter into the period of coercion which immediately precedes the contest.[38] Certain likely adherents may be spared until later, as long as the possibility of attracting them into the fold still exists.[39] Others will be convinced by the first show of violence. Many will abstain from voting to avoid further unpleasantness, and a few will break their word. The rule is that pledges which are given between man and man in the municipality should be honoured, and the local leader is probably as repelled by a man's breaking his word as he is exasperated by the treachery of former associates.[40]

But there is in all this a special morality: as pledges are not taken up on the basis of political principles but turn upon concrete things, they are valid only for one election or for a few successive ones. When the need arises for him to change his party (a move which generally signifies going over to the government side), the local boss — or the *coronel* — temporises about committing himself. Should he suffer some personal setback, or should he cease to be heeded in some matter which he considers important, the reason for the break is already there, namely that his part in the deal has not been seconded by the superior to whom he owed electoral support. When such reasons cannot be advanced, he will use the supreme argument: he has no right to impose on his friends the sacrifice of his opposition. And this argument, however insincere, is, substantially, real and logical, for the primary duty of the local boss is to win, and this means obtaining for his following support at the state-level.[41]

VII. System of compromise with the state government. Coercion of the rural electorate

The rarefaction of public power in our country greatly contributes to maintaining the ascendancy of the *coronéis*, since, because of this, they are in a position to exercise, unofficially, many of the functions which are properly those of the state, in relation to their dependants. But this absence of public authority, which has as a necessary consequence the effective mobilising of the power of the well-placed individual,[42] is now being remedied by new means of transport and communication, which are becoming more and more widespread. Today, the police, except in a few states, can reach the scene of an incident and deal with it fairly efficiently in a space of time which is becoming shorter and shorter. The rebellion of the local boss — so characteristic of a certain period in colonial times — is now no longer a means of consolidating the influence of the *coronel*, but rather tends to weaken and undermine it. But even so, as long as land distribution in Brazil keeps the rural population dependent on the big landowner, hindering direct contact between the parties and this largest section of the electorate, the party governing the state will not be able to dispense with the services of the landowner.[43] But the state authorities only yield to the landlord, their intermediary, in matters which, while they have no fundamental importance at state-level, are of the greatest significance for him in the narrow sphere of his municipality. Because of this, the *coronel* knows that his impertinence can only be disadvantageous; on the contrary, when relations are good between his private power and institutional authority, the *coronel* can, with no questions asked, arrogate a large number of the state's functions. Here we have a most important feature of *coronelismo*, namely, the system of reciprocity: on one hand, the local bosses and the *coronéis* leading swarms of electors as one drives a herd of donkeys; on the other, the dominant political force in the state which controls the exchequer, jobs, favours, and the police, which in sum possesses full power to make or break.[44]

It is clear, however, that these two aspects — the *coronéis*' own prestige and the prestige which they borrow from the public authority — are interdependent, and function at the same time as pre-conditioning factors of the situation as well as being the outcome of it. Were it not for the *coronel*'s leadership — founded on the country's agrarian structure — the government would not feel itself bound by any notion of reciprocity, and without this reciprocity the authority of the *coronel* would be considerably diminished.

Many local bosses, even when they take part in politics as state or federal deputies, are usually subordinates whose superiors, through ties of family or friendship, through natural talent, by collusion or simply by force of circumstance, have already risen to positions as heads of groups or factions on the way to state or federal leadership. But, on every rung of the political ladder, the system of reciprocity imposes itself irresistably,[45] and the whole structure has at its base the *coronel*, strengthened by the understanding which exists between him and the dominant political group in his state, by way of bosses of intermediate status.

The good and the harm which local chiefs can do to those under their jurisdiction, are determined in large measure by the extent of the support, at state level, for this or that particular undertaking. In the first place, a great number of personal favours depend, fundamentally, when not exclusively, on the state authorities. As the local boss, when friendly, is the one who has the ear of the state government in all matters relating to the municipality,[46] the very state functionaries who serve in the area are chosen in accordance with his wishes. Primary school teachers, the revenue officer and his assistants, clerks of the court, the public prosecutor, school inspectors, health inspectors, etc.: for all such posts the candidates suggested or approved by the local boss are customarily the successful ones. Even when the state government has its own candidates, it avoids nominating them if such a course would threaten the prestige of the political boss of the municipality. If any state functionary clashes with him the most convenient way out of the impasse is to remove the former, sometimes promoting him if necessary. The influence of the local boss can be felt even in the appointments to federal posts such as revenue officer, postmaster, inspectors in secondary and commercial schools etc., and posts in the autonomous administrative agencies (whose personnel has been greatly increased), because it is also customary for the federal government, in its own compromise with the political leadership of the states, to accept suggestions and requests put forward by the leaders who run them.

Not only personal favours are involved. It is well known that public services in the interior are very deficient, because the municipalities do not have the resources to meet many of their needs. Without financial help from the state government it would be difficult to undertake the provision of essential services like roads, bridges, schools, hospitals, water, drainage, electricity. No municipal administrator could hope to retain the leadership for very long if he did not secure some benefit for his district. The very landowners who lack roads for transporting their produce, and even the most rudimentary kind of medical attention for their employees, would reach the point where they would withhold their electoral support. And the state government – which, for its part, has only slim resources, insufficient for the running of the services which fall within its sphere – has to dole out its favours in matters of public utilities with great care. The most logical criterion, especially from the point of view of electoral value, is to give preference to those municipalities which are in the hands of political friends. The financial weakness of the municipalities is therefore a factor which contributes directly to the maintenance of *coronelismo* where the *coronel* concerned is a government ally.[47]

Official support is even more precious when it comes to the question of electoral expenses which the local bosses are not able to meet out of their own pockets, although many of them make considerable sacrifices in order to do so. Because of this it is also common for candidates, some of them undertaking heavy financial responsibilities, to make contributions in order to contest the seat in question. But it is no secret that it is more usually the public coffers which help both the candidates and the local bosses of the government party when they are in difficult straits. This help is sometimes given in the form of cash subsidies, or as direct payment for services and utilities. At other times, the help is indirect, through contracts which allow for a wide margin of profit, or by the loan of public buildings, transport and printing facilities, propaganda material, etc. A large part of the already meagre resources of our municipalities is spent, at election time, on the election campaign of the governing faction.[48] Among the reasons which can be given to explain the frenzy which is so characteristic of election time in the municipalities, this one is of primary significance. The state, and eventually the federal government, as well as the administrative agencies — all customarily provide funds and services to be used exclusively by government candidates.[49]

All of this is included in the category of the 'good' which local bosses can achieve when they are in charge of the affairs of the municipality and are allies of the state government.

On the other hand, the same leader who can do good becomes more powerful when he also has the capacity to do harm. In this respect the support of the officialdom of the state for the local boss, either by deed or by omission, has the greatest importance. Here the figures of the regional chief of police and his deputy come into prominence.[50] The nomination for these posts is of supreme importance for the ruling group in the municipality, and constitutes one of the most valuable commodities held by the state in its political horse-trading with the local leaders. Obstructing or otherwise hindering business enterprises owned by the opposition, turning a blind eye to the persecution of political opponents, withholding favours from and infringing the rights of adversaries — these are the different ways in which the state government can help to consolidate the prestige of its political allies in the municipality. But, the state's trump card is undoubtedly this: to place the police of the state under the authority of the local political leader.

In certain circumstances threats and violence fulfil a primary function in so far as operations of this nature can, at times, guarantee that the least powerful of the local factions can still function as the government of the municipality. But, as a rule, this does not happen: the rule is simultaneous recourse to granting favours and to wielding the 'big stick'. This is completely understandable when one considers that the controlling party in the state government is concerned to consolidate its position with a minimum of violence. Only a deranged person practises evil for its own sake: in politics, particularly, violence is only resorted to when other methods are too slow or ineffective for the end in view. Because of this the state government often supports the faction which has already achieved control in the municipality.[51] At other times it imposes an alliance, sharing out the benefits. By virtue of these arrangements — truces of longer or shorter duration — one of the opposing groups, perhaps the one which comes off best in the distribution of favours, or the one to which ostracism is least distasteful, can finally emerge as the dominant one. The preferred faction then becomes the majority one, the need for the alliance thenceforth disappearing.

It is clear, as has already been indicated, that not all leaders of local factions, nor all *coronéis* are the allies of the state government. They can be in opposition, as is the case in nearly all the municipalities. But the position of the local leader in opposition is so uncomfortable that, as a general rule, he only remains in opposition when he is unable to attach himself to the government. As has already been observed, the political factions in the municipalities quarrel with great bitterness, but usually all of them aim to secure the preference of the state government; they do not quarrel in order to overthrow the government of the municipality and so strengthen the position of a state or federal party hostile to the government; their quarrels turn on the question as to which of them will have the privilege of supporting the government and of being supported by it. In the words of Basílio Magalhães, when 'Factions arise in the municipalities, usually in fierce opposition one to the other, they all immediately begin to clamour noisily for the unconditional support of the state government.'[52] The greatest evil which can befall a local political leader is to have the government of the state against him. Because of this he ardently seeks its support. Elections in our municipalities are the occasion of such bitter controversy precisely because if any faction can prove that it carries with it a majority of the electorate of the municipality, it stands a better chance of being singled out for support by the state government. The state government, itself, is primarily concerned to secure, in the state and federal elections which follow, the greatest number of votes, while pledging as few favours and employing as little violence as possible. Supporting the local faction which commands a majority is, therefore, the best way of achieving this result;

all the more so because having control in the muncipality represents, for the local faction, as well as for the state government, a positive factor in the elections, the balance in which public money and benefits in the gift of the government weigh so heavily.

The essence, therefore, of the compromise with *coronelismo* — except in special cases which do not conform to the usual pattern — is as follows: on the part of the local bosses, unconditional support for official government candidates in state and federal elections; on the part of the state government, *carte blanche* for the local boss who supports the government (preferably the leader of the majority faction) in all matters relating to the municipality, including the nomination of state functionaries employed there.

VIII. Local government autonomy and coronelismo

When we study the subject of autonomy in the municipalities, we notice at once that it is less a problem of autonomy than of the lack of it, so consistent has been the depreciation of municipal institutions in our history, except for brief periods of reaction from the municipalities themselves. The decline of the municipalities has been the result of various processes: budgetary impoverishment, excessive responsibilities, reduction of prerogatives, limitations of the principle of elected representatives in their administration, interference of the police in local ballots, etc. The golden age of the colonial assemblies passed, to be succeeded by the practice of interference in the details of administration which occurred during the monarchy, and the tutelage which became usual during the Empire. The fresh breeze of autonomy, which sprang up in the early years of the Republic, soon ceased to blow, and strong currents from the opposite direction began to be felt in the political life of the municipalities. In 1934 there was a new surge in the direction of autonomy but this was quietened by the *Estado Novo*.[53] And so now, in 1946, the third Republican Constitution places the problem of the municipalities among the first to be deliberated, analysing principally the fundamental question, which is that of finance. The movement of 1946 is a more conscious and meaningful continuation of that of 1934, although certain details point to noteworthy differences between them. However it still remains an open question, which only time can solve, as to when and if the resurgence of a belief in the integrity of the municipalities will result in an effective strengthening of their political autonomy.

Meanwhile, in the absence of any legal autonomy, local leaders of the government party have always enjoyed a generous measure of extra-legal autonomy. As a rule their opinions carry the day in the counsels of the government in everything which relates to the municipalities, even in those matters which, strictly speaking, are within the competence of the state or federal governments only, as for example the nomination of certain functionaries, among them the chief of police and the officials of the Inland Revenue. It is precisely this extra-legal autonomy which constitutes the *carte blanche* granted by the state government to its local political allies, in fulfilment of the pledges undertaken in the form of agreement typical of *coronelismo*. It is also by virtue of this *carte blanche* that the state authority either approves or closes its eyes to all the actions of the local boss, including acts of violence and other behaviour of an arbitrary nature.

A curious inversion takes place, therefore in the exercise of local autonomy. Were it juridically guaranteed against intervention by the state government and grounded on a solid financial base, the autonomy of the municipality would be naturally exercised under a representative regime, by a majority of the electorate acting through its delegates chosen by the mechanism of the ballot-box. But with legal autonomy circumscribed in so many ways, the exercise of extra-legal autonomy is entirely dependent on the concessions of the state government. It is no longer a right of the majority of the electorate, but a gift from the powers that be. And a donation or delegation of authority of this kind will necessarily benefit the friends of the ruling party in the state government, should they, by any chance, be in charge of the administration of the municipality. When this is the case, the municipality can even achieve a measure of prosperity, relatively speaking, including the kind of prosperity which results from the introduction of basic public services. If it happens that the municipality is in the hands of a faction which has no link with the state government, it is clear that it will not be granted the extra-legal autonomy which it would receive if it participated in the distribution of the state government's patronage. It will therefore have to function strictly within the bounds of its legal autonomy, which is to say that it will have at its disposal a budget inadequate to deal with even the most rudimentary public services. Apart from this, the specific prerogatives of the state government, in relation to the municipality (especially nominations), will be exercised, not according to the wishes of the government of the municipality (the political enemies of the state government) but according to the wishes of the opposition factions of the municipality (political allies of the state government). Consequently, the question as to whether or not the state government respects the wishes of the majority of the municipal electorate, is decided on the basis of serving its own political purpose.

In these circumstances, a win by any particular faction in a municipal election is a pyrrhic victory, unless that faction already is, or becomes, an ally of the governing party in the state. Because of this complete reversal of roles, it is clear that, as a rule, candidates for municipal posts, chosen by a majority of the electorate, cannot be regarded as the electorate's spontaneous choice, but rather a selection more or less forced upon them. If candidates for the municipal government, supported by the state authorities, are the ones who have the best chance of setting up a beneficial administration, this fact predisposes a large number of the electorate to vote for the local faction which is on the state government's side. In such conditions, even the freest and most open of municipal elections frequently serve merely to rubber-stamp candidates previously nominated by the state government. This is authentic mystification under the representative system.

The much-quoted argument that local autonomy favours wasteful and corrupt administrations, unrestrained from above, is generally documented by the experience of 1891 in the majority of the states. But if the state had complete ascendency over the local leaders in 1891, why was this ascendancy not used to clean up municipal government? Why was it used only to impose candidates in state and federal elections? These questions expose the reality disguised by the argument itself. State governments have always closed their eyes to maladministration in the municipalities, declining to use their influence to eliminate corruption, and this attitude has been part and parcel of the system of compromise which exists under *coronelismo*. It was included in the *carte blanche* which the local bosses received in exchange for their unconditional support for government candidates in state and federal elections.

But it is still in order to ask: why did state governments pay such a high price for the support of local bosses while allowing waste and corruption to devastate municipal administration? The answer is not difficult: the finances and the services of the municipality were useful tools in the creation of the majority desired by the state governments in state and federal elections. Aside from this, they had no direct responsibility for the frauds perpetrated by the local bosses for their own advantage and at their own risk. The high price paid by the state in exchange for the electoral support of the local bosses was, therefore, an *objective* condition by which this support was measured in terms of the aims envisaged by the state government.

IX. Fragmentation of the social hegemony of the landowning class

If the attitude of the executive authorities — that is to say the political leaders of the state administration — in relation to the municipalities can be satisfactorily explained by the mechanism which we have described, the same is not true of the attitude of the state legislators in so far as they enact legislation relating to administration in the municipalities, and this legislation works towards the up-ending of the representative principle. How can we explain the fact that the majority of local political bosses agree to the mystification of the real choices of the local electorate, forced almost always to lean to the government side as a result of the declining power of the municipality? The primary reason is certainly the fear of being crossed off the government's 'list' and thereby losing the chance of returning to the state Congress or even reaching the federal Congress. If they are taken off the government's list, the compromises which function under *coronelismo*, as described above, will help to defeat them in their own municipalities. But apart from this purely political reason, very ponderable in itself (since the government, notwithstanding the conformity of the electorate under *coronelismo*, still uses fraud and coercion to ensure electoral victory), there is another more profound one.

The student of *coronelismo* begins by ascribing the phenomenon, naturally and justifiably, to the social hegemony of the landowning class. But it is important to understand this hegemony only in relation to the landowner's immediate dependants, who live on his property and constitute his stack of 'block' votes. His ascendancy must not be taken as extending throughout the municipality. A municipality is divided into districts: the district of the seat of government – i.e. urban – does not come under the influence of the *coronel* unless he is also, at the same time, the political leader of the municipality; and each of the rural districts is composed of a number of large estates.[54] This fragmentation of social dominance in the countryside tends to take place in areas of declining or unproductive agriculture where landowners are losing money, and, still more often, is the result of our laws of inheritance.[55]

If a single *coronel* were owner of a whole district, his social hegemony, resulting from his ownership of land, would be uncontested in that area, the same occurring in relation to the whole of the municipality, if the circumstances were repeated. However, since, as a general rule, there are several landowners in each district and an even greater number in each municipality, it would be natural if they spontaneously fell into more than one political faction, according to the various factors which determine political alliances in the municipalities. The grouping of the landowners of the district around one of their number, and that of the district leaders around the leader of the municipality – forgetting for the moment the influence of the state authorities – can be explained in a number of ways: personal reasons (greater vocation, competence or ability); by tradition (the leadership having always been in the hands of one family); by economic factors (the richest estates, with a large number of electors, or greater resources to cover electoral expenses), etc. Because of the variable pattern of motivation behind party affiliation, the balance of local political forces is very unstable, a situation aggravated by the habitual vacillation of the urban element, less submissive and therefore less predictable. Given these conditions, what would happen if the outcome of the contest for political leadership depended solely on the electorate, that is to say, on the election agents in the towns and on each of the many landowners in the rural districts? In all probability every election would be an uncertain venture, or at least a lengthy process. The risks would increase considerably, and the results would favour those leaders who in fact possessed personal qualities of leadership. But as local positions of leadership are often acquired by accident of birth, of marriage, or by some sort of protective friendship, in all these cases when the individual was found to be lacking in the relevant qualities, his political fate would hang by a thread in every new contest that he undertook.

Not every municipality presents the political picture which we have painted here, for it is modified precisely by the acquisitive force of the state government, which extends its sphere of influence in direct proportion to the declining authority of the municipality. The government's power to attract support to itself frees municipal contests of many of the risks that might otherwise be inherent, because it predisposes the electorate in favour of candidates on the government side. This perhaps explains the attitude of state legislators who fail to use their constitutional powers to revive political organisation in the municipalities and so to help in freeing the electorate from the all-absorbing influence of the government working through the local leaders and the *coronéis*. If, on the one hand, state deputies remain allied to the government on which, in the last analysis, the outcome of the election depends, on the other hand, their re-election or their promotion is guaranteed according to whether or not they can maintain good relations with the ruling party in the state.

All this indicates that the problem of *coronelismo*, apparently simple, presents great complexity in its internal structure. There is no doubt, however, that it is much less the result of the importance and strength of the great landlords, than of their decline. The weakness of the landowning class only appears as strength in contrast to the mass of the people who live meanly under its wing and cast their votes as it dictates. *Coronelismo* rests, therefore, on these two weaknesses: the weakness of the landowner who deludes himself with a semblance of power and prestige, obtained at the price of political submission; and the weakness, desolation and disillusionment of the almost sub-human beings who wrest a hand-to-mouth existence from the landlord's estate.[56]

The *coronéis* of today and yesterday — they repeatedly nowadays have to appeal to the police for help — are very far from those rebellious and powerful rural landlords of a certain colonial period, who were the government and the law as far as their underlings were concerned. The power displayed by the two types, although having certain external similarities, is the expression, in the latter case, of the force of a slave-owning and patriarchal system at its apogee and, in the former, of the fragility of a decadent rural system based on the poverty and ignorance of the agricultural worker and subject to the hazards of the world market in primary products and foodstuffs, which we cannot control.

The best proof of the contention that *coronelismo* is more a symptom of the decadence of the rural landlords than a manifestation of their vitality, lies in this fact: it is by sacrificing the autonomy of the municipality that it has nourished itself and survived.

2. Powers of the municipalities

I. Quantitative concept

It is an extremely difficult task to determine exactly what, within a good administrative structure, should be municipal prerogatives. Observations of a very general nature shed little light on the subject. When one says, for example, that the municipality should assume functions of a local nature or those which affect its own particular interests, there still remains the problem of defining what are these particularly local functions and interests. The difficulty increases when one observes that certain matters which formerly concerned the life of only one municipality may now be the concern of several, or of a whole state, or even the whole country. This variation in time of the territorial area affected by a large number of administrative problems, makes the idea of 'the municipality's particular interest' or 'local interest' a very relative one, and makes it more difficult to find a solution based on general principles.

For the rest, it is not the intention of this work to discuss what would or would not be an ideal type of municipal authority, but simply to seek to understand certain aspects of municipal power as we have known it in reality. In this sense the most important thing is to demonstrate how the municipality's sphere of influence has been widened or restricted, comparing the various phases one with the other and not with some model erected *a priori* as a definitive standard of measurement.

Within this framework we shall begin in the period of the greatest expansion of the municipal chambers, in colonial times, and we shall follow, from there onwards, the successive limitations imposed on the autonomy of the municipalities, notwithstanding the various manifestations, nearly always sporadic, in favour of greater privileges for them.

II. Apogee of the colonial legislatures

Only those places which belonged to a category no lower than that of *vila* [small town or borough], and this conferred by royal decree,[1] were entitled to municipal chambers, whose structure was transplanted from Portugal, in the beginning in conformity with the Ordinances of King Manuel, and later, King Philip. The chamber properly speaking[2] was composed of two ordinary judges each serving in turn,[3] or of a judge from outside (when one was available)[4] and three councillors. There were also officials of the chamber with special functions, the attorney, the treasurer, and the clerk, elected, as were the judges and the councillors. It was the chamber itself which nominated the parish judge, inspectors of weights and measures, trustees, guards and other functionaries.

The officials of the chamber, especially the councillors in their joint deliberations with the judge and the subordinate functionaries, were responsible, within the limits of their powers, for all local matters whether administrative, judicial or police affairs. Its standard acts consisted primarily of orders and edicts subject to the control of legality and advisability exercised by the magistrate who was head of the legal district, and who, in turn, was subordinate to other authorities in the hierarchy of colonial administration.[5] Thus, it fell to the magistrate to order the local authorities 'to execute public works, roads, bridges, springs, wells, fountains, paths, administrative offices, pillories, and any other works which might be necessary, enjoining them both to undertake new projects and to repair those which were in need of repair'.[6] Summarising the prerogatives which could be exercised locally, the Ordinances lay down that 'it is the duty of the councillors to carry the burden of the entire organisation of the administration's land and works, and to do all in their knowledge and understanding to ensure the well-being of the area and its inhabitants, and to this end they must strive'.[7] In order to carry out these duties, the chambers disposed of their own funds, generally very limited, or resorted to raising special contributions for a specific project.[8]

It is impossible, however, to understand the workings of any institution of that period, including the local authorities, without ridding oneself of the modern idea of the separation of powers, based on the division of functions into legislative, executive and judicial.[9] In this area there existed the most overwhelming confusion, the same authorities exercising public functions of every kind, limited quantitively by the often unclear definition of their prerogatives, and subject to a graduated control which ultimately reached up to the king himself.[10]

In describing the colonial chambers Carvalho Mourão observes that they exercised 'much more important functions than the modern municipalities'. It is the case that, apart from their control in matters of local interest, they exercised functions which today are the responsibility of the State Prosecutor, denouncing crimes and abuses to the judges; they assumed the functions of a rural police force and of an inspectorate of public hygiene; assisted the *alcaides* in the policing of the territory and chose a large number of the functionaries involved in general administration, such as: the inspectors of weights and measures, assistants of the chief *alcaide*,[11] the four tax receivers, the legal trustees of the orphans' fund or of the tithe, the assayers of distrained goods, the keeper of the armoury, the *quadrilheiros* — police guards of a sort — and other functionaries. In addition, the chambers had the right to nominate attorneys to the Royal Courts.[12]

Aside from the police and judicial functions, which will be discussed in greater detail elsewhere,[13] the exercise of the chamber's prerogatives was within the competence of the councillors, acting jointly with the judge, or specifically delegated to a relevant official. The attorney, for example, petitioned for and costed public works from the district's funds as was required, he paid fines, represented the district in court and acted as treasurer when there was none. The treasurer collected the revenue and undertook the expenditure agreed by the councillors, and the clerk acted as secretary and book-keeper to the chamber and as a legal scribe in matters of litigation.[14]

Under Dutch rule, the system of local government underwent some specified changes,[15] and Indian settlements administered by religious orders cannot be considered as examples of local government.[16]

It is impossible, however, to know exactly what the colonial chambers were like, simply by examining the relevant legislation. If, as Carvalho Mourão would have it, we are not yet at a stage where a primitive sense of municipal autonomy is expressing itself, the 'exorbitant claims' and the 'rebellious impulses' of the chambers, which he sees as 'accidents',[17] were, for a long time, the reflection of the social state of the colony with private power, nearly always tolerated and quite often urged on by the Crown, challenging public authority. During a long period – lasting, according to Caio Prado Júnior, until the middle of the seventeenth century, as we shall see later – the chambers exercised immense power, which developed on the margin of their legal writ and often in contradiction to it. It was not rare, however, for the Crown to sanction usurpations carried out against the chambers by omnipotent rural lords. Thus was legalised a concrete situation which subverted legal rights but which corresponded directly to the social and economic order which prevailed in these remote areas. It would be difficult to contain these manifestations of private power in a structure whose basic unit (whose mark was clearly impressed on a whole range of institutions) was the extensive rural estate, essentially monocultural and built on slave labour.[18] The king often was, or pretended to be, powerless to control the tyranny of these potentates, who dominated the chambers and through them all the territory which came under their jurisdiction. The mass of the population – composed in large measure of slaves and of so-called free workers, whose situation was one of total dependence on the landowning nobility[19] – was also powerless in the face of this private power, which at times held in check the sovereignty of the Crown itself.

It is therefore not strange that, in this period of the almost exclusive domination by the landowning upper class, the municipal chamber – instrument of its power in ths political sphere – had a wide range of prerogatives which resulted less from legal right than from the realities of life. 'If within the political system in force in the colonial period' – says Caio Prado Júnior – 'we find the only sovereignty, the *political power* of the Crown, we are going to see it, *de facto*, invested in the rural landowners who exercise it through the municipal administrations.'[20]

Referring to the chambers of São Luís and Belém, João Francisco Lisboa in a classic passage, describes 'the immense political power arrogated by the senates of the two cities':[21]

From an examination and study of its archives, from memoirs of the period, and from laws and royal letters, it is clear that the same senates, legally or illegally, fixed the rate of the daily wage of Indians and other free workers, and the price of artefacts from mechanical craftshops, meat, salt, manioc flour, *aguardente*, cotton cloth and thread, medicines and even manufactured products of the realm. They regulated the flow and value of money, levied tributes, deliberated on matters relating to the Indians: advances to them, transportation of Indian workers, missions, peace and war, and on the creation of camps and settlements. They arrested and put in irons functionaries and private individuals, made political alliances among themselves, summoned into their presence and even, finally, nominated and suspended governors and captains. This vast jurisdiction was exercised by them, on their own, in matters of lesser importance; for more serious matters, however, they convened the so-called general assemblies, in which the votes were shared by the nobility, the military and the clergy.[22]

Among the causes of this illegal extension of prerogatives,[23] which lasts at least until the middle of the seventeenth century, the most important is the inadequacy of the administrative machinery in a vast, wild and almost unpopulated territory, or, in other words, the weakness of public authority. Put another way, the basic factor in this situation was the isolation in which the rural landlords lived, free, therefore from any effective element of contrast to their own authority. Furthermore, as they constituted the Crown's vanguard in the occupation of new lands defended by warlike peoples and threatened by other European powers, there was no great margin of conflict between the private power of the territorial nobility and the public authority in the person of the king and his agents. It was for this very reason that Portugal not only resigned herself to the fact of the colonists' predominance but even conferred special privileges on them. For example, she protected the great landowners from the competition of the small producers of *aguardente* by having the latter's mini-factories destroyed; turned the chambers into the private domain of the landowners by forbidding the election of merchants; protected the patrimony of the plantation owners by ensuring that property could not be divided, etc.[24] For all these reasons single-crop, slave-owning latifundia represented, at this time, the true centre of power in the colony: economic, social and political.[25]

III. Reaction of the Crown. Strengthening of royal power after the transfer of the Court

Viveiros de Castro does not agree that the colonial chambers were able to exercise such wide prerogatives because of royal approval. In his opinion:

Because they were distant from the Court, the municipal chambers were encouraged to assume, without ceremony, prerogatives which were not their own; but when the matter came to his notice, the king reprimanded them severely, as for example in the royal letters of 4 December 1677, 12 April 1693, 20 November 1700, and 28 March 1794. In these it is formally declared that the chambers were subordinate to the governors, whose orders they were bound to carry out, *even if such orders were illegal and contrary to the jurisdiction of the chambers.*[26]

We have not the slightest intention of becoming involved in historical controversies, neither are we competent to do so, but Viveiros de Castro's observation could well be congruent with the preceding affirmations, when we notice that the royal decrees which he cites[27] belong to the period in which the Crown was already beginning to restrain the rural nobility. At this time the king was already reacting to strengthen the public authority of the state against the personal power of the *paterfamilias*, who was slave-owner, plantation-owner, and general of a private army at one and the same time. The earliest of the royal decrees mentioned dates from 1677, and it is well known that at the end of the seventeenth century and the beginning of the eighteenth, coinciding with the discovery and exploration of the mines, royal authority in the colony was tightened to an extra-ordinary degree.

Caio Prado Júnior puts the reaction of the Crown at an earlier date, suggesting that it began to be evident, in an effective way, in the second half of the seventeenth century after Portugal had shaken off the Spanish yoke and expelled the Dutch.[28] By this time the metropolitan country could dispose of greater forces to assume, on Brazilian territory, the major role in functions which now ceased to fall to the rural nobility. The increase in trade, predominantly by Portuguese, and the growth of urban centres of population, contributed to this result. As a consequence of this change the colony's economy developed at a faster pace: the faster its economy grew the more the colony felt itself to be fettered by Portugal's mercantile monopoly and by the prohibition which denied it the right to set up indus-tries.[29] The divergence of interests between the settlers and the colonisers grew wider, and the decline of trade with the East Indies increased Portugal's zeal for lands in America on which she was beginning to depend. The discovery of minerals accelerated this transformation. As long as the interests of the rural nobility left a wide margin for metropolitan activity and while Portugal itself was not in a position to demand more, the private power of the settlers was approved and encouraged by the Crown; but the latter did not hesitate to censure, contain and punish their independence when its interests and theirs began to collide more violently, and when the king felt sufficiently strong to cease to tolerate their insolence. Clearly the change did not occur abruptly, nor at a stroke: the process was gradual with advances and retreats, but having as its inevitable outcome the reinforcement of the king's authority.

The study of the struggles between families in Brazil amply illustrates, in another sector of social life, the same process of the reinvigoration of public authority and the decline of private power whose remnants still survive today but allied to political power and not in opposition to it. These struggles are, in themselves, clear evidence of the weakness or absence of public authority. The intervention of the state in such disputes, first in a mediatory role and later as an effective organ of jurisdiction, goes hand in hand with the strengthening of the political power of the Crown, in the measure in which new social and economic conditions in the colony and in Portugal permitted or hindered this change.[30]

In the first phase of this long process — in the phase of the effective imposition of royal power upon private dictatorship — the Crown had no need for radical reform of the existing legal provisions, since the expansion of the chambers had taken place by stretching the regulations laid down by the Ordinances or by breaking them. The Crown had only to withdraw concessions made to the chambers of rural landlords and put the Phillipine Code into operation, or to use the expedients already contained in the code.

Consequently, once it had annulled or reduced the concessions which had enabled the chambers to legislate widely, all the Crown had to do in order to impose its authority effectively, was to increase the importance and improve the working equipment of its agents in the colony, especially visiting judges, magistrates and governors. Unquestionably it did not limit itself to these measures, but went so far, as we shall see, as to nominate local authorities which, by law, should have been elected.

The administrative regime established in the gold-producing areas[31] sufficiently demonstrates how the pressure of a major interest made metropolitan authority more direct and more active. Because of this, the war of the foreign prospectors is highly symbolic of the hegemony of the Crown over its turbulent colonists.[32] The administration of the district of Diamantino is another example, and, precisely because it is an extreme case, is expressive and useful for an understanding of the process which produced a strengthening of the king's powers.[33]

The transfer of the Court to Brazil and later independence and the establishment of a Constitution, greatly accelerated the process of the progressive reduction of private power. Closer and better equipped, the government could extend its authority over the national territory with much greater efficiency. In the course of the nineteenth century (especially with the conservative reaction which, from 1840 onwards, established political and administrative centralisation as the basic principle of government), we witness a consistent effort to consolidate the power of the state.

The new and very significant factor which is now apparent, is that public authority, especially after the abdication of Don Pedro I, ceases to be the expression of something situated above and outside the country and begins to reflect in its composition the political forces of Brazil itself. Already the political problem can no longer be posed in terms of a dispute between the colony and the mother country or between Portuguese and Brazilian interests. April 7 (in order to understand it better, it is proper to take an outstanding event as a point of reference) was the signal for the complete transfer of power to the rural upper class, which therefore ceased to operate in the restricted area of the municipalities and began to project its economic and social, and hence its political power throughout imperial Brazil. With the mother country no longer providing an element of contrast, and with Portuguese interests too drastically reduced to influence events effectively, there will now be other contenders in the political disputes which from now on will fill the pages of our history. During the Regency — a period which still requires fuller and deeper study — the struggles assume great complexity. Beside the regional motives for discontent within the ruling strata themselves, fused by liberal ideas to which independence and the new constitution gave weight, there were violent popular revindications which produced surprising agreements within the dominant groups. Once order was restored, and this meant political centralisation above all, and the claims of the lower strata of the population were stifled, internal peace came to rest on the solidity of the agrarian structure, based on slavery, and political struggles were now joined on the national level and within the powerful class of rural landowners. The political axis will shift according to the movement of agricultural wealth, which was to be found principally in the cultivation of sugar, cotton and coffee and in the large number of slaves which made them productive.

IV. The law of 1828

During a short period, from the return of Dom João VI to the year 1828, various measures were taken in the direction of broadening the 'franchises' of the municipalities.[34] The movement undoubtedly corresponded to the same order of ideas from which our independence resulted. Nor is it strange that this was so, since, all other reasons apart, the chambers were precisely the institution which, for a long time, reflected the conflict between national interests and Portuguese ones, these last being represented by the Portuguese Crown. Nevertheless, the law of municipal organisation of 1 October 1828 shattered any illusion which still persisted as to the future widening of the chambers' prerogatives.

It is important to notice, at the outset, that the chambers were declared to be merely administrative bodies, which could not exercise any jurisdiction whatever in matters of litigation. Doubtless this separation of the exercise of administrative and judicial prerogatives represented an advance in the direction of a better organisation in the public service, because it was in keeping with the general principle of the division of work and the specialisation of functions.[35] Yet the emphasis which the law placed on the administrative character of the municipalities, on the one hand, constituted an effective mechanism for reducing their independence and, on the other, helped to prevent them from becoming centres of more intense political activity, capable of furthering the interests and aspirations of the lower strata of the population. The chambers had formerly been the instrument of the rural aristocracy in its acts of rebellion against the Crown, and had an active role, although one of doubtful efficacy, in the independence movement itself. After the heirs of those same angry colonists had succeeded in dominating political power at the centre, this ancient function of the chambers would no longer be a cause for merit, but a demonstration of a serious lack of discipline which it would be necessary to suppress with promptness.[36]

By the law of 1828, the chambers were subject to a rigid control exercised by the general councils, by the provincial presidents and by the national government. This concept was, in fact, known as the doctrine of *tutelage*, and it consisted of giving the municipality, in administrative terms, the status of the minor in civil law; its incapacity to exercise functions which properly concerned it, imposed the creation of a strict system of support and financing, the responsibility of 'adult' authorities.[37]

The administrative functions of the chambers were quite extensive and were enumerated in detail. They were responsible for the urban centres, roads, bridges, prisons, slaughter-houses, supplies, lighting, water, sewers, sanitation, protection against madmen, drunks and ferocious animals, measures to protect health against harmful plants or animals, the inspection of primary schools, assistance to minors, hospitals, cemeteries, keeping the peace, the prescriptive police, etc. Summarising the list, Article 71 declared that, generally speaking, the chambers should decide upon ways and means of promoting and maintaining the peace, security, health and comfort of the inhabitants, the cleanliness, security, elegance and external orderliness of the buildings and streets of the towns and villages.

Special orders indicating their areas of competence were published, but these were valid for one year only unless they were confirmed by the general councils of the provinces, which could alter or revoke them. Reclamations arising out of municipal decrees which dealt with 'purely economic and administrative' matters could be made, in the case of the court, to the

General Assembly; in the provinces, reclamation was made to the general councils and through them to the government. 'In relation to acts within the competence of the municipalities', Carneiro Maia observes, 'the law gave such wide jurisdiction to the provincial presidents that, in their supervisory capacity, they were entitled to unlimited information as to the deliberations, agreements or decrees of the chambers on economic or administrative matters.'[38] Decisions of the chambers concerning the exemption of elected councillors who did not wish to serve, as well as those dismissing councillors guilty of misconduct during meetings, although such acts did not deal with economic or administrative matters, were also subject to the supervision of the president (in the case of the court, of the chief minister) and of the general council.[39] Municipal autonomy was greatly restricted in financial matters, as will be shown in the relevant chapter, and a new manifestation of tutelage was witnessed later, when it became legal for councillors to be suspended by the presidents of the provinces.[40]

V. The Additional Act and the move towards greater decentralisation

The Additional Act, reflecting a substantial trend towards decentralisation as far as the provinces were concerned, simply transferred to the provincial assemblies, created at that time, the extensive tutelage which had been exercised over the municipal chambers by the presidents, the general councils, the chief minister and the parliament.[41] The president still had important powers especially as a result of the conservative reaction and the legislation of the Council of State. It is a fact that the situation of the municipalities was worsened by the reform of the Constitution,[42] but the liberals, whose idea it was, considered that the chief objective was to allow each province, taking local conditions into consideration, to find a way of establishing the form of municipal government which it considered most suitable.[43]

What seems more plausible, however, is that the main concern of the liberal political forces of the time was to strengthen the provinces *vis-à-vis* the national government. Conceding greater autonomy to the municipalities would certainly not have contributed to this result, because it could have put at risk the homogeneity of the groups in power in the provinces. With the municipalities strictly controlled by the assemblies, the provinces, as strong and cohesive units, would be better able to resist the expansionist supremacy of the centre.[44]

It was, without question, this line of argument which led to the provincial legislatures being given the right to regulate the presidents' authority to nominate, suspend and dismiss provincial employees.[45] But the clearest indication of this proposition is to be found in Article 13 of the Additional Act, which suppressed the presidents' sanction of provincial laws dealing with specific matters. Among these were laws concerning revenue and expenditure, financial control and contributions to municipal accounts, creation, suppression, appointment and remuneration of municipal posts. With such powers over the life of the districts, the ruling faction in the assembly could acquire great influence throughout the province, and thus gain the authority required to pursue its agreements and its disagreements with the central government.

Later events show, however, that the dominant figure on the provincial stage continued to be the president, the Emperor's deputy, whose most important political function was to guarantee the electoral victory of candidates supporting the government.[46] The interpretative law of the Additional Act, the reform of the Criminal Code and, in large measure, the legislation of the Council of State[47] were the chief instruments which guaranteed the pre-eminence of the provincial presidents and, through them, the consolidation of the central power, not forgetting the role played in this process by the conservatism of the Senate and the precarious financial position of the provinces. The bills which were discussed during the Second Reign[48] did not contain any proposal to alter the dependent position of the districts; some of them, on the contrary, reflected the move to make the provincial government even more active within the municipality, by means of a local executive organ nominated by the president of the province.

Hermes Lima observes that the centralising reaction of the Empire can only be understood, in part at least, by considering the fact of the existence of slavery. In a large country like our own with such diverse geographical and economic characteristics, if the provinces had been given wide powers, it could have come about that in some of them slavery would have given way to free labour. And as the coexistence, in the same country, of two opposed labour systems would have been impossible, the slave-owners who dominated the national political arena, could not fail to support centralisation in order to ensure the continued existence of slavery[49] throughout the Empire. The historians say that centralisation saved national unity. It also saved the uniform use of slave labour, according to Hermes Lima's shrewd analysis, thus safeguarding a unified economic structure throughout the country.

VI. Municipal powers under the regime of 1891

Municipal autonomy was a question which preoccupied the members of the Constituent Assembly of 1890, but chiefly as regards the elective nature of municipal administration, as we shall see in the following chapter. The prevailing ideology of the assembly was favourable to the municipality, seeing it as a theoretical double of the federal idea, which had itself finally emerged victorious with the fall of the monarchy, after a futile attempt at coexistence of the two. Given that the basic principle of federalism is decentralisation (political and administrative), then it seemed perfectly logical to extend decentralisation to the municipal sphere. It was also argued, in the Constituent Assembly and later, that the municipality lay in the same relationship to the state as the state to the Union.[50]

Carvalho Mourão wrote: 'The glory of establishing true municipal authority in Brazil was reserved for the Republic.'[51] Yet the early ardour of the supporters of the municipal idea soon began to cool. The state Constitutions were quickly reformed, and they reduced the principle of municipal autonomy to the minimum required to comply with the provisions of the Federal Constitution. Moreover these provisions were imprecise and left the states more or less free to work out the details. In this regard Carlos Porto Carrero was to observe: 'It is noticeable, when one examines the state Constitutions carefully, that initially they are all prodigal in their liberalism, recognising the autonomy of the municipalities and conceding it generously. Not long afterwards the liberal spirit of the legislators of certain states disappeared. There was a spate of reforms aimed at prescribing the rights of the municipalities, either limiting, through tax control, the conditions under which they could exercise their own affairs, or withdrawing from them the right to elect their chief executive.'[52]

Leaving aside here other aspects which will be treated in later chapters, it must be observed that many state Constitutions established a system of fiscal and financial control of the municipalities by the states. This control was frequently exercised *a posteriori*, but sometimes it was exercised *a priori*. Moreover, while in some states there was a simple legal control over the life of the municipalities (a control which clearly was exercised in limited areas), in others the control was also a matter of opportunity and convenience.[53] With these expedients the state governments could guide the municipalities, as they saw fit, in the political interest of concentrating power in the state's orbit.

From the strictly juridical point of view, it is clear that the Federal Constitution allowed for restrictions on the administrative and political autonomy of the districts. Municipal autonomy, according to Article 68, had reference to the notion of 'special interest', but this secondary concept was not defined in the text of the Constitution. It was left to the legislators of the state Constituent Assemblies and, within the limits permitted, to the ordinary legislators, to decide what were the limits of municipal competence and which matters came within it.

The federal legislature might have established a different theoretical framework, by making use of its ability to permit intervention on the part of the states in cases of infringement of constitutional principles. It chose not to do so, however. The Federal Supreme Court, with a few exceptions, also gave its blessing to an interpretation that favoured the states.[54] In accordance with the basic postulate of our political system, it was the duty of the Supreme Court to give a final and conclusive interpretation of the Constitution; it could have given a different stamp to municipal government if it had agreed that fixed principles were necessarily implied in the constitutional notion of 'special interest', as Pedro Lessa maintained. But it also chose not to do this.

Apart from the strictly legal arguments based on the letter of the Constitution and on the historical contribution of parliamentary documents,[55] there was also a political theory which justified restricting the autonomy of the municipalities. Castro Nunes, in a book which attracted much attention, argued that, in a federal system, the political unit is the state and not the municipality. Consequently, a unitary system within the states is more consonant with the theory of federalism. The sub-federation of the municipalities, if we may call it that, was more in keeping with a centralised monarchical system. For these reasons, the author proposed various measures which would impose restrictions on municipal autonomy,[56] in the interest, he argued, of improving municipal organisation.

Since the revolution of 1930, in an attempt to contribute through his studies to the re-establishment of constitutional government in the country, Levi Carneiro, in a widely read volume, has developed ideas which he put forward in two articles previously written in Castro Nunes' book. Although disagreeing with Nunes' ideas as to the position of the municipality in the Federation,[57] this jurist nevertheless denied that the municipality is to the state what the state is to the Union. He concluded by suggesting measures to restrict municipal autonomy, although his idea was to increase judicial control over the districts rather than to impose legislative or executive tutelage.[58]

Very interesting as a body of doctrine, from the point of view with which we are here concerned, were the speeches of Francisco Campos in the Chamber of Deputies of Minas Gerais on the occasion of the constitutional reforms of 1920. The thesis developed on this occasion to justify restricting municipal autonomy, was based on the idea that in modern times almost all the important problems with which a municipal administration deals, transcend the narrow limits of a single district, and therefore become the concern, either of more than one municipality or of the whole state. It was therefore expedient to furnish the state with powers to ensure that over-all interests took precedence over local ones in the area of municipal administration.[59]

The proposal for constitutional reform of 1926 was partly inspired by this line of thought, although in certain areas it did impose restrictions on the almost unlimited freedom which the states enjoyed in matters relating to municipal organisation. On the question of the intervention of the states in cases of violation of the principles of the Constitution, it was recognised that municipal autonomy was itself one of these principles. However, proposals relating directly to municipal organisation were set aside to expedite the passing of the reform.[60]

The ultimate result of the pro-municipal policy of the regime of 1891 was insignificant. In spite of this, controversy continued, some maintaining that it was necessary to show more moderation in venerating the dogma of the autonomists, while others held that municipal autonomy as we knew it was only an illusion.[61]

VII. The phase of the provisional government of 1930

The revolution of 1930 found itself at once with a gigantic problem: to dismantle the political machinery of the Old Republic, whose roots were tied up in municipal problems. Hand in hand with this task was the parallel one of setting up new machinery, a task to be carried out by the very idealistic men who, at the beginning, were the leaders of the revolution. At the same time, the preoccupation to improve the efficiency of the country's administrative procedures, never very clearly articulated, encountered seductive suggestions in favour of the administrative tutelage of the municipalities. A lack of rational methods, administrative chaos, wasteful management of resources, increasing debts, total disorder in accounts, when there were any, a defective system of raising revenue exercised according to party-political allegiance, these and other defects were rife in the municipal administration.[62]

Apparently with both objectives in view — to dismantle a corrupt political machine on the one hand, and to introduce some morality and efficiency into municipal administration on the other — the laws of the provisional government, besides instituting in each municipality a nominated prefect generally assisted by a consultative council, established a system of supervision which extended upwards from the prefect to the intervenor and from him to the head of the national government.[63] In this way, the whole sphere of municipal administration was effectively brought under the control of superior agencies, not only from the point of view of legality but also from the point of view of the appropriateness and convenience of its actions. It could not possibly be held that in the absence of any local representative body whatsoever – since the consultative council did not have this character – the prefect was immune to any supervision or control. The interests of the municipalities themselves, imposed a system of controls which, in those circumstances, could not differ very much from the one actually adopted, save that, in exceptional circumstances, the state government might have been prepared to withdraw the authority of its political agents in the municipality.

What we have here is a rigorously hierarchical system, conceived as such in its transitory phase, during the period of discretionary government which succeeded the victorious revolution. Yet, an innovation adopted in this phase, with the proposal to clean up abuses in municipal administration and improve its efficiency, was allowed to stand in the period of proper constitutional government which followed, and remained definitively part of the country's administrative system. We are referring to the *Department of the Municipalities*, a state body whose name varied, but among whose important functions were included those of giving technical assistance to the districts, co-ordinating their activities on a state level, supervising the drawing up and execution of their budgets, indicating in advance its views on a large number of administrative measures, etc. All in all, it fell to this body, directly dependent on the interventor, to exercise the extensive supervisory functions which the current legislation granted to the state government over the administrative life of the municipalities.

The experiments tried by the states of São Paulo and Espírito Santo attracted the attention of many others which were then inspired to set up similar organisations. In the Constituent Assembly of 1933–4, the São Paulo members made an eloquent defence of the new institution, presenting a balanced picture of its advantages, especially in the field of financial management. The municipalities of São Paulo had reduced their debts and improved their budgetary situation thanks to the help and supervision of the department.[64] The representatives from other states which had created similar departments, also testified to the excellence of this important administrative innovation,[65] around which there developed such a halo of prestige in the assembly, that a deputy from Espírito Santo demanded for his state the glory of having discovered such a valuable instrument of progress.[66]

It requires only a very cursory examination to see how convenient it was to create, in the states, a new political machine to be controlled, not by the worn-out forces of the past, but by the leaders of the day. It fitted perfectly with the patriotic endeavour to improve the administration of the municipalities, making it more economic and productive. By placing the emphasis on this aspect of public order, the political interest, being served by the setting-up of party machinery, could appear in the eyes of the whole country to be rooted in a solid theoretical base capable of protecting it against the defenders of greater municipal autonomy, especially as this last was so intimately associated, in practice, with the insolvency and anarchy so prevalent in the municipalities under the pre-revolutionary system. Hence, the old imperial doctrine of tutelage was revived under another name.

It is clear, and goes without saying, that to many well-intentioned people this marriage of party-political interest and the desire for administrative progress did not appear so conspicuous. The psychological predisposition of politicians always to consider themselves more able than their opponents may have contributed to the unintentional confusion between the well-being of the country and party-political convenience. A very typical example of this position was that adopted by the deputy, Gabriel de Resende Passes, in the second Constituent Assembly of the Republic. Disturbed by the chaos, waste and inefficiency of municipal administration, which he later came to observe much more closely as Secretary of the Interior in Minas Gerais, he proposed that the state be the sole judge of whatever extension of autonomy its municipalities should have.[67] Excessive autonomy – and this was how the hitherto unproductive municipal system appeared to him – was a serious evil, and one which had to be remedied by the guiding and supervisory function of the state.

We are convinced that the fact of his being a government deputy did not influence his judgement as to the over-all advantages of the points of view which he supported, although his ideas could have been equally defended by another deputy whose views would spring wholly from his position as a government supporter. So much so that in his diagnosis of the situation there was an implied condemnation of the political subjection of the municipalities. In his opinion, a serious anomaly threatened municipal organisation: while they were subject to the state in political terms, the municipalities enjoyed unrestricted administrative freedom which, as a rule, they used badly. The important thing, in his view, was to guide and supervise municipal activity in the administrative field.[68]

The ambiguity of this diagnosis lay in the supposition that the state government, which had powers – legal or extra-legal, it does not matter – to dominate the municipalities politically,[69] did not also have the authority to influence administration for the better. We think that it would have been enough for the state to have employed its incontestable prestige to this end. But, generally speaking, this was not done because the greater interest of the ruling group in the state was not administrative but electoral. *Coronel* politics lay precisely in this reciprocity: *carte blanche* in the municipality to the local boss, in return for his electoral support for candidates nursed by the state government.

VIII. The Constitution of 1934 and the departments for municipal affairs

In the Constituent Assembly of the Second Republic, three principal tendencies predominated in relation to the municipal problem. As a consequence, the principle of the elective nature of the municipal administration, with exceptions expressly sanctioned by the Constitution,[70] was guaranteed; the revenue of the municipalities was increased;[71] finally, a certain control over municipal administration was instituted, based on the experiment of the departments of the municipalities during the period of discretionary government.

The first two tendencies could have been related in some way to the dominant composition of the assembly, since a large number of deputies had laboured in opposition during the Old Republic, although, then, many had seen themselves as representatives of new governments established in their states after the revolution. Their previous experience in opposition — which allowed them to evaluate, fairly, how effective the system of nominating prefects and the smallness of municipal revenues could be as instruments of interference by the states in municipal life — can be said to have contributed to the formation in the assembly of a majority in favour of greater protection of political autonomy in the districts. The large opposition returned to the Constituent Assembly by the elections of 1933, had also been an influence in the same direction, because it had not been in its interest to strengthen state governments run by its opponents. Besides, the mechanism of reciprocity in the *coronelista* system always became more obvious and more offensive to the principle of autonomy when it touched on the elective nature of the municipal administration. This question came immediately to the fore when the problem of the municipality was discussed, and it was with reference to it that the conviction grew that the principle of electivity was indispensable to an autonomous political life for the districts.

But the same principle was not applied to administration proper. The Old Republic had always been more tolerant of extending municipal prerogatives in the administrative rather than in the political field, as has already been pointed out. But at the same time the experience of the previous regime, raised many reservations on the subject of inefficiency and irregularities in municipal administration. All this was linked to the new political situation of voting strength within the assembly which before the revolution had had an opposition majority and after the revolution a government one. It is not easy, nor indeed even possible, to determine to what extent the majority in the assembly was conscious of the fact that the departments of the municipalities, whose creation would be authorised in the text of the Constitution, would be able to influence the municipalities as political instruments for the government factions in the states. But the strong warnings that this would happen were not mistaken, and it is very probable that this very possibility played a part in the establishment of these bodies, so much so that their function came to be not only to give technical assistance to the municipalities but also to supervise their finances.[72]

In this respect it is important to observe that this supervisory prerogative provoked heated debates in the assembly. The creation of the departments was put forward by the São Paulo representatives in Amendment No. 703 of the preliminary draft, which empowered 'the states to create bodies to supply technical assistance to the municipalities and to *examine* their finances'. It would appear that Cunha Melo kept the word *examine* [*verificação*], and the proposal, differently phrased, became Article 130 of the draft legislation of the Constitutional Commission.[73]

It was Amendment No. 1945, of the powerful states, which proposed the word *supervision* [*fiscalização*] instead of *examination*, an identical proposal being made by the deputy, Soares Filho, at the same time.[74] Justifying his proposal, the representative from Rio de Janeiro said: 'The amendment maintains the same principle, making the system healthy and free from abuse, yet giving it a more comprehensive definition of its scope.' Deputy Irineu Joffily repeated the same thing in different words: 'What purpose would it serve [for the Department] to examine the affairs of the municipalities, if it did not dispose of any sanction in case of irregularity? The state must, therefore, supervise. The sanction will lie in the state law which permits this supervision.'[75]

The second reason, suggested by Cunha Melo, against substituting the word *supervision* was that this word [*fiscalização*] could be 'interpreted as more harmful to municipal autonomy' by those who had requested the suppression of the article in question. As he explained later the word *fiscalização* seemed to him to be 'far too strong'.[76]

In the plenary session the passage which substituted the word *examination* for *supervision* was specially considered with the latter term finally adopted by 157 votes to 46.[77]

This significant majority, representing the views expressed by the representatives from the powerful states in Amendment No. 1945, clearly indicated that the ruling group wanted to allow the states to give the departments of the municipalities more effective powers. But this was not passed without strong resistance. Daniel de Carvalho declared that such a body, 'designated to provide technical assistance and undertake financial supervision', would reduce 'to nothing' the municipality, which henceforward would not be able to take a step without consulting the centre and waiting for its decisions. In his opinion, the proposed measure *envisaged* [*visava*] 'surrendering the municipalities in submission to the state government'. Subject, not to a Court of Audit endowed with guarantees, 'but to a bureaucratic organisation of some government office', the municipalities would be 'ycked to the wagon of power'. And he concluded: 'The expression — municipal autonomy — is left, but its content has been removed. We have taken the kernel and left the shell.'[78] Many other deputies supported the idea of a Court of Audit, either because they were against the existence of the proposed departments, or because they opposed their supervisory function. And others declared that they would vote against the departments.[79]

Deputy Augusto Viegas, after saying that, at best, such a technical and supervisory body would in the end be able to dispose of municipal finances as it pleased, and that the provisions of the bill would permit all sorts of extravagances on the part of those administrators who 'wanted to play the political game', concluded his indictment rather lamely: 'I pray to God that I may be wrong and that my gloomy forecasts will be disproved.'[80] These prayers were not answered and the departments of the municipalities, according to the evidence of Orlando M. Carvalho, were soon to serve as a political instrument.[81]

The prohibiting of external loans without prior authorisation by the Senate and the possibility of the state's intervention on the grounds of insolvency are other aspects of the policy of financial control adopted by the Constitution of 16 July.[82]

A contradiction then occurred in the work of the Constituent Assembly of 1934: while seeking, on the one hand, better guarantees for municipal autonomy, on the other, consciously or not, it allowed the states, through the departments of the municipalities, to exercise administrative and political tutelage over the districts.

IX. The decline of the municipality under the regime of 1937

The Constituent Assembly of 1937 was more coherent, because it was unequivocally against municipal power. Not only were the departments of the municipalities retained, but municipal revenue was reduced and the principle of the elective nature of the office of prefect was suppressed. The ideas put forward for more than fifteen years by Professor Francisco Campos were embodied in the Constitutional Charter of which he was the principal author.

Relatively speaking, however, in the period of the *Estado Novo*, what the observer must examine is not the letter of the Constitution. This was never applied in those areas in which the elective or representative principle was at issue, though it was on these that the constitutional organisation of the states depended. As far as the states and municipalities were concerned what was important in this period was the system, intended as a provisional one, established by Decree–Law No. 1202 of 8 April 1939, partially altered by Decree–Law No. 5511 of 21 May 1943. Here was the culmination of the system of tutelage. The municipality continued to be deprived of any local representative or pseudo-representative body of any kind (since it did not retain even the consultative councils of discretionary government which followed the revolution of 1930), and its administration was still subject to a system of tight control that was both preventative and corrective. Besides the departments of the municipalities, which remained, Decree–Law No. 1202 established, in each state, an administrative department, designed to give help to state governments and municipalities and to exercise control over them. Without doubt, this department had a certain administrative value especially when it contained individuals with administrative experience and technical competence. Its principal task was to give prior approval to the legal decrees of the interventor and the prefects,[83] and in this it exercised control in matters of legality, appropriateness and convenience. This body, whose members were nominated by the President of the Republic, should have functioned principally as an instrument counterbalancing the interventor.[84] In practice, however, the nominations were made on the basis of the interventor's suggestions, and therefore the department became not the interventor's overseer, but his ally.

After Decree–Law No. 1202, a Commission for the Study of State Affairs, responsible to the Minister of Justice and nominated by the President of the Republic, was set up in the Federal Capital. As the legislation in question required the prior approval of the head of state for many legislative and administrative measures concerning the states and the municipalities,[85] it was precisely this body whose function it was to advise on the legality, appropriateness and convenience of such measures. The responsible minister then conveyed its findings and his own views to the President for the latter's consideration.[86] On the other hand the same legal decree established the interventor as the arbiter of municipal acts. His decisions and acts originating from the state authorities were, in their turn, subject to the final approval of the President.[87] It was the administrative department of the state which reviewed municipal acts, while this body and the Commission for the Study of State Affairs (C.E.N.E.) prepared the items which were subject to presidential review.

In a regime whose aim was to place unshakeable power in the hands of the head of government, this hierarchical organisation is no surprise. By means of it, homely acts of municipal administration, after a long journey, were, in the final analysis, decided by presidential despatch. The *Estado Novo*'s preoccupation with political centralisation, to the point that it never attempted to give any real life to the representative machinery set up by the Charter of 10 November, was so evident that the complete nullification of municipal autonomy in this period requires no other explanation.[88]

Thus, thanks to notorious political reasons, the old and persistent process of erosion of municipal autonomy was noticeably accelerated in this period. There were only two brief and insignificant pauses in the process, at the beginning of the Republic and under the Constitution of 1934.

X. The Constitution of 1946: technical assistance to the municipalities and supervision of their finances

This was the panorama which presented itself to the Constituent Assembly of 1946, which showed a greater preoccupation with the fate of the municipalities than the Second Republic had done. Its 'compassion for the municipalities' was manifested chiefly in the solution proposed for the problem of tributary status and, in the main, followed in the steps of the previous Constituent Assembly. The autonomy of the municipalities was guaranteed: by the election of the prefect[89] and the councillors; by its own administration in matters of its own special interest. It was esteemed that the municipality's special interest lay specifically in its ability to decree and collect its own taxes, to allocate its revenue, and to organise local public services.[90]

Mário Masagão argued in the assembly that the notion of autonomy was restricted to the composition of the municipal government, in other words to its elective nature. The problem of municipal prerogatives, constituting the orbit of special interest, was foreign to the concept of autonomy, which is, by nature, political. This distinction was disputed by several of his colleagues for whom the definition of the municipality's actual sphere of administration was also included in the notion of autonomy.[91] In effect, although it is theoretically possible to distinguish political autonomy from

the orbit of special administration, in practice the two concepts are inseparable if the objective be a relatively independent life for the municipalities.
The municipality can be undermined in two ways: either by the autonomous exercise of minimal prerogatives, or by the restricted exercise of
wide prerogatives. The elected administration would be valueless if it were
impeded in its slightest movements.[92]

The Constitution of 1946 allowed the states to set up special bodies
with the task of providing 'technical assistance' to the municipalities.[93]
The previous Constitution, as we have seen, also empowered these departments to supervise municipal finances. The preliminary draft had designated this task to state Courts of Audit whose members would have held
the privileges of judges of appeal.[94] The first draft transferred this duty to
the municipal chambers, any councillor having the power, in agreed circumstances, to refer to the state Court of Audit, whose members would
not in this instance have special privileges.[95] The revised draft finally
adopted the solution which stood in the definitive text: the supervision of
financial administration, especially the execution of the budget, will be
carried out in the states and the municipalities, 'according to the form laid
down in the state Constitutions'.[96] Hence, the Constituent Assemblies of
the states were left with full powers in the matter of supervision of the
financial arrangements of the municipalities. They were able to entrust it
to the technical assistance bodies themselves, thus ascribing to the latter a
fixed measure of tutelage over the districts. This was all the more so as the
supervision envisaged, according to the terms of the Federal Constitution
itself, included the working of the budget. It is true that municipal autonomy, as textually defined, embraced the allocation of the municipality's
own revenues, and that the Constitution of 1934 had also stated this, but
none of this was enough to prevent the departments of the municipalities,
by using the pretext of *supervision* enshrined in another constitutional
directive, from becoming deeply involved in the financial management of
the municipalities.

Apart from this, the municipalities' share of the taxes derived from
petrol, oil or gases, minerals and electricity, had to be used for 'purposes
established by federal law'. The Constitution also demanded that at least
half the municipalities' quota of tax revenue had to be spent 'on services
of a rural kind'.[97] There were many other potential sources of interference
in the financial life of the municipalities, and already the application of
these revenue supplements to specific projects, required federal direction
and eventually the imposition of sanctions in cases of transgression. All
this was capable of giving rise to an irksome system of supervision.[98]

Consequently, the establishment of new constitutional rules could, in the future, restore in large measure the imperial system of tutelage.

XI. Intervention of the State in the economy; its effect on municipal powers

It is clear, beyond doubt, that the conditions of modern life are not very favourable to the increase of municipal powers, or, in other words, that they are more favourable to the extension of centralised power. A growing number of administrative problems require joint solution, if not by the whole country or by a whole state, at least by a group of municipalities, which could theoretically belong to different states. Roads, for example, are already a national problem and responsibility for them will increasingly be taken away from the municipalities. Problems of sanitation too are also assuming this character. At the rate at which we are extending our use of electricity, the municipalities will not be able to undertake, individually, the construction of large electric plants, or meet the cost of the powerful generators which such a service would entail. Consequently, in the proportion in which these and other responsibilities, either for public convenience or through technical necessity, are centralised, corresponding sections of authority will be taken away from the municipalities. In the majority of cases this will be done by their own decision and in their own interest. Where this agreement is lacking, however, the interpretation of the implicit powers of the Union and the states could eventually offer the necessary theoretical solution. The association of the municipalities in a para-state organisation with responsibility for common public services,[99] is a reaction to this prescience.[100]

It is not entirely new, this idea of instituting a *regional* organisation between the municipality and the state, but attempts in this direction have always failed in the past.[101] It may be inconvenient to set up this intermediate authority with fixed territorial jurisdiction for two reasons: in the first place, the municipalities which share a common interest, may belong to more than one state. In the second place, an area which constitutes a *region* for the purposes, shall we say, of exploiting hydro-electric resources, may not necessarily be the same with an interest in other administrative problems like navigation, roads, soil conservation, re-afforestation, etc.

The institution of special agencies, with a legal character of their own, and having administrative and financial authority, seems to be the best solution and the one that will probably be adopted in Brazil. It is, moreover, the form best able to conciliate the convenience of centralising certain public services with the autonomous aspirations of the municipalities, since these would participate in the composition or selection of the four directors of the regional organisation.

On the other hand, as public intervention in economic matters increases, the municipality could acquire new powers in areas which have traditionally been the preserve of the private individual. The colonial chambers very often exercised control over the local economy. In the modern world, however, this intervention depends on a plan which goes beyond the limits of the municipality or the state, and which, for this very reason, has to remain a federal responsibility.

Under the *Estado Novo*, the machinery for public intervention in the economy more or less followed the administrative structure: while federal power controlled organisations operating on a federal basis, the states were entrusted with the control of state bodies, and finally, the municipal authority (the prefect acting individually or assisted by a commission) fulfilled this function locally. In a phase like this, with power clearly organised along hierarchical lines, the solution was perfectly normal, since the system adopted to facilitate economic intervention strengthened the powers of the interventors, i.e. the federal government's deputies, at the same time reinforcing the powers of the prefects, agents of the state government. Intervention in the economy thus operated as a considerable source of power, which helped to consolidate the political machine in the three spheres — federal, state and municipal.[102]

But is it reasonable to suppose that things will continue in the same way, when political groups in power in the states are opposed to the federal government, or ruling groups in the municipalities opposed to the state government? In such an emergency, which has not yet occurred, it would seem to be a more realistic attitude to allow the federal government to institute, in critical states, bodies designated to execute its economic plans, and these bodies (or state governments, as the case may be) should do the same in relation to municipalities controlled by the opposition. In these hypothetical cases the modern interventionist tendency would have the opposite result to that shown earlier: the presence in the municipality of extra-local authorities with such important powers as, for example, the ability to intervene in the economic activity of ordinary citizens, would doubtless create serious embarrassment, if not administratively, at least politically, for the local agencies of government.

An increase in municipal revenue can contribute effectively to the independence of their administration, but it is probable that economic strengthening of the municipalities will not be matched by a similar reinforcement of its political autonomy. Without financial stability the municipality cannot have political independence, but the first does not necessarily involve the second, because it can arrive with its own system of control. And this system, if not favoured by the Constitution of 18 September, seems, at the very least, to be permitted by it.

XII. Municipal authority and federal authority

In the twilight of the monarchy, the Cabinet of Ouro Prêto announced municipal reform as an important part of its programme, the President of the Council having studied the matter in advance. This manifestation of governmental intentions was very much neglected[103] but it is certain that the concern of the old liberal was to revitalise the monarchy by strengthening the municipalities; which is the same as saying, by weakening the provinces.[104] Yet, judging by his work of 1882, it seems unlikely that he would have obtained this result. Nevertheless, whatever new perspectives were opened up as a result of Ouro Prêto's policies, his position confirms the suspicion that the federalist movement in Brazil,[105] from the time of the concessions made to it by the Additional Act, would not be based on the political robustness of the municipalities; on the contrary, larger units would consolidate themselves at the expense of municipal autonomy, an effective expedient for creating political homogeneity in the province and, later, in the state.[106]

The process of the concentration of power in Brazil, both at the national and at the provincial or state levels, was accomplished through the weakening of the municipality. There is not the slightest contradiction in this process. It is well known that central power under the monarchy, through its practice of relating to the municipalities only by means of tutelage, based its political force on the strong authoritarian power wielded by the provincial presidents, the Crown's personal deputies. Consequently, the central power itself was consolidated through a system of the concentration of provincial power, that is, by the undermining of the municipalities. It is therefore not strange that the provinces and, later, the states, when they were seeking to combine forces to oppose the centre, continued to employ the same process. Moreover, the tutelage of the municipality had the weight of tradition on its side.

The later history of the Federal Republic fully illustrates this interpretation. In place of the all-powerful president of the province, the all-powerful governor of the state was installed. Campos Sales was not slow to inaugurate the so-called 'politics of the governors', which was more a recognition of a *fait accompli* than an invention of his political talent. The process of the concentration of power in the orbit of the state continued in exactly the same manner as it had in the provincial sphere during the Empire; but, as the election of a state governor did not depend wholly on the wishes of the centre, as the nomination of the provincial president had in the past, the head of the federal government had only two alternatives: he either had to declare war on the ruling factions in the states or come to some agreement with them in a system of compromise, which would simultaneously consolidate the federal government and the governments of the states.[107]

In order for the process to operate on the two levels, the victim inevitably had to be the municipality, sacrificed as far as its autonomy was concerned. In Brazil the federal executive was as much in favour of the concentration of power in the states at the expense of the municipalities as were the legislature and the judiciary. Moreover, the simple idea that, left to themselves, the municipalities would fall into the hands of local oligarchies who, if opposed, would maintain their position by subornation and violence – led naturally to the conclusion that it was necessary to give the state the means of obviating that possibility. Yet, a fact that usually passes unnoticed is that the state government did not employ these instruments against its friends, but only against its opponents.

The reason has already been given in the first chapter: the majority of the rural electorate – which comprises a majority of the total electorate – is completely ignorant, and depends on the landowners, whose political orientation it follows. Consequently the political reflection of our agrarian system, the party chiefs (including the government which controls the official party), had to reach an understanding with the landowners, through the local political chiefs. And this understanding led to the *coronelista* type of compromise between the state governments and the municipalities, similar to the political compromise established between the Union and the states. Hence, just as the 'politics of the governors' was dominant in state–federal relations, so what by analogy we may call the 'politics of the *coronéis*' dominated state–municipal relations. Through the compromise characteristic of the system, the local chiefs gave prominence to the electoral policy of the governors and received from them the necessary support for the setting up of municipal oligarchies. In order to ensure that it was the governors rather than the *coronéis* who derived more advantage from this exchange of services, the technico-legal method which proved most adequate was precisely the restriction of the autonomy of the districts.

Thus it becomes clear how our idealistic jurists, who claimed to be limiting the power of the municipalities to prevent the rise of local oligarchies, succeeded only in giving the governors the means by which they could set up those very oligarchies to their own advantage. Thus oligarchies at the state level were formed, and these, in turn, led to the establishment of that other system of compromise — between the states and the Union — known in our history as the 'politics of the governors'. In this wider political arrangement, the instruments which best ensured the pre-eminence of the President of the Republic, were, in the field of finance, subsidies from the Union, designed to supplement the meagre revenues of the states, and in the political field, the verification of powers (the *degola* — literally decapitation') which could maintain or expel from the Federal Congress, senators or deputies whom fraud or the local bosses deemed to have been elected. One and the other — the compromise of the governors with the *coronéis* and the compromise of presidents with the governors — were founded on the lack of awareness of the rural electorate and, by reason of this, on the type of agrarian structure predominant in Brazil.

It is clear, however, that the 'politics of the *coronéis*' was much more effective in strengthening the power of the states than the 'politics of the governors' was in reinforcing federal power. In state–federal relations, although the President had at his disposal many much blander and generally efficacious methods of convincing less accommodating governors of reciprocity, the 'final solution' for nonconformity would be federal intervention and this carried with it at least the possibility of armed conflict. It would not always be convenient for the head of state to face the possible national consequences of this measure.

Such dangers did not exist in the same proportion in state–municipal relations. When persuasive methods failed — nominations, favours, loans, public works — the police detachment, under the command of an efficient chief, could with relative ease convince the recalcitrant *coronéis*; in such an event, the wholehearted support of the other political faction in the municipality would certainly be forthcoming. Such a process of persuasion, often backed up by violence, did not have the same repercussions at state level, as intervention in the states by the federal government might have at national level, if only because the importance of the municipality *vis-à-vis* the state is not comparable to that of the state relative to the Union.

The preceding considerations seem to prove conclusively that federation in Brazil developed at the expense of the municipal ideal: the price paid was the systematic undermining of the municipality, in spite of an abundant adulatory literature not in itself enough to ease this misfortune.

3. The elective principle in municipal administration

I. The elective principle in the municipal chambers of the colonial period

The elective principle has traditionally been much stronger in Brazil with respect to the municipal chamber than to the office of prefect. The importance of the chamber increased in the colonial and imperial periods, when there was no local executive existing as a separate and autonomous body.[1] In the republican phase, with the presence of the prefect (or equivalent official of a different name), this importance diminished, but even so, political and ideological controversies raged over the question of the supervision of the powers of the councillors, a problem inseparable from the elective issue.[2]

According to section 67 of book I of the Phillipine Ordinances, the elective principle applied to the offices of the two ordinary judges, the three councillors, the attorney, the treasurer (when there was one) and the clerk.[3] Other functionaries — parish judges, inspectors, guards, etc — were nominated by the chamber.[4]

The mandate of those elected lasted only for a year, but elections were held every three years, all the officials who would serve in three consecutive years being elected at the same time. According to the ordinance quoted, the election was indirect and took place on the eighth day of Christmas in the last year of the triennium. In the first instance a vote was taken, at a meeting presided over by the oldest judge, of 'worthy men and members of the public', and those officials whose term of office was about to expire.

In spite of the expression 'worthy men and members of the public', there is no question here, as one might suppose, of universal suffrage. On the contrary, the electorate in the first ballot for the chambers was considerably restricted, since those considered to be 'worthy men' were persons who had already held office in the municipality or who 'were accustomed to play a part in the government' of the area. Cândido Mendes observed, moreover, that the Portuguese legislator employed the expression 'worthy men' with a different meaning in different places,[5] and it is difficult to ascertain how many actually voted, even in cases where the process of choosing the electors for a first election (when a locality had been created *vila*)[6] was being carried out. The process of election was described in detail in the Ordinances.

When the electors of the first ballot had met, each of them, in secret, informed the judge (and the clerk noted down) of the names of six persons capable of serving as electors in the second ballot. The shortlist was compiled by the judges and the councillors, comprising the six who had received the most votes.

The six electors of the second ballot, after swearing that they would choose for the district's official posts the 'most appropriate' persons and that they would keep their names secret, were separated by the judge into three groups of two, who might not be in-laws, or relations up to the fourth degree of kinship laid down by canon law. Each of the pairs, without communication with the others, composed its list of those who should occupy the elective offices in the three following years, in other words: six names of judges, nine of councillors, three of clerks, etc.

The lists were handed to the oldest judge and he, after swearing publicly to keep the result of the balloting secret, had to make the selection from the second round of voting and draw up the list of those elected (those with the most votes) to each office. Besides this list, the judge drew up a ballot-sheet for each office, and each sheet contained the names of those who would serve in each of the three years. 'And to allow them to work together' — as was the case of the councillors (three in each year) and the judges (two) — the law required the judge that he should place together 'the most suitable, for example those who were not related, and also the most practised with those who were not quite so capable, having regard to the abilities and habits of each one, for the better government of the district.'

The ballot-sheets were collected in a sack 'with as many compartments', says the text, 'as there are offices, and in each compartment shall be placed the title of each office, and in it shall be put the ballot-sheets of that office'. The sack was kept in a chest with three keys each one of which was kept by one of the councillors of the previous year. On the appropriate day, in public, the chest was opened, 'a boy of seven years or under' drew out a sheet from each one of the compartments relating to the various offices, and in that year those whose names were on the ballot-sheets served in the offices.[7]

In case of death, absence or other impediment in the way of any of those elected, the so-called *cap* election took place: the officials of the chamber, assembled with 'the worthy men whose names are wont to appear on the ballot-sheet', chose the substitute by a majority of votes.[8]

The principle of the elective nature of the chambers fitted in, for the most part, with what was convenient for the Crown, and the Ordinances themselves were concerned to prevent those elected from refusing the mandate which was frequently seen as a duty.[9] On the other hand, Portugal wanted to ensure that the elected chambers did not become stronger than was desirable. Thus the Ordinances prohibited re-election, generally for three years and, where the number of people capable of holding office was small, for a year only.[10] Ordinary judges were not allowed to exercise their functions before obtaining their *letter of employment*, that is to say, before the election was confirmed by the competent authority.[11] In connection with the restrictions imposed on the chambers, it is important to mention that one of the most effective ways, seized upon by the king when he undertook the task of bringing his sulky colonists to heel, was the nomination of visiting judges — delegates of the Crown — whose presence involved the lowering of the status of the two ordinary judges.[12] It must be observed, moreover, that later, when the Court was installed in Brazil, the selection for the ballot-sheet was abolished when there was a visiting judge. In places where this office existed, according to Cândido Mendes who cites directives of 1815, 1817 and 1820, once the lists of six electors had been made up, the pruned version was sent to the Royal Office of Despatch and there the functionaries, who had to serve for each year, were chosen.[13]

We must be forgiven for not giving a detailed examination of the text of more general laws. The absolutist system under which we lived gave the monarch complete freedom to intervene in municipal life, as he saw fit, or to authorise his agents to do so.[14]

II. In the Empire and in the Republic

The elective nature of the municipal chamber was maintained in the Constitution of the Empire and, subsequently, in Law No. 1 of October 1828. In the opinion of Castro Nunes, it is here that 'the truly Brazilian phase of the municipal history of Brazil' begins.[15] In this period we see the chambers already stripped of their former power and reduced to 'merely administrative bodies', but still being formed as the result of the citizens' votes.

Seven councillors in the towns and nine in the cities[16] comprised the chambers, which functioned under the presidency of the councillor who had received the most votes. In order to vote in the election for councillors, a person had to fulfil the requirements set out in Articles 91 and 92 of the Constitution. All those who could vote and who had lived in the district for at least two years, were eligible for election.[17] The mandate lasted four years.

The law of 1828 regulated the form of the election for councillors, providing for a system of a complete list drawn up on the basis of the number of votes received by each candidate, the shortlist being compiled by the chamber of the town or city in question. The electoral law of 1846 which modified the composition of the parochial boards, gave them the right of compiling the shortlist, with the chamber having the final word after consulting the records.[18] The electoral law of 1875 which instituted the system of the limited vote, also applied it to municipal elections: in municipalities with nine councillors, the voter put forward six names; in those of seven, he put forward five. The votes were checked by the parochial board itself, a fact which expedited matters in municipalities in which there was only one parish; in municipalities with more than one, the final check was carried out by the chamber basing itself on the records of the parochial boards. In cases of electoral dispute, it fell to the district judge to pronounce on the validity or otherwise of the election, with any voter having the right of appeal to the District Court of Appeal if the election was approved; in cases where the contest was annulled the appeal was obligatory and had a suspensive effect. The law also required, as a qualification of elegibility for the chamber, that the candidate meet the conditions necessary in the case of electors, as well as the residence qualification, i.e. more than two years' residence in the municipality.[19] New alterations arose with the *Lei Saraiva* of 1881, which established district elections throughout the country, increasing the number of electors by registration. Any citizen who fulfilled the requirements for registration (the existing requirement concerning length of residence in the municipality was maintained), could be elected councillor. Each voting paper would bear a single name, and those who reached the electoral quotient would be considered elected; in places where these conditions could not be met, there was a second ballot which proceeded according to special rules. In the municipalities of the Court, in provincial capitals and a few other cities, the re-election of councillors was only allowed when four years had elapsed from the end of the four year period in which they had served. The electoral boards continued to be responsible for the counting of votes, and the final shortlist remained within the competence of the chamber. The district judge, with recourse to the Court of Appeal, continued to exercise the function of determining the validity or otherwise of the election, including the checking of votes, and of making decisions on all questions related to these matters.

The elective nature of the chamber was of importance in provincial and general elections, because, traditionally, the electoral laws granted it some participation in these wider elections.[20] At best, the precarious position of the municipality in the range of administrative institutions existing under the Empire, considerably diminished the scope of the measure. In spite of this, there was no delay in seizing upon a recourse which was directly offensive to this basic principle of municipal autonomy. Article 5, para. 8 of the law of 3 October 1834, permitted provincial presidents to suspend 'any employees', in cases where such action was indicated, and the organs of the central government took this prerogative as referring to councillors as well, given that the text did not exempt any class of employees. A provincial law of Paraíba do Norte, or 23 October 1840, which declared that the contrary was true, was held to be an infringement of the Constitution, and was annulled by the General Assembly by the law of 9 November 1841.[21] It was, as we can see, a Caesarist interpretation, which subordinated the exercise of the municipalities' elective mandate to an authority nominated by the Emperor, and whose primary function was frequently nothing more than to win general elections for the governing party.

In the early years of the Republic, several states conferred the right to vote in municipal elections on strangers to the district, some states even maintaining that such individuals were themselves eligible for election. The condition that was generally imposed was that of residence in the municipality for a fixed length of time.[22] This liberality was gradually curtailed with the passage of time, but Castro Nunes, in a work of 1922, confirmed the maintenance in some states of the right of outsiders to vote in municipal elections.[23]

While the Constitution of 1891 was in force, no decision was reached as to a uniform title for the deliberative body in municipal administration, a matter which lay in the competence of the state government: *Intendancy*, *Council*, *Chamber* were the names which were chosen. Its elective nature was not in dispute, this had always been part of the Brazilian tradition, but some states deprived or attempted to deprive the municipal regime of certain areas of its territory. In Pará, for example, districts [*circunscricões*] were created which were administered by a delegate nominated by the governor, and which were raised, either totally or partially, to the status of municipalities, the determining factor being their ability to conform to certain requirements. In Minas, a law of 1897 gave the capital a special form of government, entrusting the deliberative function to the president of the state and the executive ones to the prefect who was nominated by the president. This system, known as the system of the *prefectures*, was extended to the hydro-mineral establishments by the constitutional reform of 1903, which created, alongside the prefect, an elected council, whose deliberations were later (1918) subject to the prefect's veto. The council had no say in the management of help or loans furnished by the state. The Bill for Constitutional Reform of 1920 proposed, unsuccessfully, that the state legislature should be empowered to extend the prefectoral system to any other municipalities or to all of them. In São Paulo, on the occasion of the reform of 1911, it was also mooted that a special administration be established for certain areas to be expropriated by the state. In the state of Rio, there was also an attempt to create, for the capital, a system which would not be a municipal one.[24] In Paraíba, Epitácio Pessoa, too, had the idea of 'Distinguishing from the municipality of the capital, the area covered by the city itself and any other territory which the assembly might consider necessary, and thus form a special district administered exclusively by state authorities', but he had doubts 'as to whether the measure was constitutional.' Levi Carneiro, who gives this information, compared such attempts to the behaviour of a man who, 'in Holy Week, in order not to deprive himself of meat, christens it with the name of some fish'.[25] The power to create 'special forms of government' for designated municipalities, which was contained in the proposal for constitutional reform of 1926, could eventually imply the suppression of the municipal chamber.

Yet, here and there, certain differences of detail could be observed. The Constitution of the state of Rio, for example, established in each municipality: the *municipal chamber*, consisting of councillors; the *district assemblies*, composed of the district councillor, the first justice of the peace, and of the person nearest in votes to the last justice of the peace, and the *municipal assembly*, which brought together representatives from the chamber, the district assemblies and the justices of the peace. In Minas, the law of 1891 relating to the municipalities created, besides the *municipal chamber*, the *district councils* (abolished in 1903), composed of elected councillors, and the *municipal assembly* (also abolished later), which brought together members of the other two bodies and a certain number of their major figures. Among other functions, the assembly had to review the accounts of the chamber and the council. A difference worth noting was to be found in the Constitution of the state of Goias, where the electorate was allowed to withdraw the mandate of any councillor who proved himself to be unworthy of its trust.

The Federal Constitutions of 1934, 1937 and 1946 fully guaranteed the elective principle with respect to the municipal chambers.[26]

III. Creation of the municipal executive in Brazil

We have not always had a municipal official with centralised executive functions, although during the Empire certain provinces had created one through laws whose provisions remained in force only a short time, and various other attempts were made to incorporate into the general legislation the figure of a prefect or a local administrator.

In the confusion of functions characteristic of the colonial period[27] (the king, at the top of the hierarchy, accumulated in his person all the powers of the state) almost all the municipal authorities had prerogatives of a normative, executive and judicial nature. The ordinary judge in office (or, an outside judge, where there was one) presided at the meetings of the chamber — *vereações* or *vereanças* — but this prerogative did not make the judge in question chief of the municipal executive, nor did the spirit of the times conceive of uniting the executive functions in a separate office.

The Constitutional Bill which was discussed and voted upon in the ill-fated Constituent Assembly of 1823, divided the country for administrative purposes into regions [*comarcas*], districts [*distritos*], and smaller areas [*têrmos*]. In each of the smaller areas there was to be an administration, and a chief executive known as a *decurion*, who was not allowed to exercise any judicial function. It was he who presided over the 'municipal assembly or the chamber of the area', in which was to reside 'all the economic and municipal authority'.[28]

The Constitution of 1824, having created elective chambers in all existing cities and towns and in any still to be created, enjoined on them 'the economic and municipal government of the said cities and towns', and determined that the councillor who had received the most votes should be president.[29] It was not specified that it was to this individual that the exercise of executive functions in the municipal orbit, would fall. On the contrary, the creation of this post simply lent greater lustre to the chamber as the responsible body. The law of 1828 did not, therefore, institute a municipal executive official, but left these functions to be performed by the chamber and its agents. The process employed was, at times, the creating of committees drawn from inside the chamber, among whom executive functions were shared. At other times, the executive power was delegated to various subordinate functionaries of the municipality, notably the revenue officers.[30]

The bill of 1831 which contained authorisation for constitutional reform, provided for the creation of a municipal administrator, but the item was not retained in the law of 12 October 1832, which the bill became, nor did the Constitutional Amendments, adopted in 1834, treat the matter.

Immediately following the Additional Act, several provinces, beginning with São Paulo, created the post of prefect (some also that of sub-prefect), with executive and police functions, but the General Assembly later came to regard the innovation as unconstitutional.[31] After the laws of the prefects, many bills presented to the General Assembly proposed unsuccessfully, the creation of a municipal executive for the whole country.[32]

Under the regime of 1891, in all the states certain executive functions were distinguished as falling, in some measure, to the president of the chamber himself. In the great majority of the federated units, there was a special executive post whose name varied: *prefect, intendant, superintendent, executive agent.*[33] The matter was left to the discretion of the state Constitutions because the federal one had omitted it. But all subsequent federal Constitutions referred expressly to the prefect.

IV. Elected and nominated prefects under the regime of 1891

The problem of whether or not the municipal executive should be elected assumed great theoretical and practical importance during the First Republic, owing to the frequent violation of the elective principle in various states. Already in the Constituent Assembly, in spite of the fact that, by general consent, municipal autonomy was considered inherent in the republican system, the conceptualisation of it provoked controversy, a formula favourable to the greater power of the states to regulate municipal organisation, being the one that finally prevailed. Under the Constitution of 1891, the invocation of parliamentary proceedings was one of the principal arguments resorted to by all those who, through interest or conviction, defended the right of state governments to impose limits on the autonomy of the municipalities.

Agenor de Roure summarised the debates which then ensued.[34] The bill of the provisional government, following that of the Constitutional Commission, demanded the inclusion in the text of the Constitution of the principle of the elective nature of local administration, as essential to the running of the municipalities, with a guarantee that this principle could not be overruled by the states. The Commission of 21 upheld this demand. But the representations of the Positivist Apostolate, maintaining that this principle should be left to the judgement of the state assemblies, reopened the question in the plenary session.

A pro-state faction was then established and the thinking of this group was embodied in the amendment of the Lauro Sodré, which became Article 68 of the Constitution. This proposal was based on the concept that the prerogatives of the states should not be restricted by the Federal Constitution even if these limitations, as was indeed the case, were intended to guarantee municipal autonomy against the possible dictatorship of the state assemblies. In the words of Nina Ribeiro who, with others, also subscribed to it, the amendment preserved 'the principle of municipal autonomy' and left the states with 'complete freedom to organise them as they judged most convenient to their special interests'.[35]

The other faction favourable to the basic idea of the government's bill feared that the unrestricted freedom of the states in this matter could prejudice the autonomy of the municipalities. Moreover, in his amendment, Casemiro Júnior was asking for the municipalities to be protected from interference by the state government in organising their budgets and in the management of their affairs. He was hoping, through this, to prevent states from running the municipalities 'as in the time of the monarchy, when their budgets could not be passed except with the approval of the provincial assemblies'.[36] Meira de Vasconcelos also pleaded for the inclusion in the federal text of some principles of municipal organisation among which should be that of the elective nature of their administrations.[37] Pinheiro Guedes, who introduced a complete substitute for the government's bill, also included in the text the elective nature of the municipal chamber — divided into two parts, 'one supervisory the other executive' — with the object of making this principle legally binding on the states.[38] 'This was not done', writes Agenor de Roure in his work of 1920, 'and the states are nominating governments for the municipalities.'

In reality once Lauro Sodré's amendment, which left it to the judgement of the states to define what was meant by the 'special interest' of the municipalities, had been passed, the states set about restricting the elective principle with respect to local administrations. Some withdrew the principle only in the case of the municipalities of capital cities, whose prefects were then simply nominated; others extended the principle of the nomination of the prefect to those municipalities in which there were hydro-mineral establishments, or works and services which were the responsibility of the state; others, finally, did not hesitate to make all prefectures posts to be directly nominated by the state government.[39]

Other authors have called attention to this change of attitude on the part of state politicians who were not slow to reduce to very modest limits the liberalism of the early days of republicanism.[40] Rui Barbosa condemned this tendency with the vigour characteristic of his polemic style: 'in establishing our present system', he said, 'those loyal to the new democracy were anxious to see all its hopes realised, when the autonomy of the municipalities was included in the Charter of 1891 in the serious, liberal and elegant formula of Article 68. But only time could submit to the real test, the sincerity of the patriarchy and its descendants. When men of orthodox views began to waver, Article 68 withered, and from its text, squeezed to a pulp in the hands of the regenerators, there emerged this clumsy product, this child of reaction, this sorry outcome of political usury: the nomination of the executive authority of the municipalities by the governments of the states.'[41]

In the constitutional reforms of 1926, the government tried, without ultimate success, to regulate the problem of the elective nature of the municipal administration, permitting the states 'to create a special type of administration for the municipality which was the state capital or an important seaport and those which were sanitary stations and required special works for this purpose'.[42]

The problem of the electivity of the municipal administration was discussed in the Federal Supreme Court at various times. There, Pedro Lessa, at first almost isolated, finished by leading a faction, at times a majority one, which maintained that the nominating of prefects was unconstitutional. It can not be said, however, that this legal wisdom prevailed, since the latest pronouncements of our highest Court on the matter have been contradictory.

V. Discussion of the problem in the Constituent Assembly of 1933–4

The Constituent Assembly of the Second Republic, in contrast to the period of the provisional government in which all prefects were directly nominated by the interventors,[44] adopted the elective principle as binding on the states, allowing, however, for the executive of the municipality to be chosen either by direct election, or by the vote of the councillors. The Constitution of 1934 still allowed, as an exception, that the states could place nominated prefects in the municipalities of the state capitals and in those which had hydro-mineral establishments.[45] This proposal provoked heated debates during the parliamentary discussion as we shall show later, but it was finally approved by 156 votes to 47. A request that members vote by name, put forward by Deputies Kerginaldo Cavalcânti and Leandro Maciel, was defeated along the way.[46] As a result of the controversies to which these points gave rise, several deputies declared which way they had voted after the announcement of the result. This evident concern to free themselves of responsibility, already revealed in the request that members vote by name, is further proof that the matter, far from being a simple administrative question, was loaded with political interest.

The preliminary draft of the Constitution, drawn up by a committee nominated by the provisional government and which had proposed several modifications in our municipal system, determined that local executive power should be exercised by a prefect, elected by equal suffrage, directly and by secret ballot.[47] It also proposed that the municipalities of the state capitals, and those which had revenues in excess of 2000 *contos* and whose urban centres had more than 50,000 inhabitants, should be organised by means of a special bill, which would be drawn up in accordance with general principles established by the legislative assemblies of the states and which would be approved by local referenda. In the carrying out of this precept, the general principle of the electivity of the prefect could possibly suffer restrictions, although this was not the most probable outcome, given the concern shown for consulting with the electors.

Of the amendments proposed to the preliminary draft concerning the investiture of the local administration (the point which interests us now), two deserve special attention: (I) that of Deputy Gabriel Passos, also supported by Negrão de Lima, who wanted to leave the whole problem of municipal autonomy to the discretion of the state assemblies, including the composition and investiture of local government, but employing a much wider formula than that of the Constitution of 1891;[48] (II) that of the delegation from São Paulo whose ideas were closer to the proposals which finally figured in the text of the Constitution. These deputies, under the banner of 'A United São Paulo', proposed: (a) direct election of the municipal chamber; (b) election of the prefect, either direct, or by the councillors; (c) power for the states to establish 'a different system' (including if need be, the suppression of the chamber) in municipalities which were the seat of government, or which contained weather stations or hydro-mineral establishments.[49]

The deputy who drafted the motion, Cunha Melo, while agreeing that 'the elective nature of their executive and legislative authorities' should be included in the constitutional definition of the autonomy of the municipalities, admitted exceptions to the principle, in some ways broader than the proposals of the São Paulo amendment. In his own words, these exceptions would apply in those cases in which 'there being the possibility of a collision, a clash between municipal and state interests, the latter must prevail'. The Constitutional Commission adopted his suggestion with a few minor changes.[50]

A similar innovation, which did not form part of the government's preliminary draft, gave rise to many opposing amendments and to an abundant flow of oratory, which was not completely successful. While some proposed, purely and simply, the suppression of the precept, others asked for a certain tempering of the excessively liberal model contained in the proposition. Cunha Melo who had himself supported greater restrictions to the elective principle, was to say later, in the second reading, that the Commission's proposal had considered 'the choice of their authorities the special business of the municipalities', but 'subsequently established so many exceptions that it annulled that power, and converted it into a utopian ideal . . . a power which should be considered a necessary element of municipal autonomy'.[51]

Amendment No. 1945, one of those known as a 'co-ordinated' or 'large delegation' one, guaranteed majority support for the text of Article 12, para. 1, which reduced the states' ability to nominate prefects to two cases: state capitals and hydro-mineral establishments. This proposal was accepted by the official drafter,[52] and, with no change of wording, became para. 1 of Article 13 of the Constitution of 16 July.

VI. Solution adopted by the Constitution of 1946

After the period of the *Estado Novo*, when all prefects were directly nominated by state governments,[53] the Constitution of 1946 re-established the tradition of the elective prefect,[54] spelling out the exceptions in specific terms.

In the first place, it permitted the state Constitutions to nominate prefects in capitals and in municipalities which had natural hydro-mineral establishments developed and maintained by the state or by the Union.[55] The corresponding provision of the Constitution of 16 July was more liberal (from the point of view of the states) because it did not impose any restriction whatever on the nomination of prefects for hydro-mineral stations.

The other exception to the elective principle — which did not exist under the 1934 Constitution — refers to municipalities 'which federal law, acting through the National Security Council, declared military bases or ports of exceptional importance for the external defence of the country'. In such cases, the prefect shall be, obligatorily, nominated by the governor of the state.[56] The definitive text, on the one hand, narrowed the formula of the original draft, because it required that the municipalities in question be of 'exceptional' importance for the 'external defence' of the country;[57] on the other hand, it broadened the first draft, because it did not allow state Constitutions to declare the prefects of such municipalities elective.[58]

In spite of the openly pro-municipal atmosphere of the Constituent Assembly and the long experience of nominated prefects under the *Estado Novo*, there was still no lack of dispute in the assembly on the question of the elective nature of the municipal executive.[59]

VII. The judiciary and municipal elections under the Republic

Under the regime of 1891 the qualifying requirements, the conditions of eligibility and the electoral process in municipal elections were not uniform throughout the country, because they were matters which lay within the competence of individual states.[60] But in this area, the principal restrictions on municipal autonomy — seen from the quantitative point of view and not by following an ideal model — were represented, on the one hand, by the intrusion of the state into the contest by means of coercion, favours, use of public money and other electoral abuses, and, on the other, by the interference of the dominant political group in the state in the elective composition of municipal bodies through the system of the recognition and verification of powers. Even so, it is true that our municipal elections during the First Republic, were often less corrupt than state or federal ones.[61]

Here it is the second aspect which particularly interests us. That is to say, the prerogative of political or judicial bodies of the state, to provide the solution in cases of duplicates, loss of mandate, verification of powers and other incidents relating to the composition of the municipal administration.

According to the affirmation of Castro Nunes in 1920, 'the doctrine which claims the intervention of the state in the formation of municipal bodies, or, more precisely, in their elective composition, is incompatible with the autonomy laid down in Article 68 of the Federal Constitution, and has not been upheld either in law or in the courts'.[62] The justification for this intervention was based, in part on the wide terms of reference of the constitutional provision which we have quoted, failing as it did, to define the concept of the special interest of the municipalities, and, in part on the juridical principle according to which municipal autonomy was of an administrative rather than a political nature. This meant that certain matters relating to the composition of municipal bodies were taken to be political and hence reserved by the Constitution for jurisdiction by the states.[63] It was also argued that the confirmation of the powers of deputies and senators by the Houses of the National Congress itself did not present any inconvenience, because in this case they were representatives from various regions, returned by different electors, and had to respect each other's mandates. However, in the municipal orbit, councillors put into office by 'electors of the same district and from the same social groups . . . were naturally impeded in confirming their own powers, in pronouncing on the legitimacy of their own electors and the legal propriety of their mandate'.[64]

The states dealt with the question in different ways. The commonest method, however, was to invest the state legislative assembly, or the state judiciary, with authority to decide on the issues in question. The Supreme Court supported the right of intervention of the state legislature or judiciary in the elective composition of municipal bodies (confirmation of powers and loss of mandate), when this prerogative was given to them by state law.

The ministers Sebatião de Lacerda and Muniz Barreto denied this prerogative to any state body including the judiciary.[65] But there was always a greater preference, in that Court, to give the state judiciary competence in this matter. Pedro Lessa himself, a vigorous defender of municipal autonomy, maintained that 'It is only the judiciary which has the legal right to make decisions on ballot checks and on the confirmation of municipal powers; because the judiciary judges by means of allegation and proof; and, consequently, its decisions cannot be contrary to the declared aims of the municipality in its elections.'[66]

More than once the Supreme Court declared it illegal for the state executive to intervene, since it so clearly became the preoccupation in certain states to strengthen the dominant political faction at the expense of the municipalities. 'The governors of the states', says Castro Nunes, 'have been formally forbidden to intervene in the electoral processes of the municipalities, as this practice, though legally established, is incompatible with the principle of municipal autonomy. They may neither intervene in a reviewing capacity nullifying a councillor's mandate, nor in resolving cases of duplication in chambers, dissolving Councils and appointing substitutes on their sole authority, according to the most frequent arguments which have been submitted to the judgement of our Supreme Court.'[67] Nevertheless the fact that there have been such cases — and many others, certainly, which did not reach so far as the federal judiciary — is valid as evidence of the thinking of some of our pro-state politicians.

Among the reforms of 1926, there was included in the Constitution para 5 of Article 60, which forbade the application of any judicial remedy in cases of, among others, confirmation of powers, recognition, possession, legitimacy and loss of mandate, on the part of members of either the federal or *state* legislature or executive. Although henceforward this text could be invoked to defend the opposite thesis, Levi Carneiro maintained that the constitutional revision did not prevent the intervention of the judiciary in these matters when it was a question of municipal elections. His point of view is substantiated in an exhaustive study of the evolution of Brazilian law on the subject, essential reading for anyone who wants information on the judicial aspects of the problem.

From among the arguments he invoked, we must single out the evidence from parliamentary debate. Among the amendments to the Constitution contained in the government bill, apart from the one which became para. 5 of Article 60, there was another which expressly permitted the state 'to authorise a review of the recognition of the powers of municipal authorities, except for the executive'. The rejection of this amendment, along with many others, was not due to any theoretical opposition to them, but was intended 'to facilitate the passage of more of them, by reducing their number, and concentrating them into fewer Articles'. Thus in the first

instance 44 amendments were withdrawn, and later 27, among this second
batch, one which related to the confirmation of powers of municipal authorities. 'In order to remove any doubt', says Levi Carneiro, 'as to the
reason for the withdrawal – a doubt which contemporaries did not have –
it is enough to consider that these amendments had 112 signatures, that is,
not only the support of the obvious leaders of national policy, but also an
absolute majority in the house.'[68]

The Supreme Court, even after the reform of the Constitution, had
occasion to declare legitimate a judicial review on the matter in question.
It was in the well-known case of Petrópolis, which was judged on 27
January 1928, the decision being confirmed, after some opposition, in the
session of 24 October 1928. Some state tribunals also had occasion to
reach the same decision, as can be seen in Levi Carneiro's detailed work.

The Constitution of 1934 integrated electoral law, created by the electoral code of 1932 which regulated the elections to the Constituent Assembly, into the over-all judicial system, and made the judiciary responsible
for deciding all questions relating to the checking of votes and the accreditation of those elected. The Charter of 1937 did not refer to the electoral
code, but this was restored, without being part of the Constitution, in
Decree–Law No. 7586 of 28 May 1945, and came to be included once
more among the powers of the judiciary by Article 94 of the Constitution
of 1946. Among its prerogatives, according to Article 119, are 'the electoral process, the checking of elections and the accreditation of those
elected'. It is, without doubt, the solution which presents fewest difficulties
from a political point of view, because the judiciary, in principle at least (a
rule which, unhappily, is not always respected), 'judges through allegation
and proof and, consequently, its decisions cannot be contrary to the
declared aims of the municipality in its elections', according to the words
of Pedro Lessa.[69]

VIII. Importance of the municipal executive and of the form of his investiture

Under the Republic, the most sensitive point about municipal autonomy
has been the elective nature of the executive. Around this problem have
raged, in political debates as well as in legal battles, the fiercest disputes on
questions of municipal administration.[70] It is not strange, therefore, that
the opponents of the elective principle should seek to reduce the importance of the prefect (or whatever name the relevant official bears) in the
political life of the municipality.

Levi Carneiro, defending the principle of nomination in his famous monograph, declared that the elective nature of the office of prefect was 'the most decorative aspect of municipal autonomy'. In his opinion, other measures are much more important than this if the municipalities are to be guaranteed a truly autonomous existence.[71] There is, without doubt, a large measure of truth in the observation that the problem of autonomy does not lie solely in the electivity of the prefect. This measure, unaccompanied by others, would be totally innocuous. But all who have lived in rural areas know that the investiture of the prefect by the votes of his fellow citizens, is a question of exceptional importance for local autonomy, because of the decisive role which the prefect plays in almost every aspect of the life of the district.

Another set of arguments is to be found in Francisco Campos, for whom the prefect is, or should be, the pure administrator, the technician, a specialist in the business of directing local public services. With this strictly professional character, stripped of any party-political connection and hence unlikely to support either of the rival factions in the district, the prefect, according to Francisco Campos, could then be nominated by the state government in a perfectly logical manner. Since his selection would not be dependent on local preferences, he would be better able to exercise his technical functions in an unrestrained manner. Besides, in his opinion, the prefect should represent, in the municipality, the general interest of the state, which should take precedence over local interest, and should be in a position to superimpose the general well-being over the ambitions and whims of groups. This impartial mission — a genuine magistrature — could not be satisfactorily undertaken by the prefect when his investiture depends precisely on the preference of party-political groups in the municipality.[72]

These observations on the technical character of the office of prefect, can be said to reflect a high ideal for which it would be worth while striving but which does not correspond to Brazilian reality.[73] Nor is it the case that it is the electoral procedure which has been an obstacle to the selection of good municipal administrators. On the one hand, many elected prefects have shown themselves to be good managers of the public interest and, on the other, nominated prefects have always shown themselves to be, at least in the same proportion as the others, fundamentally political beings. Even when they are strangers to the locality, they are not slow to develop a preference for one of its factions. The faction will then, because of the prefect's position, admit him as its leader and will gather around him in order to share in the advantages of power.[74] The recent example of the restructuring of parties in our country clearly revealed, even to the most unsuspecting eyes, this established national practice. The prefects in office, all nominated, constituted the natural nuclei around which groups of the governing party coalesced. Invariably, or with very rare exceptions, they were the open or hidden leaders of their local directorates. Thanks to this, the governing party enjoyed an unparalleled initial advantage over the others: its structure, which coincided with the politico-administrative organisation, was already established in advance, while its opponents had to start from scratch.

Immediately after 10 November the rule was that the individual who had come to exercise the functions of prefect as a result of elections held under the previous administration, should be chosen to continue in office. The greater part of these were, in fact, maintained in office during the period of the *Estado Novo*. This shows the other side of the observation made earlier. If, on the one hand, nominated prefects generally show themselves to be much more politicians than administrators, on the other, state governments are directed primarily by political and not technical criteria in the nomination of prefects, seeing that they put to good use the great majority of those who formerly had been local political leaders.[75]

To stress the technical and administrative character of the municipal executive in Brazil, however noble the intentions of those who do so, contrasts violently with the day-to-day evidence of the facts. Much less than administrators, prefects in Brazil have been above all political leaders. The prefecture is traditionally, along with the Council and the office of public prosecutor, one of the first steps in a Brazilian political career.

By virtue of his position as political leader, everything or almost everything in the municipality revolves around the prefect. In periods of representative government it is he who controls the majority in the municipal chamber, and in periods of discretionary government he exercises a limited dictatorship even more effective and uniform for the duration.[76] And this is not a phenomenon of the past, but of our time. In that turbulent period when the country was being returned to constitutional rule, when the government of José Linhares was seeking to safeguard the purity of federal elections, an important measure to which it had resort was the replacement of prefects.[77] And since the state elections of 19 January 1947, as was widely reported in the press, the problem of the investiture of prefects has occasioned bitter political disputes not only at the state level but also at the federal one. To cite but two examples, we may recall the cases of São Paulo and Bahia. The mass dismissal of prefects decreed by Governor Ademar de Barros shortly after taking office, and his refusal to reach a compromise with the P.S.D. of São Paulo in order to resolve this enormous problem, caused a political storm whose effect was felt nationally. In Bahia, the nomination of prefects from the U.D.N. in municipalities in which this party had a majority in the elections of 2 December 1945, constituted, as is now a notorious fact, the first step in the approaches between the U.D.N. and the federal government. The tumultuous echoes of this *volte-face* were registered in the records of the chamber, where Bahian deputies of the government party did not hesitate to label such conduct as treason. It would be unnecessary to cite any other episode as further proof that the essentially political nature of the office of prefect is still a living and significant fact in present-day Brazil.[78]

The general tendency among us to consider the prefect as an administrator, pure and simple, is one more symptom of the prestige which we attach to formulas to which Oliveira Viana alluded.[79] As legal theory, inherited from the Empire, teaches us that municipal chambers are merely administrative bodies, so it is concluded that municipal leaders are pure technicians managing the local section of the public estate. Effectively, the law of 1828 laid down that 'the chambers are merely administrative bodies', but this simply means that they had no judicial function, as was the case in colonial times; so much so that the law adds: 'and shall not exercise any litigious jurisdiction'.[80] The prohibiting of political activity on the part of the chambers was contained in another article which forbade them to make 'deliberations and decisions . . . in the name of the people', or 'to divest anyone of office'.[81]

It was always, as is clear, the memory of the colonial experience which coloured these proscriptions. But the fact of deciding that the chambers, as bodies, are merely administrative, does not necessarily imply that the municipal administrator must be purely a technician. What we must confirm is whether the reality of the situation allows the municipal administrator to be the sort of apolitical expert theoretically described. Our history — in colonial, imperial and republican times — replies 'no'; and it is still a matter of 'no' even when we are speaking of nominated prefects, those who, according to the rhetoric of the formula, should only be administrators. Referring to municipal councillors, Deputy Raul Fernandes had this to say in the Constituent Assembly of 1934: 'one of the celebrated Brazilian realities — and this is clear and incontestable — is that the municipal councillor, who is by definition an administrator, cannot cease to be a politician, closely linked to the dominant party, or in exceptional cases, to an opposition party'.[82] What he said about councillors can be applied with better reason to the prefect, who is the central figure in municipal life.

In order to verify this fact of daily observation it is enough to remember that local administration is not the sum total of municipal life. Nor is it its most important aspect. The municipality in Brazil is the basic division in electoral campaigns. On the one hand, rural inhabitants, who form 80% of the national population, are much more effectively subordinate to the municipality than to the state or to the Union, given the political links which state and federal authorities have with municipal leaders; on the other hand, no section of the rural electorate is excluded from the municipal system, which covers the entire territory of Brazil. How then, are we to consider as purely administrative figures, prefects who exercise such a great influence over the mass of people who provide the greatest number of votes in elections?

To pretend, in the face of this reality, that the elective nature of the office of prefect should be obliterated in the interest of the technico-administrative character of the post, or to consider it of little relevance to local autonomy, is to furnish, albeit in good faith, the partisan aspirations of ruling groups in the states with even more efficient weapons. For this reason, the proclaimed anti-state posture of the Charter of 10 November was entirely ineffective: if the system were set up in accordance with the text of the Constitution, where it was declared that prefects should be nominated, the practical result, in this respect, would be the strengthening of the governors and therefore of the states.[83]

Even if we look at the office solely from the administrative point of view, the role of the prefect in municipal administration is such a preponderant one that its exceptional importance for local autonomy cannot be disputed. This was one of the important arguments of Pedro Lessa in his famous polemic in the Federal Supreme Court on this issue. The executive function, in the municipal orbit, is much wider and more effective and therefore of much greater importance than the deliberative function entrusted to the council chamber; consequently, the electivity of the prefect was, in his opinion, a principle inherent in local government, since it was implicit in the constitutional concept of the independence of the municipality in managing affairs of special interest to it.[84] Pedro Lessa did not refer to financial powers by means of which the chamber could exercise effective influence on the government of the area. We must add, however, that the problem was not to know which of the two bodies — the executive or the legislative — had greater powers, but to which of them the effective political control of the municipality belongs. And in this field the prefect, historically, has dominated the chamber. Hence the fundamental importance of the form of his investiture.[85]

Rui Barbosa, defending the autonomy of the Bahian municipalities in the Supreme Court, gave great literary emphasis to the principle of the elected prefect. We cannot resist quoting his beautiful words:

A life which is not one's own, a borrowed life, a life which is not free, is not a life. To live through an outsider, to live through another, to live subject to foreign activity, cannot be called living, it is to stagnate and to rot. Bahia does not live because she has no municipalities. The Bahian municipalities are not real municipalities because they enjoy no autonomy. They do not enjoy autonomy because they have no administration. It is the government of the state which administers them by nominating their administrators.[86]

The nomination of prefects, used in variable degrees in many states under the regime of 1891, and as a general rule in periods of dictatorship, has therefore been a decisive element in the decline of the municipalities. In spite of this, the private power of the *coronéis* — which, theoretically, the system of nominating prefects was established to destroy — has not disappeared: it has accommodated itself in order to survive. The apparent death of the *coronéis* under the *Estado Novo*[87] was not due, therefore, to the nominated prefects, but to the abolition of the representative system in our country. Once the people are recalled to the ballot-box, as in 1945, *coronelismo* will rise again from its own ashes because the sap on which it feeds is the agrarian structure of the country.[88]

4. Municipal revenue

I. Municipal finances in the colonial period

The study of municipal finance in the colonial period has no great relevance to this work, but a few details are called for. Generally, local revenue was very scant: the Crown was not sufficiently modest in fiscal matters to leave greater tax opportunities in the chambers, neither did the economic system of slave-owning latifundia favour the enrichment of the district exchequer, since the landowners had to levy taxes on themselves. On the other hand, the rudimentary nature of urban settlement, and the means of communication existing at that time, could do little to convince people of the need for a huge municipal budget.

'Municipal taxes were levied', Caio Prado Júnior informs us, 'on meat on the hoof, carcasses, a tax on the scales in which all basic foodstuffs were weighed, a tax for the public cellar (or market). There were, too, checks on weights and measures, the return from fines imposed for the infringement of municipal laws, and finally the letting of "little shops" (*casinhas*) — in some places, Bahia for instance, they were called cabins (*cabanas*) — where essential products were sold.'[1] Also contributing to the revenue of the chambers was the granting of patents and privileges, concessions to sell *aguardente*, tax on the place of manufacture, tax for transport to the chamber's boat, navigation tax, privilege of priority in transport,[2] special levies (tributes known as *fintas*) for specific projects like bridges, roads, public buildings, wells for common use,[3] etc. This list should not be regarded as complete, since it would be difficult to reduce the varied administrative practices of the colonial period into a well-ordered system.[4]

Broadly speaking, it can be said that the finances of the colonial chambers were inadequate, even for the limited works which they had to carry out. All the more so as one-third of the revenue which they collected belonged to the Crown, free of any collection expenses.[5] In January 1646 and May 1649, the Chamber of São Luís do Maranhão complained of the 'miserable state of the people, and of its property, requesting the governor not to put its small income into the chests of the royal estate, since the house of the aldermen was falling to pieces and the public fountains were in ruins'.[6]

With the arrival of Dom João, the financial situation of the municipalities changed very little, judging by the revenue of the Chamber of São Paulo.[7]

Castro Rebêlo, referring to the poverty of the chambers of the North, tells us that this fact did not contradict 'the prosperity of the land'; on the contrary, if municipal tributes were microscopic, this was felt as a benefit by the inhabitants themselves, who as individuals made up for the smallness of the ordinary revenue.[8] Later, applying this observation generally to other colonial chambers, the same author explains the phenomenon as an effect of slave labour in this passage which is worth quoting: 'There was nothing strange about the poverty of some of these chambers. The inhabitants wanted a reduction of taxes owed to the metropolitan country, levied by her; while they were themselves the only contributors it would have been insanity to create other taxes levied by their local chamber. In the slave-owning economy, the interest of the landlords always lies in the general reduction of taxes. Only in a system which includes wage-earners is a tax struggle, engaged in by different classes each eager to saddle the other with the cost of the Republic, meaningful. The increase in taxes levied by elected authorities will for this reason become inevitable on the day when the colony sees an increase in free labour.'[9]

II. The scantiness of municipal and provincial funds under the Empire

Under the Empire, in spite of some partial attempts to do it earlier, it was the Additional Act which brought into focus the problem of differentiating between national revenue and provincial revenue. In Article 10, No. V, it conferred on the provincial assemblies the power to legislate on the fixing of municipal and provincial expenses, and the taxes required to meet them, provided that these did not prejudice 'the general taxes of the State'. The first law to achieve the complete separation of revenues was No. 99 of 31 October 1835,[10] which listed the general (i.e. national) sources, leaving the remaining areas of taxation to the provinces.[11]

It did not, however, deal with the intangible principle of ordinary legislation which could, at any time, add to the nation's list of taxes. The law of 1835 itself already reserved for the National Treasury almost all the then usual sources of revenue. Suffice it to say that these were distributed under 58 headings including the revenue of the municipality of Rio de Janeiro.[12]

Since the legal text had left all remaining forms of taxation to the provinces, the lot of the municipalities in financial matters, according to the spirit of the Additional Act, was entrusted exclusively to the will of the provincial assemblies, which in this matter were not dependent on the sanction of the presidents.[13]

Before the reform of the Constitution, the law of 1 October 1828 had been extremely parsimonious in relation to the municipal chambers, to whose organisation it gave a new structure. This law did not specify any taxes which the chambers were competent to levy. Nonetheless, it alludes to the sale, leasing, exchange, hire and direct exploitation of the districts' property and allows the chambers to impose fines for the violation of their laws, fixing a maximum limit.[14] Even so, the sale, leasing and exchange of property belonging to the districts, depended on the prior authorisation of the president of the province, and in the case of the municipality of the chief minister of the court, while even a simple hiring arrangement was subject to confirmation in the same way.[15] Apart from this, the chambers' laws (in which there was the threat of fines) were only valid for a year, unless they were confirmed by the general assemblies which had the power to alter or revoke them. The same power of revocation was held by the presidents and the national government, acting upon the appeal of any citizen, in the cases of laws dealing with 'merely economic and administrative'[16] matters.

In a word, the principal power held by the chambers in matters of taxation, according to the law of 1828, was that of *soliciting*: 'Normally', in the pious words of Article 77, 'they will propose to the general council of the province, means of increasing their incomes, as well as the necessity or usefulness of making an extraordinary application to them.' The consequence of such a situation is, as Carneiro Maia describes it: 'The meagre income from the district's property, when it had any, and the possible gain from fines, was all that the new municipality had as its dowry, and this scarcely served to pay the salaries of its employees. This itself was a ridiculous legacy from the Ordinances of the monarchy.' The same author mentions a ministerial decree of 1833 which advised a certain chamber of the province of Rio de Janeiro to resort to public subscription in order to build a gaol![17]

All that the Additional Act did in this field was, as we have mentioned, to grant the provincial assemblies complete competence in all matters relating to the financial life of the municipalities. And the provincial legislators did not show themselves to be very zealous in increasing municipal revenue. The proof is that they left untouched the section of the law dealing with the organisation of the districts which treated financial matters, allowing the spirit of the decree of 1828 to continue to guide them.[18]

It is clear that two very strong reasons contributed to maintaining this situation. The first was the interpretation given to the provision of the Additional Act which exacted an agreement from the chambers whereby the provincial assembly could legislate on 'police and economic affairs in the municipality'. Tavares Bastos deplores this in these terms: 'after the *coup d'état* of 1840, the assemblies could no longer legislate, by measures of a general nature, on police and economic affairs of the municipalities. They could only do so on each individual suggestion, *à propos* of every municipal law, each separate project, each individual municipal budget . . . Hence the authority of the assemblies over the chambers is felt solely from the negative side, by the excessive dependence on, and concentration of affairs in, the provincial capitals.'[19] The other reason consists in the meagreness of the revenues of the provinces themselves, since they could not, by law, prejudice the 'general taxes of the State', variable in extent according to the taste of the ordinary legislator.

In practice, the provinces began to levy taxes which caused them to risk the accusation of acting unconstitutionally. The Council of State was the most severe guardian of the tax frontiers of the Treasury against provincial incursions. Export taxes fixed by the provinces, were contested several times, but finally their legitimacy was recognised, almost pacifically.[20] Very strongly contested were transport and consumer taxes, both being held to be import duties.[21] It was not only a few very conservative individuals who restricted the taxation rights of the provinces. The Viscount of Paranaguá himself, who, when he assumed the presidency of the Council and Portfolio of Minister of the Interior, set out to implement a liberal programme,[22] suspended taxes held to be import duties in Pernambuco and in Rio Grande do Norte, and obtained, by means of an order despatched to the provincial presidents, an agreement from the legislative assemblies of the latter and various other provinces that they would abolish these taxes.[23]

In many cases, however, the condemned taxes continued to be collected, as happened most purposefully in the case of the transport tax created by Decree—Law No. 275 of 15 April 1844 in the province of Minas. This law was revoked by the general requirements of No. 347A, of 24 May 1845, but in spite of the revocation and the protests of the Council of State, the provincial assembly reproduced it and continued to collect the prohibited duties in subsequent years.[24]

The problem of the smallness of provincial revenues is treated in a long chapter by Tavares Bastos in his famous book.[25] Not only did he vindicate the legitimacy of several provincial taxes, like consumer taxes, transport and export dues, but he also advocated the transferring of national taxes to the provincial treasury. The existing system of differentiation left only modest sources of revenue to the provinces, and the National Treasury, he emphasised, 'under the pressure of incessant checks, has monopolised completely the use of duties, direct and indirect taxes, internal and even municipal revenue'. In his opinion, it was imperative to reform the system of allocation of 1835 which still existed 'almost in its entirety'.[26] The result was that even the most able local administrations could accomplish nothing worth while with such slender resources.[27]

The Viscount of Paranaguá, as Minister of the Interior, was anxious not to have to allow the provinces to exceed their own legitimate sphere, and he busied himself with increasing local revenue. In 1862 he established a special commission to draw up a draft bill which would improve the allocation and classification of national, provincial and municipal revenue. This commission, amply documenting the financial penury of the provinces, proposed various measures which the Minister summarised in his presentation of the final bill in 1883. Among them was the allocation to the provinces of industrial and professional levies and taxes derived from the handing over of property, these being the most profitable of the national revenue. The commission also upheld the legitimacy of transport taxes and provincial export duties.[28]

In spite of the eloquence with which the case for greater resources for the provinces was pleaded, the plenary Council of State rejected the conclusions of the Commission set up by Paranaguá. The majority of the councillors agreed that the National Treasury should not suffer the diminution entailed in the transferring of taxes.[29]

It is not difficult to imagine what municipal finances would be like in such a context. The municipalities were forced by the law of 1828 to depend on central powers through the general councils of the provinces, and were subordinated meticulously in detail after detail to the provincial assemblies by the interpretative law of the Additional Act. Constrained on one side by the National Treasury, the provinces responded by themselves confining the municipalities in a tightly drawn fiscal belt which allowed them to do no more than waste away in indigence.

The testimony of the Viscount of Ouro Prêto, a contemporary of Paranaguá, is given in very instructive terms. As a member of a commission set up to study the administrative reorganisation of the provinces and the municipalities, he agreed that the problem of taxation was a primary one, since it was worthless to free them from the tutelage which was causing them to atrophy 'if, because of lack of means', they were then 'condemned to vegetate'. And he described the state of local finances at that time, as follows: 'Although it is better in comparison to what it was a few years ago, the situation in the provinces is in no way satisfactory, and when the unconstitutional taxes, to which nearly all of them were obliged to resort, are abolished, their circumstances will be much more precarious, with the State perhaps having to come to their aid through its own expenditure, as happened in the period from 1836 to 1848. If the resources of the provinces fail, the cost of the municipalities will become even higher, since their penury already constitutes one of the reasons for the decline in prestige of this most useful and patriotic institution.'[30]

The allocation of the national revenue in the last budget of the Empire showed no fundamental difference from the list of 1835. Suffice it to say that the Treasury still continued to control import and export duties, taxes on the transfer of property, industries and the professions, and the house-tax.[31]

III. Tax differentiation of the Constituent Assembly of 1890

In the Constituent Assembly set up in 1890, one of the major battles on the organisation of the federal system was fought in the field of tax differentiation. Agenor de Roure describes it in minute detail giving information on the various proposals discussed and summarising the debates and the outcome of the various votes.

The great dispute centred on the two systems of sharing: on the one hand there was the system set out in a bill of the provisional government, which listed the revenue of the Union and those of the states, and left taxes from unspecified sources to fall into the cumulative competence of one or the other, requiring, however, that federal needs should prevail in cases of rivalry. On the other hand, there was the system of Júlio de Castilhos, which set out what the revenue of the Union should be, leaving all the remaining sources in the competence of individual states, whose funds could be taxed by the Union in cases of emergency.

The principle ardently defended by Castilhos and his faction was the same as that adopted in the tax-sharing system of the law of 1835, which had listed national sources of revenue, allocating the others to the provincial treasuries. Although the basic criterion was identical, 'in 1835, the division gave a great number of revenues to the Union, so much so that in 1890–1 it was considered that they should be reduced to four sources, all others being left to the states'.[32]

Castilhos spoke in support of the proposal in the 'Committee of 21' and in the plenary session. In his opinion, the bill confused different tax systems and enshrined the principle of a two-tiered fiscal organisation 'which for so long had brought the economic and financial life of the country to a state of anarchy, under the detestable regime of the Empire'. Moreover, it was anti-federal: it gave 'the lion's share to the Union, investing it with the most lucrative sources, leaving the less profitable ones to the states'.[33]

The thesis put forward by the delegation from Rio Grande do Sul, defeated in committee, was on the point of emerging victorious in the plenary session. It fell on the first reading by the small margin of 20 votes: 103 in favour, 123 against.[34]

It was Rui Barbosa who saved the system outlined in the bill. He predicted the collapse of the nascent Federation if the proposal of the delegation from Rio Grande do Sul were accepted. On the plan which was adopted, would depend the 'durability or ruin of the Union, the Constitution of the country or the proclamation of anarchy (applause), the national honour or inevitable bankruptcy. (Loud applause.) We are not', he emphasised, 'a federation of peoples until recently separately and hastily brought together. On the contrary, it is from the Union that we proceed. We were born in Union. It was in the Union that our fathers were born and died. We never cease to be in the Union. In order that the Union may be the legacy which we leave to our children, no sacrifice will be too great.' Fighting for what he called 'a federal centre incoercible at all costs', Barbosa maintained that the prime necessity for the success of the federal system lay 'in assuring the independent existence of the federal Union', since 'Federation presupposes Union and must be designed to strengthen it.' The immediate task was to found the Union 'on indestructible granite', then it would be a question of establishing the autonomy of the states with resources capable of 'preserving their individual existence'.[35]

Barbosa's warning, with its powerful political arguments and its invocation of the danger of leaving the Union incapable of defending national
sovereignty,[36] saved the tax system of the bill.[37]

At the conclusion of the voting, many members of the Constituent Assembly were convinced that the system of sharing which was approved was
unfair to the states. The comment of Leopolde de Bulhões, offered after
the proceedings, has remained famous: 'The Constituent Assembly did not
resolve the question of the Federation, and the recently-concluded work
of the Republicans is already in need of revision with regard to various
problems, among them the real and complete differentiation of revenues.'[38]
Forty-three years later, in the Constituent Assembly of the Second Republic, his comment was to be described as prophetic, and it was not mistaken
to condemn as fraudulent the tax allocation of 1891.[39]

In contrast to the great uproar provoked by the tax division between
the Union and the states, the members of the Constituent Assembly of the
First Republic did not concern themselves with municipal revenue as a
problem separate from that of state funds.[40] According to the dominant
idea, the organisation of the municipalities was a matter strictly within the
competence of the federal units, whose autonomy on the question ought
not to be limited by the Federal Constitution. It was this point of view
which prevailed when voting took place on the amendment relating to the
elective nature of the municipal administration, as we have seen in the
appropriate chapter.

The facts later demonstrated, however, that it would have been better
for the municipalities if their sources of revenue had been set out in the
text of the Constitution.

IV. Municipal revenue under the regime of 1891

Under the regime of 1891, given the silence of the Constitution, the fiscal
power of the municipalities was derived entirely from the states, and had
to be exercised within the limits determined by the Constitution and laws
of the states. Hence municipal revenue could only come from taxes
allowed to the states, there being in force, with respect to the municipalities, the same constitutional prohibitions which operated in relation to
the state treasury.[41]

Castro Nunes enumerates, in an illustrative rather than an exhaustive
list, the following sources of municipal revenue as available under our first
republican Constitution: taxes on urban buildings; on industries and professions (constituting, in some states, a source of both municipal and state

revenue); on land and water vehicles; on pedlars, inscriptions, announcements, among these the so-called publicity tax, obstructions tax, etc; remunatory charges (death duties, rates for water, sewerage, lighting, abattoirs, markets, etc., many of them, in the majority of states, levied by concessionaires);[42] revenue from church property, including the sites of former Indian settlements;[43] fines for the infringement of laws and regulations or the failure to observe contracts; indemnities, restorations, restitutions, debts or liabilities, prescribed or contingent, etc.[44] The same author warns that uniform criteria did not exist, and does not think that such uniformity was possible '[given that] the circumstances and conditions of method, varying from state to state, naturally advise a varying distribution of taxes'.[45]

Throughout the long regime of the Constitution of 1891, municipal revenues were in general minute. There is no doubt that the states' defective tax quota allotted by the Constitution was a most important factor in this, since it was from tax sources allocated to the state that the municipal revenue had to be drawn.

The states always complained of the smallness of their revenue relative to their duties. In fact it was normal for state budgets to show a deficit. In the period from 1920 to 1931 only three states (Piauí, Ceará and Paraíba) managed a small surplus; all the others showed a deficit.[46] Besides, the total of the states' external, internal and floating debt reached a sum of 4,933,465 *contos*, while the budgeted state revenue for that year did not exceed 1,166,467. The average ratio of revenue to debt was 1:4.2 *contos*.[47]

This state of affairs was due to many factors, including maladministration, but derived in large part from the unequal distribution of revenues. In each state, the Union collected a revenue almost equal, when not superior, to that of the state,[48] not always allocating it in the most judicial manner. Pinpointing this fact in the Constituent Assembly of 1933–4, Alcântara Machado observed: 'The Union is diligent in helping those federal units which are least in need of assistance, and abandons those most in need of support.' In states whose revenue was less than 10,000 *contos*, the Union at that time spent, together with the grants tied to road construction, improvements in agriculture, education and public health, 3254 *contos*. It spent 5943 in states whose income was more than 10,000 and less than 20,000 *contos*. This expenditure rose to 10,576 *contos* in those states whose revenue was between 20,000 and 50,000. Finally, in states whose revenue was more than 50,000, federal contributions reached a level of 12,793 *contos*.[49] This was only to be expected since it was precisely the more advanced states which were better placed to influence national politics. These figures were quoted by the speaker to refute, in advance, those who imagined that the excess levied by the Union was redistributed 'equitably among all the states of the Federation in services useful to the local communities'.[50]

Alcântara Machado blamed the tax deficiency of the states for the penury of the municipalities: 'From this results the purely vegetable existence of the great majority of our municipalities, struck by paralysis, rotting in the sun, incapable of providing for their most basic needs.' 'Pressured by circumstances', what do the states do? 'On the one hand, they draw wildly against the future, compromising the Treasury with ruinous operations of credit; on the other hand, they invade the tax sphere of the municipalities, drying up the sources of local life . . . Reduced to poverty by the Union, the states, in their turn, are reducing the municipalities to misery.'[51]

The speaker went on to explain that there were three processes employed by the states in this policy of compromising municipal finances in order to save their own: 'restricting the municipalities' competence to levy taxes to a minimum; taking a fixed percentage of the limited revenues which they allowed them; arrogating the right to execute certain services of an essentially local nature, like water, sewerage, lighting, even abattoirs and others which are generally profitable'. In their budgets for 1932, 16 states taxed municipal revenues to a sum of 24,277 *contos*; the receipt from the services carried out by the states in the municipalities was budgeted as 37,238 *contos* but the speaker reckoned that this figure was 'much below the real one' since various state budgets grouped these and other sources of revenue together 'under the rubric — *Industrial Revenue*'.[52]

The result to which this policy led, according to the picture given to the Constituent Assembly of 1933—4 and much discussed by that body, spoke for itself: while the Union collected 63% of all taxes, the states received only 28%, and the municipalities a miserable 9%.[53]

V. The draft of the Constitution of 1933

The draft of the Constitution, drawn up by a commission specially named by the provisional government, also contained various innovations in the chapter on taxation.[54]

It listed federal and state taxes as did the regime of 1891, but departed from it in two points: it sought to abolish cumulative taxes, creating the machinery which could periodically allocate the remaining sources of revenue; and it included a third party — the municipalities — in the constitutional distribution of revenues, outlining a municipal tax sphere which could not be invaded by the state treasuries.

Many voices were raised in the Constituent Assembly against the proposed system of distribution, which withdrew lucrative tax sources from the states (export and consumer taxes), claiming to compensate them from the much inferior resources derived from titular income tax.[55] Numerous amendments were put forward both to the draft and afterwards to the altered text of the Constitutional Commission. For the most part, however, the amendments did not posit fundamentally different criteria, but contented themselves with asking for a more equitable division which would not call upon the states to sacrifice so much.

VI. The proposal of the São Paulo delegation

As far as amendments to the system are concerned, some merit special mention in that they were fundamentally opposed to the ideas behind the draft: those of the São Paulo delegation, elected under the banner 'A United São Paulo'; the suggestions of the Minister, Jaurez Távora, made into concrete proposals by Deputy Fernandes Távora; and the proposal of Deputy Prado Kelly, supported by his colleagues in the 'Progressive Union of the state of Rio de Janeiro'.

The São Paulo delegation revived the thesis defended by Castilhos in the previous Constituent Assembly, arguing that the federal taxes should be listed and remaining sources allocated to the states.[56] Supporting the proposals in the plenary session, Deputy Cardosa de Melo Neto confessed that he had repudiated his own ideas of seventeen years before, when, in an examination thesis, he had defended the differential principle of revenues adopted in the Constitution of 1891.[57] Expounding his new opinions, he justified as follows the system which was known by the name of 'Julio de Castilhos' and which was resurrected by his faction:

For us, in the Federation . . . legal activity, that is to say, the guarantee of the unity of the country, represented by the maintenance of internal legal order and the defence of our territory against external enemies, belongs to the Union – a legal creation which is the incarnation of national sovereignty . . . but the whole development of social activity, that is to say, the sum total of the functions of the modern state, for ever on the increase, does not come within the competence of the Union but within that of the states. It is because of this that they are autonomous. Autonomy is not simply a right; it is a right with a corresponding obligation – that of development and progress. The state is autonomous to develop one activity. This activity is to stimulate progress in all its legitimate manifestations, that is, in education and instruction of the people, public health, economic order, public assistance etc.

For these reasons, he considered the system proposed by his delegation to be

the logical consequence of the federal regime, by virtue of which the Union, guardian of sovereignty, is limited to secure and fixed taxes which it alone collects, because its activity is predetermined and the states are in a position to develop all their social activity since they have, for this purpose, all the sources of revenue not specified as federal by the Constitution. For predetermined activity a predetermined revenue; for indeterminate activity an indeterminate revenue — this is the logical formula.'[58]

In his view, the major difficulty implicit in Castilhos' proposal was the threat that the Union might find itself without funds in times or war or public calamity. Hence the politician from Rio Grande do Sul had allowed the Union the right to tax state revenues to meet such emergencies. This danger had already ceased to exist, in the speaker's opinion. According to the São Paulo proposal, the Union would have sufficient resources to 'live and prosper legitimately in normal times'; in the eventualities referred to, it could raise additional resources on income and consumption taxes or a special levy for war purposes.[59]

To match their greater revenue, the states would have to meet the cost, in their respective territories, of services which the speaker called 'aspects of social activity' (transport, public health, professional training and economic stimulation). From these the Union would be exempt, just as it would be exempt from meeting the cost of local services in the Federal District (justice, civil and military police, fire service, public lighting, health, water, sewerage). The Union would only continue to render such services, in exceptional circumstances, in states which did not collect as much as 50,000 *contos* per annum.[60]

According to his calculations based on the figures which he presented and which referred to the operations of 1931, the Union would gain 32,879 *contos*; the sum received by the states would be decreased by about 5000 *contos*, but this would be hardly apparent in the light of their powers to levy unspecified taxes.[61]

VII. The proposals of Juarez Távora and Fernandes Távora

The Minister Juarez Távora, developing ideas already mooted in the Commission for Economic Studies for the States and Municipalities, put forward a point of view very different from that of the São Paulo delegates, if not directly opposed to it. The members of the majority delegation from São Paulo were, as we have seen, fierce defenders of the financial strengthening of the states, which now had to carry the greater load of responsibility in the division of labour within the Federation. They were not indifferent to the fate of the municipalities, in so far as they proposed that the states should not be allowed to tax municipal revenues.[62] They argued, however, for the suppression of the proposal relating to municipal revenue, on the grounds that 'the determining of municipal revenue, in the federal system, falls within the competence of the state legislature'.[63] In their view, a clearly pro-state one, the financial strengthening of the municipalities would be the necessary consequence of the improved financial position of the states: 'the remedy', said Alcântara Machado, 'presents itself naturally: it is to strengthen the finances of the states and of the municipalities, with the aim of effectively ensuring their political autonomy'.[64]

The Minister Juarez Távora, on the contrary, did not want the strength of the municipalities to be based on that of the states: what he wanted was a weak state flanked by a strong Union and strengthened municipalities.[65] He expressed his formula in these terms:

> within a short time, when the natural balance has been re-established between the functional activity of the municipality, as the legitimate body to assist the people in its needs and aspirations and as the driving force behind production at its sources, and that of the Union, as the organ of national sovereignty, responsible for its internal and external defence, it will be necessary for the states to assume the dignifying role of honest broker between the sovereign Union and the autonomous municipalities, with the essential purpose of adapting the general lines of conduct laid down by the Union to the local peculiarities of the municipalities.[66]

As has been shown, the São Paulo delegation and Juarez Távora placed themselves in opposing positions as regards the role which the states ought to play in the Federation. Deputy Fernandes Távora, whose opinions on the issue were identical to those of the Minister of Agriculture, whom he quoted frequently, gave his views concrete form in a forcefully argued amendment.[67] His proposal was to specify the revenues of the Union, of the states and of the municipalities. He would confer upon the municipalities, over and above house taxes, the revenues from licences and the like and, as a proportion of the total revenue, other tax measures which could be granted to them and which were not already exclusively under the control of the Union or the states. But as the basic idea was to guarantee to the municipalities, in the text of the Constitution, 'a reasonable percentage of national resources', corresponding to their duties, and also to unify the system of tax collection, Amendment No. 262 also proposed:

'For the sake of convenience, the collection of all taxes shall be undertaken by municipal functionaries, under the supervision of the state and of the Union, and the total revenue collected shall be equitably divided between the three administrative units in proportion to the duties assigned to them by this Constitution.'[68]

The proposal of Fernandes Távora, at least in its intention, was motivated by the penury of the municipalities, whose abandonment he vehemently condemned: 'What has been done in Brazil, up until this day, on the subject of municipal administration', he exclaimed, 'is a mockery of good sense, because denying the poor districts their principal sources of revenue, has decreed, *ipso facto*, their financial ruin and, consequently, their lack of economic viability.'[69]

VIII. The proposal of Prado Kelly

With his party's support Deputy Prado Kelly proposed and defended in the plenary session, with ample numerical documentation, a system of division of revenue based on entirely different criteria from the rest. He singled out four principal defects in our tax system which he thought should be corrected: the absence of a rational basis on which to differentiate the 'sources' of taxation themselves; disproportion between state and municipal duties and their respective resources; double or multiple incidence of taxation; complexity of the system of collection.[70]

Justifying his proposal, Prado Kelly referred to José Higino who, in the Constituent Assembly of 1890–1, criticised the government's bill for having distributed taxes without having similarly portioned out the respective sources, and stated that this would be 'the only way' of avoiding cumulative incidence:[71] 'Let us verify which are the real sources of taxation, in order to divide the tax revenue realistically between the Union, the states and the municipalities. Once this is done, we shall avoid the chief evil of national taxation policy, which is the double, triple or multiple incidence of tax.'[72]

In the second reading, Prado Kelly put forward another amendment. He wanted to keep the basic principle of the previous one, but the innovations which he introduced were not merely points of detail. It is very revealing that Deputy Fernandes Távora supported the new amendment, he himself having put forward his own plan in the first session, as we have seen.[73]

Defending it in writing and from the rostrum, the deputy from Rio de Janeiro explained that the fiscal rationalisation which he put forward, had four main points: incidence of taxes, collection, distinguishing who was competent to tax where, and the distribution of revenue between the Union, the states and the municipalities.[74]

On the question of incidence, the author maintained the fundamental principle of the previous amendment. He divided the tax sources into two groups: patrimony and activity. The first — patrimony — was subdivided into goods and chattels and their transfer and real estate and its transfer. In the sub-group of goods and chattels he included capital, income, merchandise; in the other, urban and rural property. The second group—activity — was subdivided into commerce, industry and other trades.[75]

With regard to distinguishing the right of the three entities to tax, he began by showing that there was no problem in the case of income or rates.[76] The difficulty arose on the matter of levies and duties. On the basis of the previous differentiation between tax sources, Prado Kelly distributed them as follows: for the Union, goods and chattels and their transfer; for the states, activity and rural real estate together with the transfer of the latter; for the municipalities, urban real estate and its transfer. But it must be observed that this second distinction is not one for the receipt of revenue *but simply of the power to tax.*[77] The sharing-out of the taxes, once collected, was another problem which the author of the amendment sought to resolve in another way.

With the solution which he suggested for the problem of the distribution of *legislative fiscal powers*, the author of Amendment No. 1847 sought to avoid cumulative taxation.[78] There still remained the difficult problem of the distribution of revenue once collected, and which is also the most important from our point of view. Here, already, Prado Kelly's system could not draw strength from its own basic criteria.[79]

On this point, his second amendment delegated to the ordinary legislator the task of righting the inequalities of the system of exclusive taxation, adopting for this purpose the criterion of Fernandes Távora, who, as we have already noted, associated himself with its proposals. The extent of the duties of each of the three administrative spheres was to be taken as the basis for this periodic composition.

In this connection, it is necessary to remember that Deputy Levi Carneiro argued that the Federal Constitution should distinguish not only municipal revenues but also the services that fell within municipal competence.[80]

It does not serve any useful purpose, for our present study, to summarise the other amendments on tax differentiation, although they were numerous.[81] It is in order, however, to mention that many of them sought to suppress the proposal relating to municipal funds, on the grounds that this was something for the states to decide.[82]

IX. The solution adopted by the Constitution of 1934

The substantive proposal of the Constitutional Commission, basing itself on 'the exhaustive partisan reports presented by Deputies Sampaio Correia and Cincinato Braga',[83] maintained the system of the enumerative division of taxes. To the municipalities it allocated levies on industries and trades, licences, income from real estate including the urban house-tax, public entertainments, and stamp duty on deeds and transactions of a municipal nature.[84]

The 'Committee of 3', charged with pronouncing judgement on this text, adopted a few alterations. Municipal monies, according to its proposals, should consist of rates on municipal services and duties on licences, urban dwellings, public entertainments, agriculture, stock-raising and related businesses. The Union and the states could create other levies over and above the specified taxes; the collection of these would fall to the states, who would give 30% of them to the Union and 20% to the municipalities in which they had been collected. Opposing the Commission's recommendations, the proposals limited the fiscal powers of the municipalities, relatively speaking, to levies on property, industries and trades and withdrew the power to take stamp duty on transactions and deeds of a municipal nature. Moreover, the municipalities would have, at most, 20% of the unlisted duties.[85]

In the plenary session, one of the so-called 'amendments of co-ordination' or 'of the large delegations', served as a basis for voting on the content of Amendment No. 1945, after a suggestion that the matter be transferred for solution to an additional act, similar to that proposed in the Constitutent Assembly of the First Republic, had been abandoned.[86] Amendment No. 1945, containing an important modification relating to export duty, was approved in the section which concerns us, the idea that the Federal Constitution should lay down what municipal revenue should be, emerging victorious.[87] The municipalities therefore received: licence duties; taxes on urban dwellings and land, the former being calculated as one-tenth of income or a promissory note against it; levies on public entertainments; promissory duty on income from rural real estate; half of the duty on industries and trades, it being the states' function to levy this; 20%, in its own territory, of taxes not specified in the Constitution but created later by the Union or by the state; rates on municipal services; and finally any other tax transferred to them by the state.[88]

In the words of Levi Carneiro, the assembly 'adopted the great and salutary innovation' of assigning their own sources of revenue to the municipalities. Nevertheless, these funds remained greatly inferior to their needs, as we shall see later.

X. Changes introduced by the regime of 1937; the startling poverty of Brazilian municipalities

The Constitution of 1937 preserved the principle referred to above, but reduced the municipal revenue by subtracting from it the titular duty on the income from rural real estate and 20% of the collection in the territory of the municipality from unspecified federal and state taxes. The states in their turn, lost the revenue from the tax on the use of fuels and explosives.[89]

Later, Constitutional Law No. 3 of 18 September 1940 forbade the states, the Federal District and the municipalities to tax, either directly or indirectly, production and trade, including the distribution and export of nationally produced coal and of liquid combustibles and lubricants of whatever provenance. Two days later, Constitutional Law No. 4 declared that it was the Union's special privilege to tax production, trade, distribution and consumption, including the export and import of the products referred to, under the form of a single duty for each type of product. The states and the municipalities would receive a quota of this, proportionate to the consumption in the respective territories, and this quota was to be spent on the upkeep and development of roads. These changes, implying as they did, a reduction in the fiscal competence of the states, were put into effect by Decree—Law No. 2615 of 21 September 1940 and, according to Barros Carvalho's observation, the only areas which profited were 'the richest states and municipalities, those with the best developed road systems . . . while the really needy municipalities received nothing and remained in a state of stagnation'.[90]

The result of this system of taxation, notwithstanding the guarantee of a minimum revenue for the municipalities written into the Federal Constitution itself, was to maintain the municipalities in their state of penury.[91] Revealing statistics on this issue were amply provided in the studies written at the time of the composition of our last Political Charter.

According to facts revealed by Rafael Xavier, 'the relative percentages of revenue collected in Brazil in the year 1942' were as follows: the Union, 48.39%; the states, 39.68%; the municipalities, 11.75%. He observed, subsequently, that 42.4% of the total of the municipal collection came from the municipalities of the state capitals excluding the Federal District. When this deduction had been made, it emerged that there remained only 6.9% of the total tax revenue of the country for the other municipalities![92]

In another study, the same expert took a more general view covering a period of twenty years and was able to prove how consistent was the budgetary poverty of the municipalities. The percentage of revenue from all taxes, falling to the municipalities over this long period were, in round figures: 1925–9, 10%; 1930–1, 12%; 1932 and 1933, 11%; 1934, 10%; 1935, 8%; 1936, 10%; 1937, 11%; 1938, 10%; 1939, 13%; 1940–2, 12%; 1943, 9%; 1944, 8%.[93]

The meanness of these resources is highlighted when one observes that, according to the census of 1940, our population was distributed in the following manner: urban, 22.29%; suburban, 8.95%; rural, 68.76%; it being worth noting that this legal criterion of classification is applied to all nuclei of population irrespective of size or situation. Deducting the urban and suburban population of the capitals, Rafael Xavier calculated that the population of the interior of the country reached a figure of 86.4% of the total, and that this rural population was allocated only 6.9% of the country's tax revenue.

This was the state of municipal finances in Brazil when the third Constituent Assembly of the Republic met. The picture was not much worse than that of 1933. And now, as then, there was no lack of enthusiastic support for the financial strengthening of the municipalities. Now, however, this campaign would produce much more concrete results.[94]

XI. The increase of municipal funds in the Constitution of 1946

Milton Campos, then a deputy, alluded to the 'physical love' which the members of the Constituent Assembly of 1946 felt towards municipal revenues.[95] In reality, this was the fundamental point in the concern of pro-municipal members of the group involved with the drawing up of the Constitution. In fact, municipal revenue was much increased by the new measures adopted.[96] As revenue derived from taxes levied exclusively by themselves, the municipalities now had: house and land taxes in towns, licence duties, taxes on industry and trades, on public entertainments, on municipal economic ventures or other areas within their competence; improvement grants; rates; any other revenues derived from the exercise of their prerogatives and from the use of their property and services. In addition they were to have taxes transferred to them by the states.[97] But the main increase in their funds comes from other sources, namely: (1) 40% of duties created by the Union and the states, in addition to those expressly granted to them by the Constitution, shall belong to the municipalities on whose territory the duty will have effect;[98] (2) at least 60% of the over-all federal tax on lubricants and liquid and gaseous fuels, on national minerals and electric power, will be handed over to the states, the Federal District and the municipalities, by means of a method of distribution to be established by federal law;[99] (3) should the collection from state taxes (save export duties) exceed, in municipalities other than those of the capitals, the total local revenue from whatever source, 30% of the excess should be awarded to them annually;[100] (4) finally, 10% of income tax and of the tax on all profits, will be divided by the Union equally among the municipalities except those of the capitals, with the Constitution requiring that at least half of the amount received should be spent on services of a rural nature.[101] This share in income tax represents the most appreciable element in the growth of revenue permitted to the municipalities. All the more so as it is income tax which will have to sustain the Union in its growing financial needs, since, clearly, those who have most, are able to pay most.[102] With the quota in equal parts, the small municipalities of the interior will have a much better proportion than the large ones. And they are, in fact, the ones most in need.[103]

With regard to the *new* taxes created by the Union and the states, the draft of the Constitution ordered that the municipalities should receive 30% of them in quarterly portions.[104] The percentage was raised to 40% in the next draft, which also ordered that the handing over should be done through the collection system, a proposal which was retained in the revised draft.[105] The restricting of the benefit to those municipalities in whose territory the taxes were collected, led to the amendment put forward by Clemente Mariâni.[106]

As for the tax dealt with in Article 15, para. 2, the first draft of the Constitution, and the second, left it to the federal legislator to fix the quota to be distributed between the states, the Federal District and the municipalities, demanding, however, that it should be proportionate to the consumption, in the respective territories, of the product being taxed, and made reference only to lubricants, liquid and gaseous fuels and to Brazilian coal.[107] The revised draft already foresaw the possibility of establishing a single tax system for all minerals and electric power produced in Brazil, and adopted various criteria which figure in the final text, as guidelines for distribution, the distribution itself being a federal matter. However, it continued the policy of leaving it to the ordinary legislator to decide the quota to be shared by the recipient units.[108] Honório Monteiro proposed that the quota should be fixed at 60%; 'at least', added the substitute amendment of Paulo Sarazate.[109]

With regard to the handing over to the municipalities of part of the taxes that the state collected in their territory when the latter showed an excess in comparison with local funds, the changes carried out in the course of parliamentary proceedings tended to limit the generosity of the initial proposal. The first draft laid down that all taxes collected in the territory of the municipality be taken into account in calculating the excess; included state capitals among the beneficiaries; and fixed the quota to be handed over to the municipal treasury at 50%. The second draft contained identical proposals.[110] Already in the revised draft it was proposed that only state *duties*, excepting export duty, should be included in the calculation and that municipalities of the capitals should not enjoy this revenue supplement; the quota envisaged was, however, maintained at 50% of the excess. The final restriction which reduced the quota to 30%, was adopted at the final voting session by means of an amendment from Pedro Dutra.[111] Finally, in the transitional arrangements, it was held that the states would be allowed ten years to adapt their budgets gradually to this diminution in favour of the municipalities.[112]

There remains the arrangement concerning the distribution of 10% of income tax between the municipalities. This was the proposal which set off most discussion. The first draft made no mention of it. It was first proposed by Mário Masagão, as a substitute for the Article of the first draft which allocated to the municipalities half of the excess of state revenues over municipal ones with respect to taxes collected in the municipality's own territory. It did not seem to him fair to impose such a burden on impoverished state finances. The Union, with a better share of tax revenue, should carry the burden. Finally, as we have seen, the municipalities were considered from both sides and the percentage proposed in the first draft was reduced. In the second draft, the formula adopted was as follows: the 10% referred to by Mário Masagão's amendment was divided among the municipalities equally, excluding the state capitals.[113] In the plenary session, two amendments, signed by more than 120 representatives of various parties, proposed that the division should be made in equal parts between the states and the territories so that each of them could distribute the relevant quota, also in equal parts, among its municipalities. This was the system adopted by the revised draft which maintained the exclusion of the capitals from the allocation. In the final voting, through an amendment by Alcedo Coutinho, it was decided that the funds should be shared out directly to the municipalities in equal portions, excluding those of the capitals. The idea of directing that at least half of this increase be spent 'in services of a rural nature' was put forward by Deputy Paulo Nogueira. He meant by this: the construction of roads, the building of schools and hospitals, etc.[114]

XII. An attempt to explain our current 'pro-municipal feeling'

If we compare the meagre results of the pro-municipal campaign in the Assembly of 1933—4 with the success which this same campaign achieved in 1946, we cannot but be surprised at the relative rapidity with which the idea of strengthening the finances of the municipalities matured and bore fruit.

It is clear that the financial anaemia of the municipalities increases their dependence on the state governments and consequently favours the political submissiveness of local chiefs. There would, moreover, be no shortage of self-interested motives and power-seeking of the sort which have contributed in the past to maintaining the budgetary weakness of the municipalities. But to look for a purely political explanation for this fact would be to attribute a complete lack of public spirit to party politicians. It would, moreover, be inconsistent with the facts, since many of the parliamentarians who had seats in the Assembly of 1946 were also members of the Constituent Assembly of 1934, and took part in the political struggles of the Old Republic. It seems clear, therefore, that besides the undoubted political reasons, there must have been other factors present which prevented the problem of municipal finances from having been given greater importance in the past. By the same token, in our own time, factors other than political ones will have contributed to the diffuse but active awareness of the need to increase municipal revenue as a means of raising the standard of living of the rural population.

This general awareness to which we refer now produced the right social climate, the lack of which had in 1933 prevented the assembly from deriving concrete results from the emotional speeches which were then delivered in favour of our disadvantaged backlands people. This lack had even prevented the speechmakers themselves from arriving at the objective conclusions which, thirteen years later, seemed more or less obvious.[115]

Until now we have done nothing but drain the public revenue of the rural areas into the larger urban centres. From the taxes paid by their inhabitants, the municipalities receive a sum greatly inferior to the amounts conveyed into the state and federal coffers.[116] Even if we had no statistics, it would be enough to consider that the last Constituent Assembly found it too much to allocate to the municipalities *half of the excess* of state taxes collected in their territory: this simple episode should put an end to any doubt. With the Union and the states receiving the greater part of the tax paid by the rural municipalities, the allocation of these resources has tended to be in favour of the capitals and the large urban centres.

In order to characterise the disproportionate development of our capitals in relation to the rest of the country, Rafael Xavier has used data referring to the years 1940 and 1944. Here are some of his conclusions:

The collection of the tax on commercial transactions, which in all the capitals reached 47.8% of the total for the country, would exceed 50% if we included from the Federal District the 40% of the federal share of this tax collected there . . . Bank dealings in Brazil occur almost totally, or up to about 90% of them, in the capitals, with the Federal District and São Paulo competing for first place with more than 72% of the business in loans and 71% of total deposits.[117] The processing industries show the same tendency towards concentration . . . Of 29,219 establishments involved in processing raw materials registered in the whole country, 10,749. i.e. 36.8%, are located in the capitals . . . 71.1% of the capital invested in the processing industries comes from the capitals of the states of the Federation . . . The Federal District and the capital of São Paulo together are responsible for 61% of the country's buying and selling, and the figure rises to 93% when only the capitals of the federal units are taken.[118]

In the light of such remarkable figures it is necessary that we should not confuse the various factors which have contributed to producing this phenomenon. It is not the action of the public authority in allocating greater revenue resources to the centres of higher population which is the primary factor in urban concentration. Urban development, by its concentration of business and industry, is usually itself responsible for the preference shown by governments in allocating greater revenues to these areas. There is no doubt that the centralisation of bureaucratic services, functions as a direct factor in the increase of city populations, the same being true for the greater comfort in living conditions, which governments create in the large cities. But it also seems beyond doubt that we have here a case of reflected phenomena. Hence the preference of governments for the large centres essential to them and originally determined by urban concentration, functions equally as one of the determining factors of that same concentration.

The preference of governments in allocating the greater part of revenue to the urban centres does not only occur in favour of the capitals and of the large cities. The phenomenon is also typical of the smaller towns of the interior. Water, drainage, road-surfacing, parks, electricity — essentially urban services — consume the greater part of the finances of the minor municipalities (not to mention the personal expenses and the costs improperly incurred in election campaigns). Highways, hospitals, schools have tended to stay in second place.[119] In a recent article, Professor Basílio

Magalhães aired doubts about the possibility of raising the standard of
living of the rural population simply by increasing municipal funds, basing
his argument precisely on 'the excessive pro-urban sentiment that works
against any tendency towards rural development' which has traditionally
been dominant in our municipal administrations.[120] And it was precisely
because it admitted this premise that the Constituent Assembly of 1946
demanded that the municipalities should be obliged to allocate to 'services
of a rural nature' at least half of the revenue increase coming to them as
their share of the 10% of income tax.

Given the picture we have described, it seems very probable that it has
been the commercial interests and, later on, interests involved in our
nascent industries, which have been most responsible for the drain of
resources from the interior to the large cities or, in other words, from the
countryside to the towns. The town is the natural commercial centre and
also the main centre of industry. And it is perfectly understandable that
the increase in the influence of commercial and industrial interests should
have led to a proportionate rise in the preference of men in government for
the development of the cities and for the well-being of their inhabitants,
especially those living in the most prosperous districts. As our economy
has been traditionally characterised by the export of a few products, the
fact that Brazil has only a few cities, chiefly sea-ports, could be said to
follow from the needs of agriculture. Even so, the coming together there
of the interests of export and import concerns — interests which, inciden-
tally, profit more than agriculture from international trade — prevents us
from seeing this case as a genuine exception to the over-all predominance
of the city.

It remains to be explained, however, how it is that governments have
been able to retain the favour of the electorate (rural for the most part
and hence dominated by the influences of landowners and ranchers) when,
at the same time, they have shown themselves to be so partisan in favour
of urban interests in commerce and industry.[121] On the purely political
level, this is explained by the constriction and falsification of the vote and
by the complete submission of life in the interior to the public authority
of the states, which in Brazil almost always means that effective opposition
becomes impossible. In the dependent situation in which rural political
bosses have traditionally found themselves, they are, in the majority of
cases, of necessity pro-government. On the economic level, it is as well to
remember that governments and regimes come and go, leaving the rural
structure of the country intact; under the impact of the abolition of
slavery, for instance, political consequences came rapidly. Aside from this,
it is well known that our economy has been based, at different periods, on

the exploitation of one or two products for export, with the resultant shift of the population — and of political influence — to the areas of cultivation of the products in question. In the periods of expansion of our foreign trade, the prosperity of the landowners in the relevant parts of the country more than compensates for the evils of the commercial and business preferences of governments. Many of them create conditions of comfort in their hometowns superior to the standard of living in neighbouring places, or make for the large urban centres to invest or dissipate their fortunes. In times of crisis in production the government comes to their help, protecting prices or granting a moratorium on debts, and a readjustment. When the depression passes, the good times return; if not, many are ruined, others move away or adapt themselves to a new way of life, and their own importance diminishes with the transfer of electoral prestige to the areas of more recent prosperity. However, in more serious collapses, the government may lose the chief basis of its political support: this occurred with the abolition of slavery; and again in the crisis of 1929.

We are arriving, however, at the point when the industrial interests are no longer content with customs favours and the devaluation of the currency.[122] Its development, greatly accelerated by the events of the two world wars, cannot now be fed on the internal market alone, whose smallness is aggravated by the continual and systematic impoverishment of the rural population. Even discounting the artificial undertakings which tend to disappear in the aftermath of war, and are disappearing,[123] the increase in our industrial output is incontestable.[124] The dilemma of a developed industry which does not command a satisfactory internal market is: export or collapse. As far as exporting is concerned, the contingency of the war, favourable for some of our products, has passed, and we can no longer look to export as a way out. We have neither the resources, the technical means, nor the political influence to compete with highly industrialised countries, notably the United States. And it is natural, on the other hand, not to want our industries to die. The only thing left for them to do, therefore, is something which hitherto had not been thought of as a realistic idea: widen the domestic market to avoid the over-production which would result from under-consumption, and continue to obtain from the government the protective tariffs indispensable to save them from the fatal competition of foreign technology on our own territory.

It is quite probable that these facts are not seen as simply as this by many of our leaders. But the gravity of the situation has already made others certain that the only possible cure lies in the widening of the domestic market, although the problem of choosing the necessary means is still being vigorously debated. The overriding nature of immediate needs over future ones could make the solution of the problem difficult and has done so. For this very reason some, with their eyes fixed on immediate profits and unable to see that they will only be ephemeral, will not hesitate to ally themselves with foreign interests, and thus prejudice the survival of the national economy. On the other hand, protectionist policies require great judgement and caution, in order to allow financial consolidation and technical improvement in a national industry which would then become autonomous within a given time. For this reason, given the deficiencies of our protectionist measures, even honest souls will not hesitate to suggest that we are opening our doors to unbeatable foreign competition, because we are over-impressed by the temporary fall in the cost of living which will result from free industrial competition.

Not all those − we repeat − not all those who will become involved in the pro-municipal attitudes of our times will be aware that the increase in municipal funds is, in all probability, an indirect consequence of the need to widen the domestic market by investing these resources to improve the living conditions of the rural population. Neither will all of them be aware that this ruralism of the present is closely linked with industrialism − itself intimately involved with commercial and banking interests.

Deputy Fernandes Távora, for example, who was a fervent advocate of backlanders in the previous Constituent Assembly, did not make the slightest allusion to the need to increase the domestic market for industrial products. His orientation was, on the contrary, expressly ruralist: 'Our real wealth', he said, 'can only come from the land.' Because of this he was deeply worried about the visible depopulation of the farms: 'it is only those who are not able to, who are not fleeing from the interior. Those who can, flee, and they are doing the right thing.' Without referring to the expansion of industry, he sought nevertheless to increase the purchasing power of the rural population, as we see in the following extract: 'The most basic commonsense is showing us the route we should follow, and it can be described in a few words: *comfort for the country-dweller.* How to provide it for him? By simply allowing the municipality to be master of its destiny, leaving it an income sufficient for its needs.'[125]

Thus, the 'logic of the facts', running counter to the intentions of men, could allow the views of Deputy Fernandes Távora to coincide perfectly with the pro-industrial objectives of the representatives from São Paulo. The meaning of the ruralist thesis was expressed with much realism in a speech which Deputy J.C. de Macedo Soares made in the name of his delegation. We have already seen, previously, that the São Paulo delegates argued only indirectly for an increase in municipal funds: it would detract from the financial power of the states which was at the centre of the *paulistas'* immediate claim.

Beginning by saying that the Constitution of 1891 'was essentially political', Deputy J.C. de Macedo Soares declared that he felt it his duty to outline 'as an introduction to the constitutional issue . . . the Brazilian economic framework within which the various theories of public law which we should adopt or adapt, must find their place.'[126] He then referred to the economic inequalities between the various regions of Brazil: 'The great differences in wealth between São Paulo and the Federal District and the rest of the country are clearly caused by an incomparably greater flow of capital to these areas than to any other.'[127] The export of certain national products (especially sugar, cotton, gold, precious stones, spices, rubber, coffee) was, in his opinion, in each respective period, the primary source of capitalisation.

These products were responsible for the formation of concentrations of capital in our country. But given that many of them have had only an ephemeral importance in our foreign trade, and others only account for a very small portion of it, for a long time coffee has been the real international currency of Brazil . . . No other Brazilian export product can be even remotely compared to coffee as a producer of wealth or an instrument in the formation and concentration of capital. It is for this reason that, in the great coffee state of Brazil, such intensive capitalisation has taken place, not only through the production of domestic capital . . . but also through the attraction of foreign capital . . . The long duration of the coffee boom favoured the economic leap forward of São Paulo, with its resultant industrialisation, the raising of cultural standards, changes in the pattern of life and technical progress . . . As for the Federal District, it is a matter here of the effect of the National Capital always drawing to itself huge funds collected by the nation throughout the Republic in the form of taxes, rates, income from industrial exploitation in the states, etc. The same reasons, although on a much smaller scale, have led to the greater concentration of wealth in the state capitals which have economic indices much higher than those of their respective hinterlands.[128]

After these observations came the proposed formula, clearly pro-industrial in its orientation: 'The São Paulo phenomenon and the Rio phenomenon have not, however, been reproduced elsewhere in Brazil with the same intensity. We must therefore synthesise our observations by saying: it is necessary to synchronise the rhythm of progress in Brazilian states, so *that the development of the Federal District and the state of São*

Paulo does not encounter barriers in the form of the less rapid progress of the other units of the Federation' [our italics].[129] In other words, it was necessary for the rest of the country to be capable of aiding the economic development of São Paulo and the Federal District, that is, to be capable of contributing to the growth of a national industry whose principal centres were those two regions. And the rest of the country could only fulfil this task if it were able to buy a greater number of manufactured products, given that the Federal District no longer possessed a viable agrarian economy and the chief agricultural products of São Paulo (coffee and cotton) were destined, for the most part, for the international market.[130]

These observations do not intend the slightest shadow of censure to Sr J.C. de Macedo Soares. We only recall his statement for the rare clarity with which it summarises the pro-industrial position of the São Paulo delegation in the previous Constituent Assembly. Through it we can also see how the positions of the São Paulo group and that of Deputy Fernandes Távora — although radically different in their subjective expression — became the same in practice, for the ruralist plea of the latter would clearly not perform the miracle of interrupting the industrialisation of São Paulo and the Federal District and, if it had any effect in relation to the under-industrialised states, would contribute precisely to industrial expansion in these same two regions, by the cessation or decrease of internal competition.

The proposals which we have just cited reveal that the defenders of municipal revenues in the Constituent Assembly of the Second Republic did not see clearly that this expedient could be tried as a means of enlarging the domestic market, and thereby contributing to the industrial development of Brazil. The rise in the cost of living, resulting from protective tariffs, always, alas, gave rise to a certain feeling against an industrialisation which benefited only a few regions. There was not a favourable climate in the earlier Constituent Assembly, therefore, because the facts had not had time to mature in the minds of men, a process which usually takes place slowly; this was probably why the assembly was so usurious on the question of municipal funds.

In 1946 the situation was different. The Second World War had not only broadened our industrial activities, but had taught us to fear the United States from this point of view. If traditionally advanced European industry could not effectively resist U.S. competition, the latter would meet only the slightest resistance in flattening Brazilian industry. As the facts became more bruising, so we developed a greater awareness of the precariousness of our industrial programme. And this was the right climate in which to look for concrete solutions.[131]

In these circumstances certain men in public life did not fail to see the importance of enlarging the home market. In one of his speeches addressed to the Assembly of 1946, Rafael Xavier included among the evils caused by the drain of the nation's wealth to the great urban centres, the following: 'the weakening of our domestic market whose capacity for further absorption is in marked decline, *when it should be the safety valve and the lever for the development of the national economy*'.[132] It was not accidental that among the sturdiest defenders of municipal rights in the last Constituent Assembly were various members of the São Paulo delegation.[133] Among these was Deputy Horácio Láfer, so closely linked to industry in his state, and who in the previous Assembly (in which he represented industry as a class deputy) had not made a single speech in favour of the municipalities. It was he who made the following significant observations in his report on the budget proposals for 1948:

> Public revenue in Brazil is nourished by production . . . It is on the domestic market that we must depend for a guaranteed outlet for nearly everything we produce. As this depends on consumption, it is in our policy over wages and earnings that the key to the problem lies . . . Hence the problem becomes solely a matter of guaranteeing and stimulating national production for domestic consumption. The classic cycle of crises is well known: lowering of prices, reduced production, unemployment. Hence to avoid unemployment, the basic measure required is the preservation, by right, of a preferential domestic market designed solely for any product of Brazilian workmanship on Brazilian soil.[134]

However, it was not only the need to preserve our industries which, in the final analysis, gave rise to the present preoccupation of men in public life with the strengthening of the domestic market. There is another factor which should not be discounted. Two important items on our export sheet now seem to have a future which, if not gloomy, at least gives cause for some anxiety: coffee, as the result of successive crises, can no longer be our great instrument 'in producing and concentrating capital', and Brazilian cotton will be hard pressed to compete with North American cotton.[135]

Whether or not the increase in municipal revenue will be effective in enlarging the domestic market, is a question which falls outside the scope of this work. Our only object was to try to understand and explain the basic factors in our present 'pro-municipal feeling'.[136] It is hardly necessary to say that our attempt to delve deeper into the reasons for this movement carries with it no intent to denigrate the generous impulses behind the current concern for the dispossessed rural population: the moral beauty of the emancipation of the slaves is not debased by the expediency which for Britain lay in the abolition of the slave trade.

XIII. Political reflection of the financial dependence of the municipalities

The financial misery of our municipalities goes back a long way, as we have seen. Under the Empire, especially after the passing of the Additional Act, and during the Republic, the question of municipal revenue remained part and parcel of the wider problem of provincial and state revenue. The provinces, like the states after them, normally had revenues which were inadequate for the discharge of their duties, and this situation was of necessity reflected in municipal finances. Let us not suppose, however, that the National Treasury was always swimming in gold; it was, on the contrary, in desperate straits also. The picture was one of general poverty at all three levels. When politicians and publicists refer to the lion's share of our public revenue, this does not imply abundance for some and scarcity for others: it is simply a term of comparison which expresses an improper ratio between the three categories of funds: municipal, provincial or state and general or federal.[137]

On the problem of tax allocation our parliamentary annals record, as we have seen, great and learned assemblies which fully illustrate the popular saying: 'when there is no bread, everyone fights, no one is right.' Even so, the division of poverty could have been more equitable than has been usual among us. It was the municipalities which experienced greatest poverty. Without the resources necessary to meet their own expenses, their political autonomy could only be precarious.[138] Financial assistance is, as we all know, the natural vehicle for interference on the part of a superior authority in the independent government of lesser political units. The surrender, at least temporary, of certain prerogatives is usually the price of an aid which is not always inspired by considerations of public interest, being often motivated by considerations of political militancy.

A typical example of a loss of powers brought about by the need for financial aid is to be found in Law No. 546 of 27 September 1910, passed in Minas Gerais. This law, known by the name of the president who sanctioned it — Bueno Brandão — allowed the state to make loans to the municipalities for water supplies, drainage systems, and power stations. These loans were, however, conditional on the signing of an agreement which would empower the state to collect municipal revenues in order to guarantee the service of amortisation and interests. Previous loans, also by means of the agreement, could be taken together with the later ones and subjected to the same system.[139] The demand for an agreement was a bow in the direction of the legal principle of municipal autonomy, but, in certain cases, this proviso reminded one of the freedom which the worker has to discuss wages in times of unemployment.

Another example with graver consequences is to be found in the Bahian Law, No. 2229 of 18 September 1929. In municipalities with services that were the responsibility of the state, or where there was a contract guaranteed by the state, the prefect and the district administrator were not elected but nominated and dismissed by the governor. Of the same general import, although of a more limited scope, is Article 28, para. 1 of the current Federal Constitution, which has the power to nominate the prefect of municipalities containing natural hydro-mineral establishments, serviced by the state or by the Union.

Many other examples could be cited, but it is not necessary.[140] We recall, however, and only as a curiosity, the Decree—Law No. 1205, of 10 April 1939, which conferred on the Bank of Brazil and on the National Savings Bank the right to collect directly the revenues of those states and municipalities who did not regularly repay loans borrowed from them.[141]

The examples quoted fall within the legal field, that is to say, they represent the limitation of municipal autonomy by law, but it was in the area outside the law that the meanness of municipal funds contributed most to making them dependent on the favours of the state governments for the discharge of their most indispensable duties. And this phenomenon, as we have already stressed, was largely responsible for the feature so characteristic of political life in the interior, namely a tendency to conform to the wishes of the ruling parties in the states.[142]

5. Organisation of the police and the judiciary

I. Up to the Constitution of 1824

As has already been pointed out, during Brazil's colonial period Portuguese law imperfectly demarcated the prerogatives of various functionaries, showing no concern — as was generally the case at that time — to separate functions according to their nature. Hence, an accumulation of administrative, police and jurisdictional functions, in the hands of the same authorities, related to each other in a hierarchical system which was not always rigorously maintained. The confusion between judicial and police functions persisted for a long time.[1]

From the point of view which interests us here, we must mention in the first place the ordinary judges and the outside (visiting) judges who had police and juridical functions as well as administrative ones.[2] There were also in some places special judges for orphans[3] and criminal judges.[4] The chambers, for their part, retained certain juridical functions although much reduced by the Phillipine Ordinances.[5]

Under the judges already mentioned were to be found the inspectors of weights and measures and the parish judges [*juizes de vintena*]. The inspectors, apart from infringements of the council's bye-laws, also presided in certain cases of royal law relating to works or buildings, and imposed penalties, there being a right of appeal to the judges.[6]

The parish judges, also known as pedestrian judges, with a small court, presided in settlements remote from the towns or the cities; they had no jurisdiction in criminal matters but they could arrest someone *in flagrante*, or by means of a writ, or through a formal accusation, presenting the detainee to the competent judge.[7] We must also mention, as functionaries with proper police duties, the junior *alcaids*[8] and the guardsmen.[9]

Above these officials were the magistrates of the legal district[10] and, above them, the general magistrates,[11] all nominated by the king. In hierarchical order they functioned as appeal judges and set up courts in the areas in which they held jurisdiction.[12] Higher up the pyramid we find at the head, the lords of the provinces, with full civil and criminal jurisdiction, in certain cases, jointly with the magistrate,[13] and later, the 'captains' or governors of the minor captainships or provinces, the captains-general or governors of the major captainships and the governor general, later known as the viceroy.[14] All exercised functions of a juridical nature, although their prerogatives tended to vary, frequently according to the personality of the official nominated for the particular post.[15] There were also the Courts of Appeal, the highest legal authority in the colony, whose powers included many that would today be classified as both legal and administrative.[16] Various other bodies, as for example fiscal ones and those entrusted with the exploitation of gold and diamonds, also exercised functions of a juridical nature. To give a complete list it would be necessary to describe the entire colonial administration, in view of the fact that it was not usual for specifically juridical functions to be distinguished as such.

The governor was the supreme representative of the king, but many things did not come under his jurisdiction. This fact can be observed on a large scale in the business assigned to judicial bodies or, better, to bodies coming under the general rubric of the judicial system, although their functions, according to modern criteria, might also be administrative. Various legal measures from different periods, some collected by João Francisco Lisboa, affirm explicitly or implicitly that 'the administration of justice is

independent of the governors'.[17] In this regard it must be observed, according to information given us by an expert, that the governor was not superior
to the Court of Appeal in the hierarchy but was only one of its members,
with the function of president *ex officio*.[18]

In Lisbon, the affairs of the colony were submitted to the Overseas
Council (which replaced the Council of India), to the Board of Law and
Order, to the Royal Court of Appeal and to the Court of Entreaty. This
last named judged as an appeal court 'cases falling outside the competence
of colonial justice'.[19] Moreover, in the words of João Francisco Lisboa,
'the interference of the metropolitan country in the most insignificant
colonial matters reached almost fantastic extremes'.[20]

Elective justice, as it functioned in the municipalities, was an important
factor in the dominance of the rural nobility, who used their influence in
the election of judges, councillors and lesser functionaries to the chambers.[21]
For this reason, as we have already seen, to the extent that ordinary judges,
who were elected officials, were being replaced by outside judges nominated by the king, the Crown was appropriating a considerable part of local
government.[22] In joint discussions the opinions of the elected officials of
the chamber might, in the event, prevail,[23] but there still remained the
question of individual action on the part of the king's judges who in addition generally had the advantage of being 'men of learning'.[24]

Official inquiries, on the other hand, played an important role in the
retrospective supervision of ordinary judges, since each new judge had to
review the work of his predecessor.[25] These inquiries – general or specific,
according to whether they dealt with unproven abuses or known errors –
covered not only ordinary judges but also other authorities and individuals
against whom the presiding judge had to act immediately, within the limits
of his authority, and determine who was in the right in cases which demanded it.[26] The results of inquiries on the conduct of judges were submitted to the magistrates.[27] The awe-inspiring qualities of this inquisitorial
process can be easily estimated[28] when we consider that under the Ordinances torture was allowed as a means of determining the facts.[29] Even
judges and councillors could be subjected to the rack when certain offences
were involved.[30]

It is not difficult to imagine, in the situation that we have described,
how the juridical and police functions of the colony's authorities complemented by an unfair legal process, helped to build the pre-eminence of the
rural nobility and later, chiefly through the magistrates and the outside
judges, worked for the submission to the power of the Crown of these
same rebellious colonists.

The period stretching from the transfer of the Court to the promulgation of the Constitution of the Empire greatly accelerated the process by which royal authority was strengthened, along with the considerable development which occurred in the judicial and police system. Dom João established various higher courts in Brazil,[31] increased the number of magistrates and outside judges[32] and created the post of Intendant General of the Court and State Police of Brazil,[33] whose functions were not only police ones but judicial ones as well.[34]

II. During the Empire

During the Empire, police and judicial powers remained concentrated in the hands of the same officials to a very large extent, and the law of 1871, which will be discussed later, tried to remedy the situation.

The Constitution of 1824 declared the judiciary to be independent and as a consequence district judges were to be appointed for life, subject to dismissal by a court verdict only. Nevertheless this same law allowed for the suspension of judges by the Emperor, and entrusted to the ordinary legislator the task of regulating their removal 'from one place to another'.[35]

The principle of appointment for life only benefited district judges, operating in the larger legal divisions, and did not extend to the municipal judges, who served in the smaller subdivisions and were nominated for four years.[36] Nor, obviously, did it cover the justices of the peace, who were elected and whose jurisdiction was limited to the municipality.[37]

An important reform of our police and judicial system, inspired by a movement towards decentralisation, was carried out by the Criminal Code of 29 November 1832 which gave extraordinary importance to the justice of the peace, who was now invested with wider powers.[38] Until it was changed in 1841, this was one of our most discussed laws. Its ineffectiveness as a preventive or restraining measure was held responsible for all the outrages, disorders, riots and revolts which characterised the troubled period of the Regency. The work of the liberals, it was not spared by their opponents, and even within the ranks of its supporters criticism was not slow to appear. Alves Branco himself, foremost among those responsible for the drafting of it, took the initiative in asking that it be revised.[39]

The reaction against the Code of 1832, which conferred such wide powers on the local element, began to take concrete form in the spontaneous action in certain provinces after the promulgation of the Additional Act. We refer to the so-called *laws of the prefects*. The first move was made in the Provincial Assembly of São Paulo through the law of 11 April 1835, which was recommended to other provinces by the Regent Feijó in his well-known circular of 9 December of the same year.[40] Other assemblies —

those of Pernambuco, Sergipe, Paraíba, Maranhão, Alagoas and Ceará – did
not hesitate to follow São Paulo's example. The prefects created by these
provincial laws were to function in the municipalities; they were freely
nominated by the presidents of the provinces, and police prerogatives were
included among their functions.

It is immediately clear that this innovation transferred police control
from local to provincial authorities, with the consequent strengthening of
the provincial presidents. As the police have been traditionally a most valuable force in electoral struggles, the reason given for the General Assembly's
reaction against the law of the prefects, is not very understandable.[41] To
accept it, however, implied the recognition of wide legislative competence
on the part of the provincial assemblies. It is possible, therefore, that this
fact, disagreeable to politicians believing in centralised control, did not
seem to them to be sufficiently compensated for by the possible increase
in the authority of the provincial presidents – all the more so as the assemblies (there was still no interpretative law to the Additional Act) might
in time wean these officials away from presidential influence. In containing the claims of the provincial legislatures, the assembly lost a slight
temporary advantage and avoided a major disadvantage in the future.[42]

It is undeniable that conservative elements did not consider this frag-
mentary reaction embodied in the law of the prefects, to be sufficient; its
extent escaped them. They urged reform of the Code of 1832 at a national
level and the granting to the executive of extensive powers to maintain
public order and national unity; public order and national unity to be con-
strued according to criteria held dear by the conservative and centralising
school of thought. This proposal was accepted by Law No. 261 of 3
December 1841.[43] A short comparison of the two texts is in order.

According to the Code of 1832 each legal division had a district judge,
and in the most populous divisions there could be as many as three, one of
whom would be the chief of police;[44] district judges were nominated by
the Emperor. In the subdivisions there was a council of jurors – drawn up
annually at a special assembly – which functioned as two juries: one which
presented the accusations and the other which passed judgement; a municipal judge and a public prosecutor, nominated by the national government
in the case of the district of the Royal Court, or by the presidents in the
case of the provinces, from three lists drawn up by the municipal chambers;
a clerk, who was an executive officer, and minor court officials. In each
district there was an elected justice of the peace, a clerk and, for each
neighbourhood, an inspector, all nominated by the chamber on the advice
of the judge. In addition, there functioned in each legal division, assemblies

of justices of the peace, which brought together larger or smaller groups of them under the presidency of one of their number, to inform themselves about possible appeals against verdicts which any of them might hand down.[45] Police duties fell principally to the justices of the peace, and progressively to the municipal judges and to the district judge who was also the chief of police.[46]

By contrast with this decentralising law, that of 3 December 1841 established, in the municipality of the Court and in each province, a chief of police, under whom were two ranks of police officers (sheriffs and deputies), as many as were necessary, all being nominated by the government in the case of the Court, and by the presidents in the provinces. The individuals concerned had no right to refuse these duties. At the base of the pyramid remained the neighbourhood inspectors but they were nominated by the sheriffs. The chambers' three lists were dispensed with as a basis for the nomination of municipal judges and prosecutors,[47] the domain of the district judges was extended and the powers of the justices of the peace were limited. Still more significantly, the sheriffs and their deputies were entrusted with judicial as well as police functions. Finally, the law abolished the assemblies of the justices of the peace and the jury of accusation, and made other provisions which were implemented by the enabling legislation.[48]

To give some idea of what this law was like it is enough to reproduce the observations of a detached historian like Otávio Tarquínio de Sousa:

> To a true liberal, the law of 3 December can only be considered a scandal . . . And even a cold man who examines it with detachment will find some cause for serious anxiety . . . The reaction against the principle of a policing judiciary, which the liberals introduced in 1832 by giving police functions to elected justices of the peace, was certainly excessive and in its turn produced the converse principle, that of a judicial police force, when police authorities were accorded functions which were clearly of a judicial nature.[49]

The indignation caused in liberal circles was so great that the reform of 1841 became one of the reasons for the revolution of 1842.[50] But it was revealed as such an efficient instrument of government for whoever was in power that, in the words of Deputy Mateus Casado, the 'Liberal Party, when it came to power, not only failed to repeal the law of 3 December but a committee drawn from this party and including Teófilo Otôni himself, the most passionate opponent of the law, said that experience advised against reforming it'.[51]

During parliamentary debates concerned with the discussion of the law of 1871 the conservatives returned to the fray with the well-known argu-

ments that the law of 1832 was throwing the country into a state of anarchy;[52] the law of 3 December 1841 was the instrument which re-established
order and maintained the government's authority.

Although there was some truth in this accusation, it seems an exaggeration to hold the law of 1832 responsible for the disturbances of the
Regency period. These demonstrations might easily have occurred under
another more rigorous law, by reason of the excitement of a section of the
populace who were looking for new forms of political expression in the
agitation and confusion of the time.[53] It is enough to bear in mind the fact
that the law of 3 December was neither a simple procedural code nor
simply a matter of judicial or police organisation; it was above all a political instrument, a powerful mechanism of dominance, capable of giving the
government crushing electoral victories, whichever party was in power.[54]

The principal effect of Law No. 2033 of 20 September 1871,[55] was to
forbid police authorities to formulate the offence or the indictment of law-
breakers, an important point in the earlier law. However, minor offences
continued to be put through the legal process by the police,[56] and police
chiefs retained the power to formulate the offence and the indictment in
certain cases. The law took no steps to make police officials independent:
although they now had reduced powers, they continued to serve as agents
of the ruling political group, especially at election time.[57]

We do not believe that merely granting guarantees to the police would
have the effect of removing abuses, preventing the police from interfering
in party-political battles, especially when the same individuals who have
previously been corrupted, remain in office.[58] The problem is much more
complex, because corruption does not result only from the constraint
imposed by insecurity but also from favours which security does not
altogether rule out. Nevertheless, just as constitutional and legal guarantees
contribute to more ethical behaviour in the magistrature and in the public
service, so they should be able to raise standards of conduct among the
police, if at the same time there exist other measures conducive to this end.

It is clear from this brief résumé that police arrangements under the
Empire were deplorable, and that they were always dominated by party-
political considerations. The organisation of the judicial system, on the
other hand, while it showed marked progress in comparison to what it had
been earlier, left much to be desired: the corruption of the magistrature,
by reason of its political ties, was a notorious fact, bitterly condemned by
many contemporaries.[59] As the problem is not of an entirely legal nature,
one easily encounters even today the figure of the corrupt judge, careful
with authority, ambitious for honours and privileges, although the guarantees of which he makes a mockery are much more extensive.[60] And it is

precisely in rural areas that the effects of partisan policing and partisan justice are most keenly felt.

III. Police organisation under the Republic

It would be difficult to examine in detail police organisation as it has existed in the Republic. The federalism of 1891 left police functions under the control of the states and each one of them was given complete freedom to set up its own police system.[61] In general, the principle of nominating police chiefs, sheriffs and deputies was adopted,[62] and this was maintained under the discretionary government of 1930, under the Second Republic, under the *Estado Novo* and persists even to this day. The result was the persistence of a partisan police force, which had already become accustomed in imperial times to be used regularly as an instrument of political action: the difference was that, whereas it had earlier obeyed the dictates of the central government, it now served the interests of the ruling groups in the states. This is still the picture which exists in our time,[63] although here and there a tendency towards making the police more professional can be observed, and this does have the effect of removing them from involvement with party politics.[64]

In dealing with the police machinery of the states, we must not forget the military police organised along the same lines as the army. The high command is entrusted to officers who have frequently distinguished themselves as deputies. The policing of the states basically rests with those militias, whose soldiers, captains and sergeants are sent out into the municipalities under the orders of civil or military sheriffs.[65] These troops receive military training, have well-defined guarantees in the relevant legislation and their promotion to higher posts is decided according to fixed criteria.[66] An appreciable portion of state budgets is used to maintain these militias, veritable armies, whose exploits would fill volumes.[67]

The duties of the military police are not limited to the maintenance of law and order in the state. Its role as part of the police machinery in preparing for election campaigns is of greater importance than its regular function of maintaining order, and very often takes precedence over it. Finally, the military police have helped in supporting the position of the states within the political balance of the Federation.[68] Today, with the development of the Air Force and the general improvement in weapons, the importance of the state militias in the event of an armed uprising is much less than it used to be. Even so, if the federal forces were divided in the dispute, their influence could be decisive.

The state character of police organisation under our system of government suffers from two serious limitations: the military police constitute a reserve of the army,[69] and throughout the country it is the Federal Department of Public Safety which acts against crimes involving political and social institutions and which exercises, among others, the functions of a sea-borne and air-borne police force, and is responsible for the security of national frontiers.[70]

During the First Republic the organisation of the police was one of the most solid props of *coronelismo*; still today, to a lesser degree, it continues to carry out this function.

IV. Legal organisation under the regime of 1891

With the Republic came the institution of two legal systems: the federal one, concerning the organisation, procedure and legislative competence of the Union, and the local one, organised by the states, which also had power to legislate on the legal process within each state.[71]

Leaving aside the Federal Supreme Court and military jurisdiction, federal justice comprised the following institutions as courts of first instance: sectional judges, one for each state and for the Federal District; puisne judges, one for each section; and deputies of the puisne judges, later extended to all municipalities;[72] Federal Courts with judge and jury in the principal centres of the sections. The office of the Federal Prosecutor headed by the Attorney General, chosen from among the ministers of the Supreme Court, exercised over-all control over the sectional prosecutors, assistant prosecutors and solicitors.[73] The sphere of influence of federal justice was defined in the Constitution,[74] with all remaining powers of jurisdiction coming under the umbrella of local justice.

The judicial system of the states is of particular interest for our purposes, and there was moreover little variation in basic features from one state to another. The following bodies operated: courts of second instance in the capitals;[75] district judges in the divisions;[76] jury courts; municipal judges in the subdivisions;[77] justices of the peace, generally elected,[78] in the districts. For the purpose of privileges only the district judges and the members of the courts of second instance were considered members of the bench.[79]

In defining the privileges of the bench, the Federal Constitution only referred to Federal Judges. Some states, interpreting the constitutional rule very strictly, placed limitations on the rights of their own judges, or their governments committed violence and abuses against them.[80] Those who were not prepared to submit to such treatment took legal action, and the declaration that state magistrates were eligible for the privileges of life tenure and the preservation of their salaries intact. All this was implicit in the precept which laid down that the constitutional principles of the Union were binding on the states.[81] The constitutional reforms of 1926 emphasised this principle by making it explicit in the text, and strengthening it with the sanction of federal intervention.[82]

These privileges, however, were not applicable to temporary judges whose investiture was designed, according to the justification given at the time, to give them a professional apprenticeship for ultimate entry into the ranks of judges.[83] There remained, therefore, a large category of judges at the mercy of the exigencies and seductions of ruling groups and less mindful of the independence and dignity of the judiciary.

Although their authority was limited, temporary judges stood in for the permanent ones at many points in the legal process and even passed sentences when the permanent judges were prevented from serving. The scale of substitution went down as far as the justices of the peace, whose authority was thereby sometimes stretched beyond their intellectual capacities, and this situation was aggravated by the notorious liaisons between these lay judges and the local political faction on whom their election depended.[84] The general rule of appeal to the permanent judges, limited in cases of substitution, was only relatively effective, since it was frequently true that the upholding of the appeal did not make amends, or only imperfectly, for the injury suffered by the individual in question. Finally, the mechanism of promotion by merit, of re-posting and removals to better divisions or subdivisions, accentuated the precariousness of the position of temporary judges and reduced the independence of the permanent ones. Moreover, there were various measures taken by state governments to keep the magistrates in a state of submission, such as allocating, altering the boundaries of, or abolishing, judicial territories, withholding salaries etc.[85]

As for the local legal officers, they were generally nominated to their posts and as easily dismissed, so that the prosecutors and their assistants habitually became agents of party politics.[86]

Through these large doors the judiciary passed to collaborate unscrupulously in the party politics of the states, a situation directly reflected in the mechanism of *coronelismo*.

V. Under the Constitutions of 1934, 1937 and 1946

Leaving aside the numerous provisions relevant to legal organisation, which have no special significance for this work, let us note that the Constitution of 1934, following the example of the constitutional reforms of 1926, also sanctioned with federal intervention the privileges of the state magistrature, and established various obligatory rules on remuneration, investiture, promotion, retirement, etc.[87] The Constitutions of 1937[88] and 1946[89] adopted the same orientation, but they suppressed the category of common Federal Judges of courts of first instance.[90] It must be observed, however, that these privileges were little more than illusory during the *Estado Novo*, in view of the compulsory and arbitrary retirement, with remuneration proportionate to years of service, permitted by Article 177 of the Constitution of 10 November.[91]

Both the Constitution of 1934 and that of 1937 maintained the elective nature of the justices of the peace, with the authority given to them by state law, safeguarding the right of appeal against their decisions to the formally invested magistrature.[92] But throughout the entire period of the *Estado Novo*, which never put representative machinery into practice, the justices of the peace were nominated by the state governments.[93] The Constitution of 1946 also retains a system of justices of the peace whose elective nature has not been declared obligatory.[94] They have been forbidden, however, even when acting as substitutes, to hand down final or irrevocable judgements, 'in order to avoid the notorious improprieties of the system until recently in force', as Deputy Milton Campos, author of the amendment, has emphasised.[95]

Apart from the justices of the peace, the Constitutions of 1934, 1937 and 1946 continued to allow the states to create temporary judges with the important function – among others – of standing in for permanent ones.[96] The Constitution of 1946, however, took the precaution of giving these judges life appointments 'after ten years of continuously exercising their function'. Even so, there will be room for abuses, either by their being removed before the ten year period has run, or by some interruption in their service required by the Constitution to be 'continuous'.

As for the department of justice, under current regulations there are certain innovations designed to improve the situation: entry by examination and an organised career structure, with members being guaranteed tenure after two years of service and relative freedom from dismissal; rules governing promotion have also been established.[97]

Nevertheless, the judiciary has not been altogether removed from participation in politics, although such activity has been expressly forbidden to judges: the continued existence of temporary judges, the machinery for promotion and removal, and the use of various methods of seduction and various types of pressure difficult to avoid or suppress – all these things contribute to the fact that it is still possible, especially in the interior, to meet partisan judges and prosecutors, not to mention junior officials who are almost always impassioned militants.

VI. The jury

The jury deserves separate treatment, by reason of its notorious links with politics in the rural areas. The jury system was adopted in Brazil by a decree of 18 June 1822[98] to judge offences committed by the press. With this same function, it was the subject of a bill discussed in our first Constituent Assembly, the proposals of which were approved by a decree of 22 November 1823. The Constitution of 1824 incorporated it into the judicial system, with power of decision in both civil and criminal cases.[99] As a press tribunal it was reorganised by the law of 20 November 1830 and underwent more significant reforms in the Criminal Code of 1832, which brought almost all offences within the competence of the jury, which was now to function as two separate councils: one of accusation and the other of judgement. The first was abolished by the law of 3 December 1841, which entrusted to the police the power, subject to correction, of deciding whether or not an offence was indictable. Enjoying wide powers and partially reformed by the laws of 1850, 1860, 1871 and 1883, the jury continued to be used in criminal cases up until the time of the Republic.[100]

The Constitution of 1891, although it omitted the provisional government's bill, contained a succinct regulation according to which 'the institution of the jury' would be 'maintained'.[101] The Federal Jury had previously been set up by Decree No. 848 of 11 October 1890, which established the Union's legal system. In the interpretation of the constitutional text there were two bodies of opinion: one, with the added lustre lent to it by Rui Barbosa, believed that the jury should be maintained with the organisation, powers and characteristics which it possessed at the time of the proclamation of the Republic;[102] the other, having more adherents and finally victorious, argued that the Constitution had not fossilised the jury, but left room for its renewal, as long as its fundamental features were respected.[103]

The states, in their Constitutions or criminal codes, and the Union itself, in legislating on the federal legal system[104] and on the legal system which would function in the Republic's Capital,[105] introduced several modifications in the institution as it was inherited from the Empire, especially in regard to its composition and competence. As a rule its powers were reduced and the number of crimes to be tried in magistrates' courts increased. The law of Rio Grande do Sul of 16 December 1895, whose innovations were upheld by the Supreme Court, went so far as to forbid unmotivated challenging of jury membership, and to make it possible to reveal publicly how members voted.[106] The code of Minas Gerais of 1926, following the example of the Federal District and Pernambuco, gave the Court of Appeal power to annul a judgement handed down in contradiction to the evidence and to bring the defendant before a new jury.[107] The state of Ceará reached the point of allowing the official magistrature to revise juries' decisions when necessary, but did not thereby win the approval of the judiciary.[108] As to the composition of the jury, a great variety of solutions was adopted.[109]

The Constitution of 1934, although it explicitly declared that the jury system was to be maintained, delegated to the law the task of defining its 'organisation and its powers'.[110] The law, as it happened, was to be the federal law in view of the power granted to the Union to legislate on the legal process,[111] but the Constitution of the Second Republic was revoked before the national codes of legal processes could be promulgated. While it was in force, however, it retained, as far as the jury was concerned, the system inherited from the previous regime.

The Charter of 1937 said nothing on the subject, and the ordinary legislator was thus given freedom to suppress or preserve the jury system, organising it and defining its competence as he saw fit. Decree—Law No. 167 of 5 January 1938[112] was not long in coming. Its principal innovation consisted of allowing courts of second instance to revise jury decisions on their merits 'in order to decide on a fair penalty or discharge the defendant, as the case might be', when the decision arrived at was in 'complete divergence' from the evidence produced, or when 'no support' (for the decision) could be found in the minutes of the case.[113]

Later, the federal legislator said that this reform would restore the public's confidence in the jury system by putting an end to its 'systematic indulgence';[114] notwithstanding, the Constitution of 1946 re-established the sovereignty of the verdicts of the popular tribunal, requiring that it should have an odd number of members, that it should vote in secret and that there should be ample defence for the accused. As to its powers, these were by statute not to include crimes of violence against the person. The inclusion of others was left to the discretion of the ordinary legislator.[115] The legislation in force at the time was adapted to the new constitutional precepts.[116]

Ever since its introduction into Brazil the jury system has been the target of many criticisms and has also had strong defenders. The apologists themselves do not deny that it has defects, but hope that time and the education of the people will correct them.[117] However, our legislators have not had the patience to wait; rather, they have sought to collaborate with time by 'perfecting' the jury. The result, in the best of hypotheses, has been the reduction of its powers.[118]

It is not our purpose to take part in the polemic on the splendour and misery of juries, but merely to observe their relationship to the system of *coronelismo*. The popular tribunal, during the long period preceding Decree–Law No. 167 of 1938, was also one of the key points of activity in local politics. The relative impunity of the *coronéis'* thugs can be explained in large measure by the influence exercised by local political bosses over the jury. To put on the street or condemn someone who has committed a crime has, traditionally, been an important problem in local politics, especially when the criminal, his henchman or the victim, has a position of importance in local party politics. In this task decisive roles were played by police connivance in investigating evidence; by the tolerance of the public prosecutor in watering-down the charge or refraining from appeals; by involving lawyers affiliated to municipal parties, sometimes the leaders of them, or called in from outside when the importance of the case demanded it. The influence of the local leader was most keenly felt in the drawing up of lists of jurors and in the 'preparation' of those belonging to his side. Given the all but intransigent nature of municipal political conflict, it is easy to understand the importance always assumed by the principle of peremptory challenge of jurors, so ardently defended by Rui Barbosa.[119] It was not only the 'logic of feeling'[120] which informed the decisions of the jury but also 'partisan logic', which did not always work towards acquittal but also towards indictment.

In the influence of local politics on the legal judgements of jurors we can clearly see how the authority of the *coronéis*, derived from their economic and social ascendancy, is reinforced by a borrowed authority given by the state government through the compromise typical of *coronelismo*.

VII. Private power, the Ordinances and the National Guard

Very clear examples of the deals between private power and public authority are to be found in two other important institutions, among whose duties is included the exercise of police functions: we refer to the militias and the National Guard.

The growing interference of the Crown in colonial life, chiefly by means of the visiting judges and the magistrates, revealed its preoccupation with the effective exercise of its powers, but social conditions in the country did not allow it to dispense with the disciplinary strength embodied in the rich landowners. For this reason, Portugal sought to attract these natural leaders to her service by granting them positions of command in the corps of militias, a third line of reserve for the army, which embraced the entire male population between 17 and 60 years of age not enlisted in the troops of the line or in the state militias.

Caio Prado Júnior, to whom we owe this passage, carried out interesting research on the role played by the general militias, which developed on the margin of the law as a direct result of the social and economic conditions of the country. In his own words:

> If as an armed force the militias occupy an obscure place in our history, on another level, and one not foreseen by the laws which created them, they have an unparalleled function. It can be affirmed without exaggeration that it is they who made law and administrative order possible in this vast territory with a scattered population and a scarcity of regular public functionaries. Through them, the administration extended its network over this whole area. The meagre body of officials which we had, would have been incapable on their own of getting a grip on the country; concentrated as they were in the capitals and larger centres.[121]

In the maintenance of law and order, in the carrying out of public works, in the collecting of financial resources, in numerous administrative problems, Caio Prado Júnior found evidence of the interference of these citizens' militias, sometimes by spontaneous action on their part, often in response to requests from the authorities. The way in which the mother country achieved this result consisted not in launching the representatives of public authority against the local landowners but, on the contrary, in incorporating the latter with their great social prestige into the administrative machinery of the state by giving them posts of command in the citizens' militias.

The formation of these auxiliary forces and the extra-legal duties which they were generally asked to perform reveal quite clearly that conditions in the colony imposed a compromise between the Crown and the rural leaders, even at a time when the private power of the latter, though already very significant, could not present any serious challenge to royal authority. Around the rural leaders, who were the natural pivots of social and economic power at the time, there revolved, besides slaves and subdued Indians, a large number of household servants. From this dependent population was drawn, in the main, the private armies which made the landowner's authority effective and played such an important part in inter-family disputes. At the outset of colonisation, the Crown itself demanded from those who were allotted land, a minimum of armed force under their command for the defence of the land and the centres of settlement against hostile tribes.[122] In addition, in the raiding and exploration parties, the backlanders commanded military forces trained to fight against the Indians. Later, the wisdom of the Crown was revealed in its decision to invest with legal authority, chiefly through the citizens' militias, this spontaneous preempting of power by the landowners, thus placing it at the service of law and order and the aims of the government.

The National Guard was in later times to be a modernised version of the citizens' militias. Created by the law of 18 August 1831 as a permanent organisation, its task was, in Max Fleuiss' summary, 'to defend the Constitution, the liberty, independence and integrity of the nation'. Its ordinary work, 'inside and outside the municipality', consisted 'in having detachments at the disposal of justices of the peace, criminal judges, presidents of the provinces and the Ministry of Justice on the request of the civil authority. Service in it had to be performed by each individual male over 18 years of age', with specific exemptions.

The National Guard provided detachments for duties outside the municipalities in defence of garrisons, coasts and frontiers, as an auxiliary force of the army. In the event of a shortage of troops of the line, or of police, it provided the required number of men for the safe conduct of consignments of money or any other effects belonging to the nation; the transporting of prisoners or condemned persons; help to municipalities in times of conflict or civil disturbances.[123]

Before the establishment of the National Guard, and until it could be organised, the law of 6 June 1831 had created municipal militias and made other provisions for the purpose, according to the Viscount of Uruguai, of maintaining public security and of punishing those guilty of indictable offences, since 'the revolution of 7 April had only just taken place and anarchy was beginning to raise its head'.[124] The National Guard would therefore replace 'the defunct militias of municipal guards and the citizens' militias'.[125] The law of 10 October 1831 'created, in the district of the Court, a body of municipal guards, infantry and cavalry, to maintain public order and help the forces of justice, with agreed remuneration', and authorised the provincial presidents 'in Council' to create similar bodies where they deemed them necessary.[126] Several provinces made use of this authorisation, organising police forces, fixing their numbers, regulating their discipline, defining penalties and determining their application, creating institutions of a legal nature and even giving the presidents power to enlist recruits to make up the numbers of the volunteers.[127] Another general law of 7 October 1833 authorised the creation of police guards in each district, their numbers and remuneration to be decided by the municipal chambers after prior consultation with the justices of the peace. These guards remained under the control of the elected judicial authority, which had power to dismiss or replace them, substituting others whom it considered more trustworthy. The cost of the guard was met by voluntary subscriptions from the inhabitants of the district, who often had a voice in the fixing of the various salaries. In the district of the Court, the Minister of Justice, and in the provinces the presidents 'in Council', could 'delay the setting up of the guards, reduce their number, dissolve them and replace them by some other force' when they considered it necessary, with the justices of the peace to take over responsibility for any abuse which might occur.[128]

This last law and the one which originally set up the National Guard are a clear reflection of the decentralising tendencies revealed in the Criminal Code and in the Additional Act. In both, public authority demonstrates its decision to use private power to its advantage by institutionalising it. This preoccupation was revealed in characteristic fashion in the process for the investiture of officers of the National Guard, who, with certain fixed exceptions, were elected from within the ranks of the institution itself, with the local element predominating.[129] Later, however, when a tendency towards centralisation had prevailed in the government, election was abolished: by the law of 19 September 1850 nominations and promotions came under the control of the public authority.[130] By this time the central government had come to dominate the entire police organisation, either directly or through the provincial presidents, and the National Guard was doomed to suffer the same fate.[131] Accordingly, it very quickly became predominantly honorific and decorative and later altogether so.[132] With its ranks given only to political allies, rebellion was prevented and devotion ensured. The prestige of rank often proved to be an irresistible attraction in the technique of capturing the loyalty of local leaders. The Republic would continue to employ these methods for a long time.[133]

From the point of view of our present interest, the basic point to stress is the progressive strengthening of the judicial and police machinery, especially the latter. This began at a certain point in the colonial period, became more noticeable after the transfer of the Court, and increased still further after the law of 1841. This strengthening of public authority in colonial times suited the interests of Portugal; during the Empire it obeyed the principles of centralised government, which were so closely linked, as Hermes Lima observed, to the survival of the monarchy and the preservation of slavery; under the Republic — the failed experiment of the first years of the working of the Additional Act being tried again, this time successfully — the same process would serve to consolidate the ruling political parties in the states.[134]

The decline in the prestige of the citizens' militias in the last years of the colonial regime (when royal authority had already been strengthened), and later the discrediting of the National Guard in the second half of the nineteenth century — these are merely reflections of the same phenomenon:

the progressive decline of private power, which by a compromise — and this in itself is a sign of decline — found in these organisations an institutional means of expression.

We can still observe today in the interior, especially in the most remote areas, very visible manifestations of private power, notably in the influence which local leaders and landowners exercise over their dependants. And as the legal and police machinery of the states becomes more efficient, so this informal magistrature becomes more subordinate to public authority and the pro-government attitudes of local leaders are reinforced. This political conformism, an essential aspect of the compromise of *coronelismo*, brings in its wake, among other advantages, the nomination of police sheriffs and deputies according to the wishes of the municipal leaders, or instructions to police officials to work in conjunction with them. i.e. to 'do justice' to their friends and 'apply the law' to their enemies. Hence the indissoluble bonds which exist between the system of *coronelismo* and the police system.

As far as the courts are concerned, this bond used to be much closer than it is today, and it has diminished as the privileges of the judiciary have increased. Even so it is still evident with respect to the justices of the peace, and continues to manifest itself appreciably with respect to temporary judges, who have not the same rights as career magistrates. Occasionally there are shocking expressions of partisan attitudes even among the permanent judges. Legal guarantees do not always supplant human weaknesses: being transferred to more comfortable places, access to higher grades, the placing of relations, a taste for prestige — these are the principal factors in the political predisposition of many judges. On the other hand, the members of the departments of justice of the states do not have the same guarantees as magistrates, and in the most backward municipalities lay individuals continue to function as assistants to the public prosecutor, and these are almost always chosen for party-political reasons.

These weaknesses in the police and judicial systems are the result of the isolation and poverty of the country, the scarcity of public funds, human weakness and, in large part, of the less than scrupulous concerns of the ruling groups of the states. It is, above all, this party interest which determines the involvement of judges, prosecutors, minor justice officials and police chiefs in the general system of compromise characteristic of *coronelismo*.

6. Electoral legislation

I. Electoral legislation until the end of the Empire

An examination of Brazilian electoral legislation is very important for the study of *coronelismo*. Some indications have already been given with reference to municipal elections,[1] but they are not enough.[2]

The first electoral decree of Dom João VI was that of 7 March 1821, which ordered that the election of deputies to the Portuguese *Côrtes* be governed by the relevant rules laid down in the Spanish Constitution. As the system was a complicated one — indirect suffrage in four stages — there quickly followed the circular of 23 March, authorising the captains-general and the governors of the captainships to make the necessary modifications. New instructions of 19 June 1822 regulated the election of deputies to our first Constituent Assembly in two stages, by means of indirect suffrage.

The same system, with a progressive computation from the first to the second stage, was welcomed in the draft to the Constitution, which was discussed and voted upon in that abortive congress[3] and in the Constitution confirmed by Dom Pedro.[4]

The first elections which took place for senators and deputies, were regulated by instructions handed down with the decree of 26 March 1824.[5] In order to proceed with the elections of the first stage, electoral boards were set up, composed of the outside judge (or the ordinary one, or someone acting on their behalf), the parish priest, two secretaries and two examiners. The last four were chosen by acclamation of the electoral assembly[6] meeting in the church, and on the proposal of the judge seconded by the parish priest. The board had very wide powers, ranging from the qualification of voters and the decision as to the length of time allowed for the receiving of documents, to the checking of votes and fixing of the number of electors in the parish.[7]

This system, in which the electoral board was the key to the election, lasted until 1842 with deplorable results.[8] The composition of the electoral boards continued to be of fundamental importance until the electoral code of 1932, because they had the precious duty of checking the votes.

The last chamber, elected according to the rules of 1824, was dissolved, as is well known, before being installed. New electoral rules were handed down by the cabinet of 23 March 1841, and by the decree of 4 May 1842 whose principal innovation was the prior qualification of voters and candidates by a group composed of the justice of the peace, the parish priest and the police authority. The electoral board came to be nominated by sixteen citizens chosen by lot from among those eligible for election. At this time, the sheriffs and deputies of the police were the mere creatures of the central authority, owing to the terms of the law of 3 December 1841. Their influence on the qualifying of the voters of the locality thus totally distorted the results of the contest by completely unbridled violence.[9]

In an endeavour to prevent the gross interference of the police in the registration of voters, Law No. 387 of 19 August 1846 reorganised the qualifying board, which was now to be composed as follows: the justice of the peace remained, but he had to be voted into office as the president of the board, and four members were selected by a complicated process from among the electors.[10] The parochial board, given the task of checking the identity of voters, receiving and checking votes, making decisions on incidental problems and uncertainties, was set up, using the same formula as applied to the qualifying board. This system of qualification laid down by the law of 1846, deficient as it was, persisted with minor alterations until the law of 1875, contributing thereby to the failure of the laws of 1855 and 1860.[11]

The most discussed reform and the one to which many politicians of the time attached great hopes, since it had been regarded as a matter of trust by Honório Hermeto,[12] President of the Council, was the so-called Law of the Constituencies (No. 842 of 19 September 1855), which divided the provinces into districts each with one deputy. It also ordered that substitute or assistant deputies be elected at the same time as the deputies themselves, the second vote immediately following the first. As the results did not live up to expectation, the law was quickly reformed. In the first place the substitute deputies – who, since 1822, had been those receiving the second highest number of votes, and who often turned out to be members of the opposition – began to be representatives of the same local factions, generally pro-government ones, which elected the deputies.[13] On the other hand, the changes introduced in the organisation of the qualifying boards and the parochial boards were only minor ones. According to the previous law the parochial electors and a certain number of their substitutes met together to choose the members of the two bodies; by the law of 1855 the group of electors and of substitutes were to choose their own representatives for these bodies, separately.[14]

Then came Law No. 1082 of 18 August 1860, also called the *Second Law of the Constituencies*. This abolished the substitutes, determining that a new election would take place should a vacancy arise, and enlarged the constituencies so that each now had three deputies elected on a system of proportional representation. Apart from this, the changes introduced into the registration system and the electoral process were too slight to achieve any noticeable improvement in the way the ballot was conducted.[15]

A new reform came with Law No. 2675 of 20 October 1875. The adoption of the limited vote, or the incomplete list, in elections of the first and the second stages, was the principal innovation. The theoretical intention of the system was to guarantee the representation of minorities, it being supposed that a third of the representatives, not supported by the votes of the majority, could be elected by minority elements. However, those skilled in electoral mathematics did not hesitate to introduce shady practices to tamper with the *Law of the Third*. By substituting the names of candidates on the voting papers, by means of a prior calculation of the number of electors, the majority cheated in order to suppress minority representation, or to reduce it below the legal third.[16] In spite of other modifications and precautions adopted by the law of 1875, including cases of ineligibility,[17] the inadequate system of supervision continued in force: supervision continued to be undertaken by political bodies, from the electoral board of the parish to the legislative chambers at the final stage.

Hopes for the introduction of direct election also helped to condemn the *Law of the Third*. The attempt to introduce it by a provision of the Constitution came to nothing under the Sinimbu Cabinet. Counsellor Saraiva may claim the glory for having achieved the most honest elections of the Empire in the first experiment of the law which took its name from him; he had carried out the reform through the ordinary legislative process. Reducing the voting process to one phase only, Law No. 3029 of 9 January 1881, based on a bill proposed by Rui Barbosa, demanded an annual minimum income of 200,000 *cruzeiros* as the requirement for inclusion on the electoral register, hence the name *Law of Annual Income*. It re-established uninominal districts for the election of deputies to the General Assembly, sought to guarantee the secrecy of the ballot and increased the cases of inelegibility and incompatibility.

Other provisions of the law are of greater significance for our study. In each legal subdivision the question of qualification was entrusted to the municipal judge, while the final drawing up of the list of electors of the entire division was left to the district judge. The register was to be revised annually by the inclusion of new electors or by the exclusion of names in specifically-defined cases. The electoral boards — a measure of fundamental value — were composed of the justice of the peace of the parish who had received the most votes, as president, and of four board members who were the two justices of the peace nearest to the first in terms of votes, and two citizens who had obtained the next highest number of votes. In any case, these boards continued to have the important task of checking the votes.

The final check, based on the boards' own records, was to be carried out by a group composed of the district judge of the legal division in his capacity as head of the electoral district, as president, and by the presidents of the electoral boards of the area. The greater involvement of judicial authorities in determining qualification and in the final phase of supervision, represented beyond doubt a step forward, but its effect was reduced by the political dependence of the municipal judges and even of the district judges, as has been stressed in the preceding chapter.

The first experiment with the Saraiva Law returned to the chamber 47 conservatives, and 75 liberals of the governing party; among those defeated was the Chief Minister of the Empire, Baron Homen de Melo.[18] A few days after the opening of the new chamber, the Cabinet repaid its temerity by dismissing it, and the grandiose spectacle presented by the contest of 1881 was not reproduced in subsequent ones.[19]

In spite of successive reforms, the elections of the Empire always left much to be desired. To form an over-all judgement of them, one only has to observe the peculiar functioning of our parliamentary system, with the rotation of parties being predominantly, when not exclusively, dependent on the personal judgement of the monarch. In the phrase of Martinho Campos, 'the right to elect representatives of the nation' was in the reign of Dom Pedro III 'the best and most considered prerogative of the moderating power'.[20] Nabuco de Araújo summarised this situation with rare felicity in his much repeated sallies: 'The Moderating Power can summon whom it wishes to set up ministries; this person calls the election because he has to; this election produces the majority.'[21]

II. Electoral legislation of the First Republic

The Republic, by departing from the principle of the direct vote and suppressing the high income qualification of the Saraiva Law, and in every other way, went back to the beginning again. Of the numerous legal texts on electoral matters issued by the provisional government of Marechal Deodoro, two hold special interest for us.

The first – No. 200-A of 8 February 1890 – entrusted the question of qualification[22] to district committees composed of the justice of the peace who had received the most votes, the deputy police chief of the parish and a citizen elegible for registration, nominated by the president of the municipal chamber. The definitive lists were organised by municipal committees, including the municipal judge of the subdivision, the president of the chamber and the police chief (with minor alterations in specific cases). Appeal against these exclusions could be made to the district judge of the division.

The second decree to which we referred – No. 511 of 23 June 1890 – regulated the electoral process. Its name, the *Alvim Regulation*, was derived from the countersigning minister. In each district the electoral board was composed of five members. In the district of the municipal seat it was presided over by the president of the chamber, who selected the four board members, two councillors and two electors. In the other districts all the members were nominated by the president of the chamber. Uncertainties and incidental problems were resolved by the president before the composition of the board, and by the board itself by means of a simple voting majority after it was constituted. The electors of the section could only raise or discuss questions with the agreement of the board. The election was carried out on the basis of a relative majority and the incomplete list. The electoral board checked votes and drafted the report, and was responsible for the subsequent burning of the papers, save those which were checked separately, these being sent to the Ministry of the Interior. The municipal chambers of the Federal District and of the state capitals made the final check, using authenticated copies of the original reports. The elections for the Constituent Congress were carried out in accordance with these regulations, and the government, with such efficient weapons at its disposal, achieved a spectacular victory.[23]

The Constitution of 1891 maintained the broadly-based suffrage: in principle all citizens over twenty-one who registered themselves in accordance with the law, were electors.[24] The legislative competence of the Union was in this respect limited to the power 'to regulate the conditions and the procedure for the election as regards federal duties', while the states retained the power to legislate on state and municipal elections.[25]

The first federal electoral law which followed the Constitution, was No. 25 of 26 January 1892, which instituted the system of the incomplete list in districts of three deputies. A single assembly composed of councillors and an equal number of those who, next to them, had secured the largest number of votes, was empowered to divide the district into sections and elect the five serving members of the sectional committees and their substitutes. These committees were empowered to carry out the registration procedure, there being a right of appeal to a municipal committee consisting of the president of the municipal government and the presidents of the sectional committees. In certain well-defined cases, appeals against the decisions of the municipal committee could be made to the electoral commissions (*juntas*), which in each state were composed of the Federal Judge, his substitute, and the Federal Prosecutor for the section. The checking of votes continued to be in the hands of the electoral boards, which were set up in the same way as the sectional committees for registration. The final check, based on the reports, was carried out in the municipality that was the seat of the section by a committee composed of the five councillors who had received the highest number of votes, and the five citizens who came next in order of votes, under the presidency of the chief of the municipal government.[26]

Leaving aside the numerous partial alterations, it was Law No. 1269 of 15 November 1904, also known as the *Rosa and Silva Law*, which replaced the system set up by Law No. 35.[27] The new process of registration was extended to state and municipal elections,[28] the number of deputies for each district was increased to five,[29] the system of the incomplete list was retained and that of the cumulative vote was added to it.[30] The final check on the voting reports was to be carried out by the presidents of the municipal chambers of the electoral district, presided over by the Federal Judge's substitute or his deputies, depending on the nature of the locality,[31] and he, whoever he was, would have only a casting vote. The counting of the votes, however, continued to be in the hands of the electoral boards.[32] This law really favoured the representation of minorities but was soon cheated of its objectives.[33]

There followed the legislation of 1916, which with partial alterations[34] lasted until the end of the First Republic. It introduced the reform, which took the name of Senator Bueno de Paiva, with two laws. The first − No. 3139 of August 1916 − recognised the competence of the states to regulate state and municipal registration,[35] annulled previous registrations, and entrusted the qualification procedure for federal elections exclusively to the judiciary: only district judges decided petitions for qualifications, which could be made on any business day of the year, with right of appeal to a state commission, comprising the Federal Judge, his deputy, and the general prosecutor of the local judicial system; in those municipalities which had no district judge the municipal judges simply prepared the documents. The second law − No. 3208 of 27 December 1916 − maintained the earlier system of voting: constituencies with five deputies, incomplete list, cumulative vote. The general checking was done in the capitals (no longer in the district centres) by a supervisory commission composed of the Federal Judge, of his substitute and of the representative of the department of justice, together with the local court of second instance. The organisation of the electoral boards merited special care,[36] they retained, however, the right to check the votes immediately following the close of the ballot. The legislation of 1916 had many points of merit but failed to put an end to in-grained electoral frauds, which were partly due to deficiencies in the judicial system.[37]

Two very important types of fraud dominated the elections of the First Republic: the stroke-of-the-pen system (*bico de pena*) and *beheading* or *purging*. The first was practised by the electoral boards in their capacity as supervisory commissions: names were invented, dead persons were resurrected, and people who had been absent at the ballot were marked as present; in compiling their report, the all-powerful pen of the board members achieved miracles. The second metamorphosis was the work of the legislative chambers in the recognition of powers: many of those who escaped in the preliminary ordeals had their documents cancelled in the final examination.

The story is told of Pinheiro Machado who once told a young member of his own party of shaky allegiance: 'You will not be recognised for three reasons. The third is that you have not been elected.' True or false, the anecdote reveals that the number of votes placed in the ballot boxes was of little significance in the question of recognition, if there were political interests in keeping or omitting a representative. Even procedures which ensured that both the government and the opposition were represented on the electoral boards and in the supervision of the votes, were very similar in the end result. To win in this situation you had to have the police and the public treasury on your side, since you would then be in a position to remunerate or persecute. And these instruments functioned in favour of the federal opposition itself when it happened to be the ruling group in its own state. When this particular hypothesis was not verified, the presumption of legitimacy doubtless favoured the certification of opposition members, but this presumption was inverted when it came to recognition, as will be seen later.

Summarising the various phases of electoral fraud under the Constitution of 1891, Assis Brasil had this to say in a speech delivered to the second Constituent Assembly of the Republic: 'Under the regime which we over-threw by the Revolution, no one was certain that he could qualify or that he could vote ... The voter was not certain that his vote would be counted ... Once the vote was counted, no one could be sure that the person elected would be recognised by a system of supervision carried out inside this house and, very often, by orders from above.'[38]

'In Brazil', said Levi Carneiro, speaking in the same Assembly, 'when the President of the Republic wanted to cancel the qualifications of the elected deputies and senators, those who surrounded him would say: "Your Excellency can do better than this." And the *Anais* record: *cheers, applause*.'[39]

III. The electoral codes of 1932 and 1935

Having set up the purification of our representative system as one of its principal ideals,[40] the glorious revolution of 3 October sought to fulfil its promises with the electoral code approved by Decree No. 21,076 of 24 February 1932,[41] which gave women the right to vote,[42] lowered the voting age to eighteen, and made the secrecy of the ballot effective. Its principal innovation consisted of entrusting registration, the checking of the votes and the recognition and proclamation of those elected, to the electoral branch of the judiciary. As its system of representation, the code adopted the procedure of two simultaneous ballots, in the first instance proportional through a system of electoral quotients, and in the second party-based by a simple majority.[43]

It was in line with this legislation that the election of 3 May 1933 took place. This election resulted in the popular representation of the second Constituent Assembly of the Republic. Professional representation, which also figures prominently in the same assembly, obeyed other rules, as was natural.[44] The basic principles of the reforms were incorporated into the text of the Constitution.[45]

Criticisms of this electoral code, raised by the contests of May 1933 and October 1934, led to the promulgation of the other one — Law No. 48 of 4 May 1935 — which introduced slight alterations to its predecessor and remained in force until the *coup* of 1937.

The electoral branch of the judicial system had (apart from the High Court and the regional courts[46]), in each judicial area, the local life judge (or one of the life judges chosen by the regional court when there was more than one) as the electoral judge of first instance, and supervisory boards (to check votes) in specific places. Each supervisory board was composed of three local life judges, under the presidency of the one who held jurisdiction in the municipality of the chief town.[47] The electoral branch of the judiciary, besides having the power through its higher bodies to draw up instructions complementary to the electoral legislation, was responsible for all the business of registration, supervision and recognition, and even for the division of municipalities into electoral sections, the distribution of electors in the various sections and the formation of the returning boards. These, one for each section, were composed of a president, a first and a second subordinate, all nominated by the electoral judge, and of two secretaries chosen by the president of the board. The law set out the incompatibilities and preferences relating to the exercise of the function of board members, and allowed the proceedings of the board to be inspected by the fiscals and delegates of the parties.[48]

The returning boards lost the power to check votes, that permanent source of false records. The counting of the votes was henceforth to be done by the regional courts and in municipal elections by the supervisory boards composed, as we have already said, of life judges. On the other hand, with the proclamation of those elected and the issuing of documents now in the hands of the regional courts and the Higher Court, the shameful recognition functions of the legislative assemblies were abolished.

The secrecy of the vote, despite having been proclaimed on several occasions in previous legislation, was still undermined in different ways. One of the most common was for the parties to use envelopes of different size, shape and colour. By this means, when the voter placed it in the ballot-box in full view of all, the vote was perfectly identifiable. When the more cunning electors began to put the voting papers of one party into the envelopes of the other in order to elude the surveillance of the board and of spies, a system was adopted whereby the elector was handed the closed envelope with the appropriate vote already inside.[49] To prevent such abuse the codes of 1932 and 1935 sought to make the voting 'absolutely impenetrable', and punished by nullification not only the effective identification of the vote but also the mere possibility of it.[50] When the polls closed, the ballot-boxes, sealed and labelled, were handed over to the counting authority together with the reports, various precautions being required by law.[51]

Under the code of 1932, the solution offered by the High Electoral Court to the controversy over the filling of seats designed to complete the party quotient permitted a vicious practice which was described by Deputy J.J. Seabra as a 'waterspout'. The solution in question permitted the votes of one party to be added to those of the other and for spoilt ballots to be counted as well.[52] This expedient was employed in supplementary elections when the position of the various candidates was already known. With the power to influence the classification of its adversaries, each party sought to harm the most effective of them or to favour those with whom it had greatest affinity. It was a reproduction of the system of fabricating non-existent opponents which operated during the period of the incomplete list.[53] This defect was corrected by the law of 1935,[54] which also altered the existing criteria for the allocation of places in the second ballot, seeking in this way to obtain a fairer system of representation.[55]

In spite of the praise it deserved, the code of 1932, perfected by the reform of 1935, did not succeed in putting an end to the habitual coercion of party officials. We are not referring to direct and physical coercion taking place on election day or during the act of voting itself. Nor was this the most frequent means of compulsion used under the old system. We are alluding to the subtle but effective types of coercion, which in many places preceded elections in the rural areas of the country; to the atmosphere of insecurity intentionally created for the electors of the opposition, who in the smaller municipalities would be known to everyone; to the preliminary violence, actual or threatened, demonstrated persistently in big and little ways, for days, weeks and sometimes months on end.[56] The code had no remedy for this type of coercion in view of the limited interpretation put upon it by the Higher Electoral Court.[57]

In spite of the excesses and frauds which can occur in one place or another, the great mass of evidence is favourable to the experiment of the electoral laws of 1932 and 1935. It would have been sufficient for them to have forbidden recognition to be undertaken by the chambers themselves to have eliminated the most serious accusations as to the falsification of political representation in Brazil. Ruling groups in the states were defeated and large opposition factions, subsequently swollen by the dispute over the succession to the presidency, took their seats in the Federal Chamber.

Notwithstanding the appreciable increase in the parliamentary opposition, the predominance of the government group in the Constituent Assembly of 1933, and in the ordinary chamber which succeeded it, was notorious. We need not mention the Senate (a smaller body and therefore more easily controlled by the governing group), whose first investiture was by indirect election; nor need we mention the class representatives, who were in the main obedient to the government, as was proved (to give just one example) on the occasion of Antônio Carlos's dismissal from the presidency of the chamber. Consequently, the principal cause of our incorrigible pro-government stance must not be sought precipitately in the electoral legislation, however deficient this may have been in the past, since the legislation itself reflected general conditions in the political life of the country.[58]

IV. The Agamemnon Law and the Constitution of 1946

When the discussion of the constitutional problem was reopened at the beginning of 1945,[59] the government came under pressure to reform the Charter of 10 November at several points by calling elections for the Presidency and for both Houses of Parliament, so that they could revise the Constitution which had been authorised according to the established procedures.[60] Decree–Law No. 7586 of 28 May quickly followed. It regulated registration, the electoral process and the organisation of parties, hoping to encourage, by means of legal constraints, the creation of these on a national basis.[61] The new law also re-established the electoral branch of the judicial system (the Charter had made no provision for this), empowering it to direct the content, check votes, recognise and proclaim those elected. It also dealt with the question of speeding up proceedings and of lowering the qualifications, even at the risk of damaging certain guarantees contained in previous legislation.[62] The Constitution of 1946 integrated the electoral courts into the structure of the judiciary proper, and gave the district judges the right to exercise full jurisdiction in electoral matters, although it allowed the law to give other judges 'powers to carry out functions of a routine nature'.[63]

Leaving aside many details, the law of 1945 safeguarded the secrecy of the ballot by the same method laid down in the codes of 1932 and 1935, omitting only the numbering of envelopes from one to nine.[64] The checking of votes, in municipal as well as in state and federal elections, remained the function of the supervisory boards, presided over by a life judge and including two other citizens 'well-known for their moral integrity and independence', appointed by the regional courts. As far as the system of representation was concerned, two simultaneous ballots were to determine the election of federal and state deputies and councillors: each party elected as many representatives as the party quotient indicated, in the voting order of the candidates presented under the same label, all the other seats falling to the majority party. This method of disposing of the surplus seats was later discredited in the light of the Constitution of 18 September, but the High Electoral Court declared the law valid.[65] A curious phenomenon occurred: the state branches of the same party defended or opposed the law according to whether they had profited or been harmed by its method of allocating the surplus seats.

In spite of the defects of the new legislation, inferior as it was to the codes of 1932 and 1935, the federal and state elections carried out in accordance with it were very satisfactory from the point of view of the freedom of the contest.[66] The same cannot be said of the municipal elections of 1947 in some states. The remarkable results, from a formal point of view, of the contests of 2 December 1945 and 19 January 1947 were, however, due in large measure to exceptional circumstances in our political history.

In the first place, in the period of the 'rule of the judges' the Chief of State and the interventors usually recommended their subordinates to conduct federal elections in a very perfunctory manner.[67] These orders were not always carried out, but it is fair to remember that the infringements were usually committed by lesser authorities, conscious of the transitory nature of that particular order and fundamentally hopeful that winning would erase all their errors. In this conviction, ex-prefects (leaders of the local directory of the governing party), police chiefs and other holders of public office dedicated their strength — and sometimes dispensed with their scruples — to the organising of a redeeming victory. The long ideological preparation of public opinion by the official propaganda of the *Estado Novo*, and the discontinuance of electoral clashes, which had been abolished in our country, also contributed to the falsification of the expression of the ballot-box. Nevertheless, as they generally lacked support from above, the despots of the lower ranks of the hierarchy did not succeed in obtaining the results they hoped for. Even so, the victory of the governing party on 2 December 1945 was spectacular.[68] Nereu Ramos, then majority leader in the Constituent Assembly, could exclaim with pride to his opponents: 'Your political campaign was centred on the Constitution of 1937. Yet you have not won; those who have won are those who contributed to, collaborated with, or served in, the regime of 10 November in the certainty that they were serving Brazil . . . The campaign was waged precisely against the Constitution of 1937 . . . And we, who supported this regime, have been preferred by the people of Brazil.'[69]

The second exceptional circumstance to which we referred concerns the state elections of January 1947. At this time moves towards inter-party agreement, which was later formally achieved in order to strengthen the President of the Republic in the name of national salvation, were already advanced.[70] Already in the Constituent Assembly, despite a few skirmishes — whose principal instigator was ex-President Getúlio Vargas — relations between the government party and the largest opposition party were exceeding the bounds of cordiality on the road towards the longed-for agreement. In this climate of understanding, it was with rare exceptions of little interest to the head of the government whether the state elections favoured the government party or one of the larger opposition parties. Whether he was simply inspired by political motives or not, the President of the Republic certainly revealed a laudable impartiality in the contest of 19 January.[71] This explains to a large extent why the ruling groups in certain states were defeated in the gubernatorial elections.[72] Nevertheless, the result was not reflected in the composition of the respective constituent assemblies, one of the reasons being the legal provision for disposing of the surplus seats.[73]

V. The fallibility of Brazilian elections and coronelismo

Electoral corruption has been one of the most notorious and deep-rooted scourges of the representative system in Brazil. In the colonial period representation was limited to the government of the municipality, and in the very simple social structure existing at the time, the rural nobility exercised undisputed dominance over the unformed mass of slaves and servants — a dominance limited only by the absolutism of the Crown in matters which affected it closely; even so, disagreements between these nobles could lead to bloodshed in electoral contests, as happened in the famous case of the Pires and the Camargos in São Paulo. During the Second Republic and in the elections which followed the collapse of the *Estado Novo*, the electoral scene was incomparably better from the point of view of correctness and lack of constraint on voters, but in several places coercion and fraud still occurred. Nevertheless, the taint of corruption, which all students of our institutions without exception censure, spreads across the entire history of the Empire and the First Republic, outlined in sharp relief. And the interruptions in this chain of fraud and violence were either of mere local significance or of very short duration.[74]

The representative system was so clearly defective in practice that statesmen, legislators and political writers of the Empire and the First Republic habitually ascribed all the evils of the regime to it. In this climate of opinion it was not surprising that successive electoral reforms were rendered ineffective by malevolence and truculence. As disenchantment with one experiment set in, it would be followed by a new reforming impetus, kindling new but short-lived hopes. In this seemingly tireless series of reforms we annulled and re-established registration systems; altered the mechanism for qualification on several occasions, as well as the composition of the electoral boards and the supervisory bodies; included the magistrature and the police in the electoral process and then excluded them from it; held indirect and direct elections with the open vote and with the secret vote; enlarged and contracted constituencies from an area corresponding to a province or state to that of a single deputy; experimented with balloting by the list, the uninominal vote, the incomplete list, the cumulative vote and even proportional representation; and, the most curious fact of all, we even repeated in the Republic experiments which had failed under the Empire.

Through all these initiatives, received trustingly by some, with a lack of conviction or with pessimism by others, the representative machinery continued to reveal deficiencies, at times serious ones. In the final stages of the Empire, we had without a doubt made great progress towards removing the worst formal abuses from electoral contests. The Republic worsened the situation and had to follow its own road in search of the elusive ideal of clean and genuine elections. But even in those periods when the electoral process seemed least tainted by fraud and violence, men of clear judgement were always impressed by the artificial nature of this type of representation which almost invariably took the form of massive support for the government. Nevertheless, the persistence of certain external or formal abuses, notably the corrupt way in which the confirmation of powers took place (always carried out by the legislative assemblies and operating consistently to the disadvantage of the opposition), made it easy for the defects in our representative system to be attributed to factors of a purely or predominantly political nature. For this reason, the attention of observers was almost always deflected away from the profound social and economic factors which were, and still are, more responsible for pro-government attitudes, and thereby for the intrinsic falseness of our representative system.

Given this view of Brazilian political problems, it is very understandable that the perfecting of the electoral legislation was one of the most effective campaign slogans arising out of the revolution of 1930. It is also understandable that the code of 1932, entrusting the entire electoral procedure to the magistrature, from qualification to the checking of the votes and the proclamation of the names of the successful candidates, should have been hailed as the most precious of revolutionary victories. In fact, of all the elections held up until that time those of May 1933 were the most correct in terms of the machinery of registration, voting, checking and recognition. At the head of the system was the High Electoral Court, which decided doubtful cases and disagreements in judicial style, that is to say by means of allegation and proof, and reputedly without the interference of party politics. In spite of this, the deputies who represented the governing party in the respective states were much greater in number than those from opposition parties.

The formal genuineness of elections did not therefore prevent the occurrence of pro-government results, and the factors involved could not be considered exclusively or predominantly political. Evidence to this effect was given in statements of major importance in the Constituent Assembly of the Second Republic.

In reality, besides the abuses of fraud and coercion (much reduced in the elections held under the regulations laid down in the laws of 1932, 1935, 1945 and 1947[75]) and the defects inherent in the electoral system finally adopted — allocation of the surplus seats to the majority party — it is not possible to understand the exaggeratedly pro-government character of state and federal representation in our country without considering certain influences which would contribute to this result in one way or another, even under the most perfect electoral system.[76]

It is necessary to observe, in the first place, that the census of 1940, although it adopted broad criteria to define urban and suburban areas, found the rural population to be 68.76%, the urban population 22.29%,

and the suburban population 8.95%.[77] The calculation made by Rafael
Xavier, who deducted the figures for the Federal District and the capitals
of states and territories, revealed that 84.36% of the inhabitants of the
country live in municipalities of the interior,[78] where it is well known that
the rural element predominates except in those rare cases where there are
cities of the interior with important industrial establishments. Hence the
predominance of the rural electorate[79] in political contests, this electorate
'of the caves' on whom rested the frustrated hopes of a well-known politician from Minas Gerais in the last state campaign. The literacy requirement which should increase the percentage of urban electors in relation to
rural ones is not enough to make much difference, since an illiterate
peasant always can with patience and goodwill scribble his name, or tor-
tuously reproduce a requirement of qualification.[80] The recent official
campaign for adult literacy will also contribute to an increase in the rural
section of the electorate.[81]

I have already emphasised in our first chapter the dependence of this
majority section of our electoral body, a dependence made more acute by
electoral expenses which it has not the means to meet. The necessary consequence of this sad picture, already repeatedly stressed in the course of
this work, is the manipulation of the vote by the local leaders. These,
leading as they do municipalities of diminished authority which traditionally have been able to count only on very meagre public resources, cannot
find a satisfactory outlet for their personal interests or further those of
their locality unless they conform politically to the ruling groups in the
state. The final result of this control of votes by the governors, who determine the composition of the Federal Houses and the election of the President of the Republic, is the compromise which is established between the
federal and state governments, and with it the strengthening of the whole
system, which, in the final analysis, rests on the agrarian structure of the
country.

Among us, this has been nicknamed the 'politics of the governors', and
the primary link in the chain is the 'politics of the *coronéis*'. This all-
important reality is symptomatically reflected in the life of the parties,
aggravating the difficulties which result from the federal structure itself.
Anyone who observed the multiplicity of alliances made in the last state
and municipal elections could not fail to conclude that our parties are
little more than labels or pegs on which to hang the legal and technical
exigencies of the electoral process.[82]

The creation of the 'politics of the governors' has been attributed to
Campos Sales, from whose understanding with the leaders of the various
states with the largest representation in Congress resulted the reform of the

chambers' regulations as they affected the confirmation of powers.[83] In this way, an ingenious method of *purging* or *beheading* opposition candidates was evolved. No other result was possible: with the rights of their affiliates recognised thanks to the ruling party in the federal government, the governors exacted from their deputies and senators strict conformity with the plans of the President of the Republic;[84] habitually, on the eve of a presidential succession the waters of this tranquil lake would be ruffled when certain governors would diverge in their choice from the official candidate.

Recognition functioned therefore as an instrument which complemented the domination of the electorate by the ruling groups in the states. In the Constituent Assembly of 1933–4 interesting debates on the 'politics of the governors' took place. Deputy Morais Andrade, who so ardently defended Campos Sales and attributed to him the simple aim of making the process of recognition a legitimate one, did not hesitate to declare: 'It was said, everywhere, that a candidate not supported by the governments would never succeed in being elected, and if, by chance, he were elected, he would be purged.'[85]

We have no intention of accusing or exonerating Campos Sales; however, perhaps it would be more appropriate to say that he did not create but that in a certain sense he institutionalised the 'politics of the governors'. At the root of this political situation was the control of the governors over the vote, and because of this the President sought to reach an understanding with them in order to avoid following a course of intervention. This control was based on the compromise with the local chiefs, since, with slavery abolished and the rural workers incorporated into the body of the electorate, the electoral importance of the landowners increased. On the other hand, governorships being themselves elective offices, their political situation *vis-à-vis* the central government improved considerably. Nevertheless, the control of the ballot by the government through the municipal leaders and with the help of fraud, violence and gifts was not a new phenomenon appearing for the first time under the government of Campos Sales. It dated from as far back as the Empire when the provincial presidents always had the winning of elections as their foremost function. At that time, however, a broader and more solid arrangement on the part of the national government was not necessary because the presidents were nominated and dismissed by the national government. If, in later times, a conflict between a state government and the federal government could only be solved by agreement, by intervention, or by revolution,[86] under the Empire a simple decree could install a delegate more capable of leading into Parliament the deputies preferred by the Cabinet of the day.

This was the very reason that led Deputy J.J. Seabra to ask the following question in the Constituent Assembly of the Second Republic: 'What could this statesman [Campos Sales] do, if the "politics of the governors" already existed from the time of the Alvim Law, just as the politics of the interventors is being brought into being today?'[87] In this observation the Bahian representative was emphasising precisely the fact that the ballot-box obeyed the orders of the state governments: it is this which constituted the basis of the so-called 'politics of the governors'. And the same phenomenon, verified during the Empire with the provincial presidents, did not exist only under the regime of 1891: it persisted, though in an attenuated form, under the provisional government of 1930 and under the constitutional regime of 1934 and reappeared, again with some differences, from the interregnum of the *Estado Novo* until the elections of 1945.[88] If in the state contests of 1947 its anomalies were more serious in this or that state, this was due in large measure to the preliminary moves towards the agreement later entered into by the three major parties, at the inspiration of the leader of the government.

In this long period we have had various political regimes and numerous electoral reforms; nevertheless, the fundamental fact of the pro-government influence in electoral results has persisted, although to a lesser extent in the elections which succeeded the revolution of 1930. The explanation of this phenomenon lies in the pro-government attitudes of local leaders, already analysed above, and in the subjection of the electorate of the interior, especially the rural element in it, to these same leaders, as a direct consequence of our agrarian structure, which leaves the rural worker ignorant and abandoned.

This picture shows us that *coronelismo* in Brazil has been inseparable from a broadly based representative system. Its influence did not fail to be reflected in the very defects of the electoral legislation which only reached a satisfactorily high standard after a profound political upheaval, the revolution of 1930. Given the close links between *coronelismo* and the representative system, the delegate to the Constituent Assembly of the Second Republic was not far off the mark in suggesting that universal suffrage should be replaced by 'professional suffrage', a phrase which envisaged exchanging the traditional political mentors of the man from the interior for the leaders of the relevant occupational category.[89] Others were subsequently to go further and ask crudely for the suppression of the representative system: this is the attitude of those who made or supported the *Estado Novo*. But the man who put forward the real alternative was also right: either legalise *coronelismo*, or seek to create social conditions different from those which produce and nurture it. This was the position of

Deputy Domingos Velasco, proposing indirect elections in 1934 and also proposing to limit direct elections to the municipal sphere. In his own words: 'it is the only honest solution for liberal democracy in Brazil, because it gives legal recognition to the *de facto* institution, which is that of caciquism. If this repels my fellow members, we shall then have to proceed by the method of liberating the rural masses, guaranteeing them the right to live, the right to work, the right to assistance, so that they can in reality be politically free.'[90]

7. Conclusion

Evaluation of coronelismo: its consequences. Signs of crisis in the system. Perspectives.

On the basis of the preceding observations, we are already able to summarise in a confident fashion the principal characteristics of *coronelismo*, whose apparent simplicity thinly disguises an underlying complexity.

Although its consequences are felt all through the country's political life, *coronelismo* operates in the limited field of local government. Its habitat is the municipalities of the interior, that is to say the rural or predominantly rural municipalities; its strength is in inverse proportion to the development of urban activities like commerce or industry. Consequently, isolation is an important factor in producing and maintaining this phenomenon.

If we take isolation to mean the absence or sparse representation of public power, *coronelismo* can immediately be seen as a form of incursion by private authority into the political domain. Hence the temptation to consider it merely as a legacy of survival from the colonial period, when manifestations of the hypertrophy of private power were frequent, disputing prerogatives which should properly belong to institutional authority. It would be wrong, however, to identify the patriarchalism of colonial times with *coronelismo*, which was at its most powerful during the First Republic. It would also be out of the question to give this name to the powerful influence which large economic groups have exercised over the state in modern times.

It is therefore not possible to reduce *coronelismo* to a simple (if abnormal) assertion of private power. It is also this, but it is not only this. It does not correspond to the golden age of private interest: the system peculiar to this phase, already superseded in Brazil, is patriarchalism, with the concentration of economic, social and political power in the family group. On the contrary *coronelismo* presupposes the decline of private power, and functions as a way of preserving its residual content.

We thus arrive at the point which seems to us the central one in the evaluation of *coronelismo*: this political system is dominated by a relationship of compromise between private power in its decline and a much strengthened public authority.

The simple fact of compromise presumes a certain degree of weakness on both sides, hence public authority too has its weaknesses. But, during the First Republic — when the term *coronelismo* was incorporated into the language of the time to denote the peculiarities of our rural political life — the machinery of the state was already sufficiently developed, except in sporadic cases, to contain any rebellion on the part of private power. It is therefore necessary to discover what sort of weakness it was which forced the public authority into the compromise with *coronelismo*.

A short parallel will help to explain the situation.

In the colonial period, leaving aside the election of representatives to the Portuguese *Côrtes*, the representative system was limited to the membership of the municipal chambers. The electoral problem was not therefore of any fundamental interest to the Crown, particularly as the laws then in force allowed it the complete control of public administration through bodies of its own choosing. It is for this reason that the frequent submission of the metropolitan country to the arrogance of the rural nobility, and the various expedients by which it tried to reach an agreement with them, can be explained quite naturally in terms of the insufficiency of public authority and its inability to carry out its functions to the full.

In later times, the election of the Constituent Assembly of 1823 and the representative composition of the General Assembly, the country's permanent organ of government, gave enormous importance to the electoral question. In spite of this, the right of suffrage was based on economic revenue, and agricultural work continued to be the job of slaves who had no right to vote. The body of electors was therefore very restricted: fraud, violence and bribes could thus play a decisive role in the outcome of ballots. Furthermore, the provincial presidents, who played a prominent part in the running of political campaigns, were nominated and dismissed by the central government. All this helped to simplify the mechanism of rural politics during the Empire, although there were the usual compromise relationships similar to those which were ultimately to become typical of *coronelismo*.

Finally, the abolition of slavery and the later extension of the right of suffrage under the Republic gave a major importance to the votes of rural workers. The political influence of the landowners therefore increased, owing to the dependence of this section of the electorate, the direct result of our agrarian structure and the way it maintains the fieldworker in a lamentable state of ignorance and neglect. We are, in this respect, legitimate heirs of the colonial system of large-scale agricultural enterprises cultivated by slaves and producing raw materials and food products for export. Freedom to work in the legal sense did not profoundly alter this structure, dominated even today by the large estate, and characterised as far as class composition is concerned, by the subjection of a huge mass of wage-earners, sharecroppers, leaseholders and smallholders to a tiny minority of big landlords who are still powerful in relation to their dependants, although themselves in an increasingly precarious position in the national economy as a whole.

The superimposition of a broadly based representative system on this inadequate economic and social structure incorporated into the body of active citizens a numerous contingent of electors incapable of carrying out their political duty with any sense of awareness. Those holding public power were therefore very closely tied to the leaders of this electoral herd. Hence the special weakness of public authority which led it to reach an understanding with the residual private power of the landowners in the particular compromise of *coronelismo*. By pouring all their votes over the government candidates in state and federal elections, the political leaders of the interior become entitled to a special reward, which consists in their being given a free hand to consolidate their authority in the municipalities. This electoral function of *coronelismo* is so important that without it we should find it difficult to make sense of the *do ut des* on which the whole system hinges. The federal system has also contributed to the growth of the phenomenon in an important way: by making the state governments entirely elective, it allowed the setting up of solid electoral machines in the former provinces; those stable electoral machines which led to the institution of the 'politics of the governors' relied precisely on the compromise of *coronelismo*.

Thus the phenomenon, as we have studied it, is characteristic of the republican regime, although several of the elements which help to make up the picture of *coronelismo* were already present during the Empire, and a few even date from the colonial period. It has already been noted, and more than once, that an excursion into the Brazilian interior is equivalent, in a certain sense, to a visit to the past.

The dependency of the rural electorate could in theory benefit the opposition as well as the government, and it is true that *coronéis* supporting the opposition may be found everywhere. Nevertheless, *coronelismo*, as a political system, is markedly pro-government in complexion. To obtain this result the state government had to guarantee its position as the senior partner in the political compromise.

The ascendency of state leaders naturally results in the strengthening of public authority, but has been traditionally consolidated by the reflected use of this power for party-political ends. The precariousness of the guarantees for the magistrature and the public service (or the total absence of them) and the easy availability of the police have always played a major role in this respect, clearly influencing the falsification of the ballot – a practice which still exists though in an attenuated form. The use of public money, services and functions as a customary part of party-political action has also been shown to be very effective in achieving the same objectives. Finally, the submission of the municipality was a very useful expedient for guaranteeing a position of strength to the ruling parties in the states in their dealings with local leaders. With insufficient revenue, their hands tied by various forms of tutelage, hampered at times in the composition of their own governments, the municipalities could only gain advantages when they had protection from above.

It is therefore not strange that *coronelismo* is an essentially pro-government political system. With the police as part of the machinery, badly protected by a precarious legal system, without money and without power to carry out urgent local improvements, destitute of resources for electoral expenses, and unable to offer public posts or official contracts as rewards for their supporters, opposition municipal leaders have hardly ever had any alternative but to support the government. However, as it is not possible to extinguish local rivalry completely, there are always opposition *coronéis* to whom everything is denied, and on whose heads public authority descends guided by their political opponents. Hence the chronic truculence of the local pro-government faction, often accompanied by reprisals; hence, too, its favouritism in relation to the friends of the government, a practice which is very pernicious from the point of view of regularising municipal administration.

Within this framework the municipality's lack of legal autonomy has never been felt as a crucial problem, because it was always compensated for by an extensive extra-legal autonomy, conceded by the state government to the local party of its choice. This counterbalancing by the state in the compromise of *coronelismo* explains, in large measure, the support which state legislators — the majority of them men from the interior — always gave to legislation designed to diminish municipal power. Only their opponents could be really harmed by such measures: on the one hand, the local pro-government faction would always obtain from the state what was considered indispensable and, on the other, the greater the dependence of the district, the greater the probability of victory for the pro-government faction in the municipal elections themselves.

The strengthening of public authority was therefore not generally accompanied by a corresponding weakening of *coronelismo*; it has, on the contrary, helped to consolidate the system, guaranteeing to the controllers of the official machinery of the state a substantial portion of the bargain which it arranges. Paradoxically, it is the very instruments of constitutional power that are employed to rejuvenate along party lines the residual private power of the *coronéis*, which rests basically on an agrarian structure in full decline.

This decadence is indispensable to an understanding of *coronelismo*, since as the 'natural' influence of the landowners becomes fragmented and diluted, so official support becomes all the more vital if the steady predominance of a single, local, political group is to be guaranteed.

In this attempt to evaluate *coronelismo* we have sought to emphasise its most general and lasting features, of necessity omitting occasional and regional peculiarities. Within the same general orientation it is impossible to ignore the new factors which in recent times have been undermining the system of *coronelismo*. These have become more evident since the implementation of the electoral code of 1932. The clearest symptom of this change is the decline of government influence in elections, including the defeat of certain ruling factions in the states — a phenomenon which would have been inconceivable during the First Republic. However, we cannot yet say that we have a perfect system of political representation: currents of opinion are more faithfully expressed, but even today the weight of the government on the rural municipalities, by means of the alliance of *coronelismo*, is still an incontrovertible fact of life.

Certainly, the improvement of the electoral process is contributing to the abolition of *coronelismo*, although increased registration is operating in the reverse direction by raising electoral expenses. Nevertheless, given that it is only since 1932 that we have had an electoral code appropriate to the proper functioning of the representative system, the conclusion to be drawn is that conditions in the country had altered sufficiently to require the promulgation of this code, and that in the wake of a successful revolution.

In reality, the Brazilian economy in 1930 could no longer be seen as essentially rural, because industrial output was rivalling agricultural production and the coffee crisis had reduced the economic power of the large landowners in relation to that of bankers, merchants and industrialists. Concomitantly the urban population and electorate had grown, and improvements in the means of transport and communication had increased contact with the rural population; this was inevitably reflected in the political behaviour of the latter. All these factors had been at work for a long time corroding the economic and social structure on which *coronelismo* depends, but a revolution was necessary to transpose to the political level the basic changes which had been taking place unheeded. The political framework of the Old Republic pulled against this adjustment as much as it could, and it finally broke through lack of flexibility. But the adjustment itself was incomplete and superficial, because it did not touch the basic source of *coronelismo*, namely the agrarian structure. This structure continues to decline because of the corrosive action of several factors, but no political act of wide applicability has sought to change it fundamentally — witness (and this is symptomatic) the labour legislation which cautiously holds back at the door of the large estates. The result is the persistence of *coronelismo*, which adapts itself here and there in order to survive, abandoning its rings to preserve its fingers.

Coronelismo — the point has already been made — presupposes the decline of our rural structure; it is necessary to observe, however, that in this process of decline there is an optimal point at which the system functions best. The system in its turn seeks to stabilise this favourable situation and to consolidate by political means the residual private power which characterises it. However, more powerful forces have pushed the disintegration of our agrarian structure beyond this ideal point, with effects on the political level which have thus caused a crisis in *coronelismo* itself.

It therefore seems very probable that the new electoral principles adopted from 1932 onwards and which affected *coronelismo* so directly, resulted from the same economic and social factors which were undermining the bases of the *coronelismo* system. The political consequences of these factors were being stifled, disfigured or simply covered up by the power relationships which the institutions of the Old Republic were seeking to perpetuate. The revival of the municipality, the frustrated preoccupation of the second republican Constituent Assembly — which however, bore better fruit in the Assembly of 1946 — is part of this same process, and should also help to weaken *coronelismo* provided that new ways of subjecting local leaders to the control of state governments are not found. We can even imagine an unprecedented situation, namely the establishment of direct contacts between the municipalities and the Union. Should this happen, the way will be open for a new type of compromise, no longer in favour of state governments but expressly against them. The increase in the guarantees of the magistrature and the public service is also in line with the new developments, but the police apparatus has shown greater resistance to the changes which threaten its participation in the mechanics of *coronelismo*.

It seems clear that the erosion of *coronelismo* will only be complete when a fundamental change has taken place in our agrarian structure. The uninterrupted disintegration of this structure — brought about by various factors, among them the impoverishment of the soil, the vagaries of the international market, the growth of cities, the expansion of industry, the legal guarantees of urban workers, the mobility of manpower, the development of transport and communications — is a slow and unreliable process, sometimes counterproductive, which does not offer a satisfactory way out of the impasse.

Just as the agrarian structure contributes to the survival of *coronelismo*, so *coronelismo* helps to preserve this structure. Up until now Brazilian governments have always been drawn from the dominant classes and with the vital concurrence of the machinery of *coronelismo*. This is one of the reasons for their bewilderment in the face of the problems of a country whose economy is characterised by a still precarious industrial sector and an already outdated agricultural system. This bewilderment has inevitably led to the adoption of contradictory measures. In order to protect industry, governments ought to try and expand the domestic market by taking effective and decisive measures, but they have not done this because such policies would harm the interests of the dominant rural class. They have therefore opted, exclusively or at least principally, for a purely fiscal protection in order to please both Greeks and Trojans: the price of industrial products has remained high and the agrarian structure has persisted intact.

The results are the following: the domestic market does not grow, because the cost of living is rising, and the rural population continues to lack the means of consumption; with no market to speak of, industry does not prosper, does not raise its technical standards and continually has to ask for official protection; finally, agriculture, unable to stabilise itself at a high level within its old framework, becomes progressively and inevitably less efficient. Thus the vicious circle is closed: on the economic level, traditional and decadent agriculture, backward and burdensome industries, each systematically impoverishing the country; on the political level, the survival of *coronelismo*, falsifying political representation and discrediting the democratic system, permitting and encouraging the habitual use of force for and against the government.

We cannot deny that *coronelismo* corresponds to a phase in the political development of our people which leaves much to be desired. Had we been more richly endowed with public spirit things would have developed differently. For this reason all measures aimed at removing abuses from public life are undeniably useful and deserve the applause of all those who long for a higher level of political activity in Brazil. But let us not have too many illusions. The poverty of the people, especially the rural population, and in consequence its intellectual backwardness and lack of civic sense, will be a serious obstacle to the most noble intentions.

We were not venturing to put forward solutions with this simple contribution to the study of *coronelismo*; we were merely trying to understand a small area of the evils which beset us. Others, more competent than ourselves, should undertake the task of showing where the remedy lies.

Notes

1. Notes on the structure and functioning of coronelismo

1 'I do not know the other Brazilian states and I can speak only of São Paulo. Here we had several categories of political leaders. At an early stage they came to be divided into *coronéis* and *doutores* (doctors). These were in many cases two quite distinct groups, the *coronel* dominating his estate and acting in conjunction with other landowners, many of them with influence in the towns, since the business community depended on them for supplies, the lawyers and doctors needed them as clients or patients, and civil servants were subject to arbitrary nomination and dismissed by them. Other people, in other walks of life depended on them for similar reasons. The *doutor* was influential through the power of intelligence and learning, through his command of language, or through professional services — legal or medical — rendered to rich families or to the poor. In many other cases the two existed in symbiosis: the *coronel* contributing personal influence or that of his clan, money and tradition: the *doutor*, in alliance with him, contributing technical skills such as those required on the journalistic side of campaign, in speechmaking on important occasions, in registration matters, in dealing with voting frauds, the actuals poll and records of it, election funds and debates in the municipal chamber in times of opposition.' (Rubens do Amaral, 'O Chefe Político'.)

In some places it is the priest who acts as intellectual leader allied to the *coronel*, in the role more normally played by the *doutores*. In such cases the moral influence of the Church contributes to the individual's political prestige. Also not to be forgotten is the political activity of the chemist or businessman, both closely linked to the landowners.

2 In chapter VII of *Sobrados e Mucambos*, Gilberto Freire has a long discussion on the 'rise of the university graduate and the mulatto'. 'The political rise of the graduate, within families', he says, 'is seen not only in the case of sons-in-law but also, and chiefly, in the case of sons . . . If we have emphasised the rise of sons-in-law, it is because in their increased influence lies the clearest evidence of the phenomenon by which the power of the rural nobility, or a large part of it, was being transferred to the intellectual *bourgeoisie*. From the plantation houses of the countryside to the mansions of the towns.' (p. 315)

'New conditions forced the old kind of local leader to beat a strategic retreat: The *coronel* was pushed backstage. But, shrewdly, he left in the foreground, as political leader of his fief, his diploma-ed son-in-law, the modern face of *coronelismo* as a political force.' (Emil Farhat, 'O Genro, O Grande Culpado'.)

Family ties do not exclude the possibility, though it is rare, of rival parties in the area being led by members of the same family. Alfonso Celso, referring to the electors in his electoral district in the penultimate decade of the last century, wrote: 'Father-in-law and son-in-law, brothers-in-law, brothers would fight in opposing factions while maintaining their personal ties. However, it was customary for the victors, when proclaiming their victory, to send off a special kind of rocket which, when it rose, emitted a shrill whistle, a form of booing.' (*Oito Anos de Parlamento*, p. 22.) There are cases in which rivalry inside the same family is more apparent than real: according to circumstances, the leadership passes from one to the other remaining substantially unchanged.

3   Local leadership in the rural or predominantly rural municipalities, is the prerogative of the dominant classes and their allies. If in the larger towns there are already leaders of working-class origin, the phenomenon is still unknown in rural society where it would not enter into anyone's head to give political leadership to a wage-earner, incapable of controlling even his own vote.

4   The role of thuggery and banditry in local political contests used to be very important, although it has diminished with the development of the police force, which itself quite often uses similar methods. Djacir Meneses focuses on this issue, in so far as it affects the region which he studied, in various passages of his work on the formation of Northeast society. (*O Outra Nordeste*, pp. 82, 176, 228 etc.) He observes that the problem is at its most acute in agricultural areas: 'Effectively, agriculture, in certain parts of the Northeast, bound strata of the population to the soil, avoiding or restricting the banditry which resulted from the early nomadism of the more pastoral economy of the first three centuries. But in the scrublands of the Northeast, in the characteristically pastoral areas, there persist these cliques organised around local leaders.' (p. 159) In political reprisals and crimes and in struggles between families, the activities of hired thugs is of major importance.

5   A phenomenon which functions at the same time as cause and as effect of the situation is the high percentage of minors in agriculture: 'The highest proportion of adolescents in the labour force is found for obvious reasons in the areas of cultivation and stockraising. In this branch of the Brazilian economy, for every 100 persons of 20 or more, there are 44.17% between 10 and 19 years of age; next come the extractive industries with 31.03%. The great majority – 78.2% – of working adolescents in Brazil are employed in agriculture.' (L.A. Costa Pinto, *A Estrutura da Sociedade Rural Brasileira*, unpublished work based on the census of 1940, and generously placed at the author's disposal.)

6   'Although he does not always have great wealth, the *coronel* is held to be rich by the poor majority who have no difficulty in applying this epithet to him, given their relative situations.' (Aires da Mata Machado Filho, 'O Coronel e a Democracia'.)

7   Nabuco de Araújo, defending indirect elections in certain districts in the interior, had this to say in 1871: 'between the masters and the slaves, the intermediate class is a totally dependent group'. (A. Tavares de Lira, 'Regime Eleitoral', p. 340.) Today, the situation is almost the same, as will be seen later.

8   'It is the landowner, the *coronel*, who helps the peasant in times of need, gives him a plot of land to plant, supplies him with medicine, protects him from arbitrary acts of government, is his intermediary in his deal-

ings with the authorities. Thus, since colonial times, this kind of power has grown, a kind of power which has no sanction in law but which is a real power and a stable one, imposed as it is by the uncertainties of rural life.' (Domingos Velasco, *Direito Eleitoral*, p. 127; cf. the passage from Oliveira Viana cited by the author in the same place.)

9   'The majority of the national electorate, as we know, is in the countryside and is formed by the rural population. Now, nine-tenths of the rural population – thanks to our economic structure and our civil law – consists of pariahs, landless, homeless, without justice or rights, all completely *dependent* on the great territorial landlords, in such a way that even if they had any *awareness* of their rights (and, really, they have none . . .) and wished to exercise them in an independent manner, they would not be able to. And this is why even the slightest suggestion of independence on the part of these pariahs would be punished by immediate expulsion or eviction by the big landowners.' (Oliveira Viana, *O Idealismo da Constituição*, p. 112.)

Father Antônio d'Almeida Morais Jr, analysing in a Jesuit publication the reasons for the exodus from the countryside and the ways of stopping it, attributes the resignation of the countryman to religious sentiment: 'according to the latest statistics, 77.5% of our rural people are Catholics. Herein lies the secret of their admirable resistance to suffering and poverty!' ('O Êxodo da População Rural Brasileira', p. 393.)

10   Caio Prado Jr, 'Distribuição da Propriedade Fundiária Rural no Estado de São Paulo', pp. 696–8.

11   Caio Prado Jr, '*História Econômica do Brasil*', pp. 261 ff.

12   Jorge Kingston, 'A Concentração Agrária em São Paulo', p. 36.

'In a large area of those states included in the regions, North, Northeast, East and Middle West the tendency towards a greater concentration of property became more marked between 1920 and 1940, while the reverse occurred, especially in Rio Grande do Sul, Santa Catarina and Paraná, precisely those states in which most recent settlement has taken place.' (Tomás Pompeu Acióli Borges, 'A Propriedade Rural no Brasil, p. 11.)

'Single crop latifundia', says Gilberto Freire, 'even after the abolition of slavery, found ways of continuing to exist in various parts of the country. Many became even more extensive and exercised an even more pernicious effect than under the old system . . . creating a proletariat whose living conditions were even worse than those of the slaves.' (*Casa Grande & Senzala*, vol. I, p. 45.)

13   Costa Pinto, *A Estrutura da Sociedade Rural Brasileira*; T.P. Acióli Borges, *op. cit.*, p. 11.

14   At the present time the concentration of landholdings can be seen taking place in the valley of the Rio Doce, the reason being the inability of smallholders to finance the legitimisation of their claims. A high level of concentration was carried out by the sugar establishments of the Northeast, especially in Pernambuco. (Cf. Gilberto Freire, *Casa Grande & Senzala*, vol. I, pp. 45 and 46, and note 40.)

15   This last case can be observed in certain properties in the Zona da Mata (Mines), where land already rendered useless for the profitable cultivation of coffee was given over to pasture. The recent appreciation in the

value of cattle which preceded the present crisis in the industry favoured this process.

16   Caio Prado Jr, *História Econômica do Brasil*, pp. 297 ff.

17   Costa Pinto, *A Estrutura da Sociedade Rural Brasileira*, already cited.

18   Caio Prado Jr, in his study, 'Distribuição da Propriedade Fundiária Rural no Estado de São Paulo', classifies as small, any holding up to 25 *alquieros* (using the São Paulo measure 1 *alquiere* = 2.4 hectares); as middle-sized, from 25 to 100; as big, over 100 (p. 693). Aguinaldo Costa adopts the following criterion: small, up to 50 *alquieres*; middle-sized, from 50 to 100; big over 100. (*Apontamentos para uma Reforma Agrária*, p. 122.)

19   The census does not refer to property but to 'agricultural establishments'. (*Anuario Estatístico* of 1946, p. 84.)

'For the purposes of the census, the category of agricultural establishment was taken to include, without any limitation by area or by the value of production, all those which are concerned with the direct exploitation of the land for commercial purposes, and, by extension, those, like farms and country seats which, while not being commercially exploited, are worked with the aim of meeting running costs and being self-sufficient.' (I.B.G.E. *Sinopse do Censo Agrícola*, p. VI)

20   According to information collected by the I.B.G.E., the 'actual population', as recorded by the census of 1 September 1940, broken down as to 'place of abode', was distributed as follows: urban − 9,189,995 (22.29%); suburban − 3,692,454 (8.95%); rural − 28,353,866 (68.76%). It should be noticed that even in small basically rural districts, the population in the commercial centres were considered 'urban'.

21   From the Presidential Message to Congress in 1947, we give the following extract: 'A primary feature of the agrarian question was shown by the last census, which confirmed the high level of concentration in land-holding in rural Brazil. This basic aspect of the social and agricultural structure is a reflection of the traditional use of land adopted during the period of the colonisation of Brazil, and from which arises the situation currently existing in rural areas, namely, millions of Brazilians submitted to an age-old process of stultification, their physical and intellectual powers unused, vegetating without purpose, denied good health and education, and living on someone else's land, whose speculative value removes any possibility of their ever acquiring it. On the other hand, the high concentration of agricultural land explains, likewise, the low wage of the rural worker, the bad use of land in Brazil, the slow progress towards mechanisation in agriculture, the shameful waste of human resources, the unwillingness of the worker to remain on the land, the smallness of our internal market, the shift of population to the cities, the diminished density of traffic on our railways and the staggering deterioration of arable land.'

The agrarian problem posed by the President himself in his message was already the subject of parliamentary inquiry. Deputy João Nangabeira, appointed to report on matters coming within the sphere of the Joint Committee for Complementary Legislation, referred to the subject in these terms: 'Agrarian reform − in a semi-feudal society with its latifundia, leases and emphyteuses, and its rural workers unprotected, illiterate, wretched −

is the most serious problem which Brazilian democracy has to face and resolve.' (*Diário do Congresso*, 23 September 1947, p. 5994.)

22   Excluding the extractive industries which, for the purposes of this study, are for the most part intimately linked to agriculture, as Professor Costa Pinto has observed.

23   Everything indicates that the margin of error due to the existence of middle-sized properties is very small.

24   Cf. José Higino, *Análises de Resultados do Censo Demográfico*, no. 376.

25   This conclusion also appears admissible in the light of the following passage from the *Análise*, no. 376, cited above: 'in the examination, besides the classes of employees, employers and self-employed, another, that of "members of family", was treated separately, and taken as *including persons* belonging to the families of the "self-employed", who worked for them without receiving a fixed wage'.

26   Hypothesis based on the other census definition referred to in note 24.

27   The Electoral Register of 1945 – excluding the territories – gave 5,319,678 electors from the 'interior' (73%), as against 1,966,797 from the 'capital cities' (27%). (*Anuário Estatístico* of 1946, p. 515.) These figures are subject to confirmation in view of the cancellations referred to in the first table published in the *Diário de Justica* (section II) of 15 March 1948, p. 61. We are unable to make the deductions because the new official publications do not make the distinctions referred to above. The difference however is small.

28   Cf. note 70, ch. VI.

29   The depositions made by Juares Távora and Domingos Velasco to the Constituent Assembly of 1933–4 are very informative on this point. The former said: 'I know, as do few in this House, the reality of life in the rural areas of the country. I am a child of the backlands, I was raised there, and after having studied in a centre like Rio de Janeiro, fate drew me once more, during more than a year's travelling, to some of the most remote corners of the country . . . We are a country in which the elector, as a general rule, has no means of transport from his house to the seat of the municipality where he must go to cast his vote. If any of you took a pencil and calculated how much transport costs for millions of electors in the rural areas you would see how easy it is to justify the disgraceful practice, long in use, of paying for elections with public funds.' (*Anais*, vol. II, p. 355, and vol. XV, p. 555.)

Domingos Velasco, after referring to the damage resulting from the lack of services, and to expenses like the transport, accommodation and registration documents of the rural elector, observed that 'it would be impossible to form the electorate if the local leader was not there to entice the elector and pay his expenses'. And he added: 'Once the elections have arrived . . . the spectacle which we all know so well unfolds itself. The economic life of the municipality suffers an hiatus. The local bosses organise transport, arrange lodgings and provide food for hundreds and, at times, thousands of electors. This 'hospitality' is expensive, because in rural districts the electors arrive on the eve of the contest and only leave on the day following the election; and during this time they do not spend a penny of their own, not even for the entertainments regarded as obligatory in the towns at election time.' (*Anais*, vol. VII, p. 323.)

30   The growth of the Brazilian electorate can be attested by the following figures: for the election to the Constituent Assembly on 3 May 1933, 1,466,700 electors were registered. This number had risen to 2,659,171 in the election to the federal legislature on 14 October 1934. The new register made in 1945 showed a total of 7,306,995, rising to 7,710,504 in 1946, excluding all the territories except Iguacu. (*Anuário Estatístico* of 1946, pp. 514–15; *Diário da Justica*, section II, of 15 March 1948, p. 61.)

31   Oliveira Viana observes: 'Serfdom on the land . . . whose existence can only be explained in terms of the scarcity of land, will not appear here. Given the miraculous lavishness of space which we have, this form of slavery is impossible. Our peasants escape easily, by flight, by wandering and by the nomadism so common even today in the backlands.' (*Populações Meridionais do Brasil*, p. 164.)

32   See ch. VI, section IV.

33   His first task was the institution of the rule of law and then the establishment of peace in the district. He strove hard for this, bringing all his authority to bear, in order to ensure a better reputation for his municipality, enhanced by the introduction of the formal judicial process. The local gaol and the interests of the local schoolchildren were two matters which required frequent visits to São Paulo. Also the matter of state and federal taxes, rural schools, roads. Pleas for a grammar school, a normal school, a professional institute. All this he had to ask for and obtain, either because of his own love of his home-town and his desire for progress, or under pressure from public opinion, which demanded these improvements from the local boss and from no one else. The latter had to wrest them from the government or be regarded as a failure, incapable of carrying out his function.' (Rubens do Amaral, 'O Chefe Político', pp. 57–8.)

34   Here is a complete list: arrange work; lend money; legalise titles; obtain credit in shops; secure a lawyer; influence juries; persuade and 'prepare' witnesses; provide a doctor or hospital treatment in emergencies; lend animals for travelling; secure passes on the railway; give lodging and food; prevent the police from seizing his protégés' weapons, or bribe them into returning them; be godfather to children and patron at weddings; write letters, receipts and contracts or ask his son, accountant, book-keeper, manager or lawyer to do so; receive correspondence; collaborate in the legalisation of land rights; settle disputes, compel marriage when children under legal age have gone astray; in short, an infinite number of services of a personal kind which are his responsibility or that of his servants, employees, friends or superiors. When the local boss is a lawyer, doctor, notary, priest, etc., many of these services are rendered personally for a derisory fee or completely free.

Among the favours which the local authority can grant, fiscal consideration ranks as one of the highest. According to the evidence of Deputy Luis Cedro in 1934, 'Taxation in the municipalities has a serious drawback: that is the privileged distinction which arises at the time of tax assessment, distinctions between political allies and political opponents.' (*Anais*, vol. XI, p. 557.)

35 Saying attributed to a politician from Minas, preferred here to this one, more elegant perhaps, ascribed to another state leader: 'He does justice to his friends, he applies the law to his enemies.'

36 This hostility is evidenced by the absence of social contact (separate clubs and cafés); in malicious or mean gestures (commemorative parties, 'booing' rockets, changing of the names of public parks, works and other establishments); in acts of provocation (putting into certain jobs thugs or persons of low qualifications); by exclusion from public services (dismissal of officials, failing to pave or clean the street near one's opponents house); in fiscal severity (exaggerated tax assessments in comparison with those of friends, excessive fines and penalties); in police severity (seizure of weapons, questioning under pressure); in acts of sabotage (winning over or threatening merchants' customers, doctors' patients, lawyers' clients); and in many other ways, reaching the level of physical violence and more serious crimes, perpetrated not by the two leaders themselves, or rarely, but frequently by their less conspicuous followers.

Referring to the state of Espírito Santo, Judge Ataualpa Lessa declared in 1932: 'The revolution has arrived but its spirit, its permanence and its high ideals have not yet been understood by the rural population and perhaps will not be for some time. They all therefore assume that only the actors have changed and the play has remained the same. Generally, each man reasons as follows: "When I was at the bottom I was beaten left and right; now that I'm on top, I have to beat in the same way." ' (Sobral Pinto, 'Crônica Política', *A Ordem*, 18 January and 17 February 1932.)

37 Discussing the concept of coercion in the electoral process, Domingos Velasco has this to say: 'We have observed that the constraining party rarely acts on the day or at the moment of the contest to coerce the elector. The process employed most frequently is to create, before the ballot, a climate of apprehension and insecurity which keeps the electorate away from the voting booths. It is true that it is possible to secure a writ of *habeas corpus* to prevent this, but as it is generally the government which is doing the coercion, it is the federal authorities which would have to make the *habeas corpus* effective, and in the majority of cases they are unable to transport themselves to the place to carry out this function . . . Apart from this, it is often impossible to offer enough proof to justify the granting of the writ.' (*Direito Eleitoral*, p. 119.)

38 Clearly, circumstances differ from one place to another. We are referring to an average type. Rubens do Amaral in this regard has the following comment on the local leaders in São Paulo: 'The *coronéis* as well as the *doutores* can be subdivided into various types. There were the autocrats, totally intolerant, for whom an opponent was an enemy to be eliminated by social and economic boycott or even by assassination. There were others, equally autocratic and equally intolerant, who regarded a vote against themselves as a personal insult, but whose electoral fights did not transgress the limits of the law or the moral code, because of their force of character. As a rule, they were tractable throughout the year, getting on well with everyone, including the opposition, reserving their hostility for election time when they would assume aggressive attitudes, but only in respect of the vote: and in this field they were capable of any degree of shrewdness and dealing, convinced of the fact that in politics the only shameful thing is to lose.' ('O Chefe Político', p. 56.)

39   From one of the bulletins distributed in a certain municipality of Minas, in the campaign for the municipal election of 1947, we take the following extract: 'Those . . . the true friends of the municipality, and patriots, who were our opponents in the past, are now lending support *to the government, to the U.D.N.* There are still some good and loyal men who have not yet decided. We await them with open arms . . . This is a general invitation to all those who, *at present alienated from the government, wish to join with it.*'

40   'Your landowner will consider himself dishonourable on the day when, without just cause, he breaks his word. To keep his pledges, he will sacrifice his comfort, his fortune and even his life.' (Oliveira Viana, *Populações Meridionais do Brasil*, p. 48.)

Alfonso Celso, referring to the electors of his district and the strength of the *Lei Saraiva* commented: 'However much they classify themselves in this or that party, less for ideological reasons than by accident of birth, ties of friendship, gratitude for favours and reasons of dependence, they always remain faithful to their chosen flag. They are so firm in keeping their word that the result of any electoral college can be confidently forecast, surprises being rare.' (*Oito Anos de Parlemento*', p. 21.)

'The given word is sacred', writes Aires da Mata Machado Filho. 'Once a pledge has been undertaken, a man will go all out to honour it. No change of attitude will make a turncoat of him.' ('O Coronel e a Democracia'.)

41   'The burdens of this position were heavy. The political leader, while seeming to be the owner of everything, finally came to be himself owned by everybody. From the beginning, he undertook responsibilities on the party's behalf, taking on the obligation of leading it to victory whatever the circumstances . . . Running the risk of being accused of softness if he was not sufficiently strict in his leadership; of oppression if he imposed the necessary discipline . . . If he compromised to save his party from going under, he incurred the disgrace of being a turncoat; if he resisted out of loyalty to his friends or his old allegiance, taunts of his incompetence and obstinacy were thrown in his face.' (Rubens do Amaral, 'O Chefe Político', p. 57.)

42   Nestor Duarte, *A Ordem Privada e a Organização Política Nacional, passim.*

43   With the reservations and clarifications indicated, these observations of Emílio Willems are relevant: 'In Brazil, paternalism put down roots in the local political structures dominated by the big landowners. The old and well-known competition between the power of the state and "private" power is generally favourable to this. The metropolitan government and later the imperial and republican government are obliged to compromise with so-called private power. With the relative democratisation of the country, the power of local landlords tends to increase, because of the electorate which they dominate and which they can hold in the political balance.' (*Burocracia e Patrimonialismo*, p. 6.)

44 'It even happened sometimes that the *coronel* also displayed great enthusiasm for Rui . . . But . . . he would go faithfully to fulfil his pledge and vote for the government. His pledge was made on the basis of an exchange of powers, state or federal power for the government, and municipal power for the *coronel*.' (Emil Farhat, 'O Genro, o Grande Culpado'.)

45 'Paternalism in local political structures has survived and manifests itself in a curious manner. If an individual comes to occupy a position of importance in the political and administrative field, it is by no means rare for one to witness the rise of a great many of his people. Not only relations of all kinds but also childhood friends, former colleagues, neighbours, relations and friends of neighbours, all occupy positions of responsibility or trust in the entourage of the new leader. All forms of nepotism may be classified as aspects of paternalism. Given that this is based on relationships of loyalty and trust, it is clear what advantages can be derived by showing preference to relations, friends and associates exposed to the control of the same local structure.' (Emil Farhat, *op. cit.*, p. 7.)

46 Deputy Fábio Sodré, in the second Constituent Assembly of the Republic, called attention to 'municipal dictatorship'. In Brazil, the system of checks and balances would not work in the municipalities, 'because the prefect and the governor indisputably exercise direct action over the electorate. Only with great difficulty could a municipal chamber be in opposition to the prefect.' However, in his diagnosis of this condition Sodré gave exaggerated importance to the fact that the municipal executive has a mandate of fixed duration: 'Elected for a fixed term, the prefect will totally dominate the municipal chamber.' He will be a minor dictator. (*Anais*, vol. XX, p. 401.)

47 'As a rule', said Deputy Raul Fernandes in the Constituent Assembly of 1934, 'the municipal councillor supports the government. Only in this way can he obtain for his municipality the bridges, roads and schools which the government gives out with preference to its own party, and which it passes on to its allies. It is the *do ut des*, honest, if you will, because it works in the interest of the people. In exceptional cases, municipal councillors may be of the opposition.'

After reminding his audience that a telegram-circular from a few political leaders in Minas, whom he named, was capable in the space of twenty-four hours of achieving unanimity among all the municipal councillors of the state (more than a thousand) 'in favour of an idea or of a candidate', he warned that the same phenomenon could occur in any other state: 'In each one a few leaders control all the municipal chambers, which are all chosen along party lines and obey a single discipline.' (*Anais*, vol. XII, p. 240.)

Very interesting too, is the following passage from a pamphlet distributed during the last municipal elections in Minas: 'The *National Democratic Union* (U.D.N.) takes pleasure in bringing to the notice of the people of this municipality that the *leadership of the municipality* is, at this moment, composed of the persons who have signed this pamphlet . . . These persons *are on the side of the government* . . . Yesterday many of these worthy comrades were our opponents, but . . . they have *resolved to support the government*, which in less than *six months created more than twenty schools in this municipality*, while the *prefect who fell* on 19 January, and who represented the *opposition party*, created *only 17 schools in seven years.*'

Let it be said in passing that, in the municipality referred to, the P.S.D. *as the government party*, won the elections of 19 January 1947, by 1050 votes; and the U.D.N., in coalition with the P.R., *as new government parties*, won the municipal elections which followed by about 400 votes. Thus, from one election to another, the party which lose the support of the state government also lost nearly 1500 votes in an electorate of little more than 6000. This change was largely brought about by a barbarous crime, the victims of which were U.D.N. supporters, and which shocked local opinion.

48   In a speech in 1923 Basílio de Magalhães called attention for the need 'to prevent revenues from falling prey to the greed and ambitions of party politicians, or from being diverted into the electoral machinery by their rise to positions of authority.' (*O Municipalismo em Minas Gerais*, p. 19.)

Great publicity was given to the action of Governor Milton Campos when he challenged several ex-prefects of Minas on the correction of their accounts, which included large items of electoral expenditure. The Director of the Department of the Municipalities said in this exposition: 'Numerous prefects have already lost any sense of public money, confusing it with their private means or with the official party funds.' In a leaflet published by the Department under the title *Regularização das Contas Municipais* we find specific details of suspected items of expenditure.

49   On this matter, Orlando M. Carvalho wrote: 'the dominant factions in the Brazil of yesterday and today always used the state coffers for their electoral expenses without this practice giving rise to the passing of any law to restrict the use and abuse of public money to maintain their particular group in power . . . Expenses for party conventions [of the P.S.D.], qualification, transport of electors for registration, transport of groups of supporters for propaganda purposes by means of special trains or official cars, all this came out of public funds with no concern to pretend otherwise on the part of those managing the party's affairs. In Minas, even the rent for the party's headquarters is paid by the state.' ('Despesas Eleitorais'; other interesting information from the same author in 'Transportes e Aquartelamento de Eleitores no Interior'.)

50   Djacir Meneses, after referring to an incident from the colonial period, comments: 'So it will be repeated under the monarchy and under the Republic: the government forces, the political prestige of the victor at the elections, supporting a family which ruled the municipality by alliance with the governing party, and by the persecution of its opponents . . . prefects dominated by banditry, supported by the blunderbus of the backlander, taking refuge with the government party in a mutual exchange of benefits.' (*O Outro Nordeste*, p. 82.)

'Politics in Brazil', says Vivaldi Moreira, 'is a question of: the police for you, votes for me.' (*Fôlha de Minas*, 25 June 1948.)

The following was told to the author: the late Sr Luis Martins Soares, leader of a dissident wing of the P.S.D. in Minas, after listening to a long speech by Sr Virgílio de Melo Franco, president of the state branch of the U.D.N., replied: 'The matter is very simple. What you want is the deputy [*deputado*]; what I want is the police chief [*delegado*].'

It ought to be observed that the nomination to minor police posts generally falls to the leaders themselves, who usually appoint them in large numbers, thus investing with public authority men who become electoral agents for the party concerned.

51   In the words of Domingos Velasco, 'the state authorities, after the rigid presidentialism of 1891 had forced the establishment of the state governorships, always had the political wisdom to rely on the municipal chiefs. The leaders of the states were interested in this only in so far as the municipal chiefs could form a unanimous block of seats which would not fail to support them. Hence the care they took not to interfere in municipal politics, holding themselves apart from disputes, in order to maintain links with all factions and to receive their unanimous vote at election time. To this is due the Brazilian phenomenon of fraudulent state and federal elections and genuine, hard-fought municipal ones.' (*Anais*, 1934, vol. I, pp. 297–8.)

These assertions are valid but with certain reservations. In many cases, the government of the state has not been willing to hold itself aloof in this way from local politics. Examples of interference are very frequent, sometimes involving the use of force to tilt the political balance in the municipality. But the important thing to notice is that this does not occur simply through love of violence, but through the contingencies of the local struggle itself, bitter, personal, without truce or pause for deliberation. Most of the time it is not possible to be for one faction without being against the other. And being against, as it turns out, includes denying the enemy any good turn, and doing it harm.

The author of the deposition cited says this implicitly when he includes the fear of violence as one of the factors disposing local leaders to support the government: 'On the other hand the leaders of the municipalities, in their historical role as willing or unwilling protectors of the masses, were unanimous in their support for governments not only in order to obtain improvements for their municipalities but also to avoid interference by force. This was the general rule.' (*Ibid.*)

52   '*O Municipalismo em Minas Gerais*', p. 10. Sr Cromwell Barbosa de Carvalho's book, published in 1921 (*Municipio* versus *Estado*), symptomatically reflects the picture of political struggles in the municipalities and how these relate to the state government. This work, complete with theoretical generalisations, deals with a fierce dispute as to who would administer the district of Caxais (Maranhão). The author himself was involved, being a prominent member of one of the warring factions, both led by *coronéis*, although we do not know whether they genuinely hold this rank or not. It is curious to observe that Sr Cromwell Barbosa de Carvalho, a militant in

local politics, vigorously supports many restrictions on municipal autonomy, as the book's epigraph indicates, including the state's right to nominate prefects whom he regards as being representatives, at one and the same
time, 'of the district and of the state' (p. 88). These restrictions would, as
it happened, have benefited his faction, according to what we can deduce
from the author's position (public prosecutor for the district), from the
fact that his book was printed in the government presses and from the
laudatory and respectful manner in which he refers to the government of
the state. In section IX of this same chapter we treat more extensively the
question of the interest which at least one of the local factions has in undermining the authority of the municipality.

53   It is clear that in some provinces or states the process has been less
evident than in others. In spite of this the problem of municipal autonomy
in Brazil follows the broad outlines which we have drawn. Beginning with
the almost sovereign assemblies of certain colonial times and terminating
in the municipalities of the *Estado Novo*, mere administrative dependencies
with no political life of their own – these, the two extreme forms, shaped
by special circumstances – we have a long process of the slow and continuous narrowing of the municipal sphere, more marked here and there
and sometimes interrupted by pro-municipal movements of little depth
and short duration.

54   In 1940, for 1572 municipalities and 4833 districts (*Quadro dos
Municípios Brasileiros Vigorantes no Qüinqüênio de 1 de Janeiro de 1939
a 31 de Dezembro de 1943*, p. 3), the census registered 1,904,589 'agricultural establishments', 148,622 of which had an area of 200 hectares and
more (*Muáfio Estatístico*, 1946, p. 84). There was therefore at that time
an average for each district of 30 properties of the size mentioned.

55   The role of inheritance in the breaking up of property is not to be
neglected, although it is very difficult to determine the exact extent of its
influence, especially as properties may have been subsequently re-unified.

Gilberto Freire says: 'in the special sense of Sorokin's terminology,
colonial society in Brazil was mobile horizontally as well as vertically. This
is attested by the often sudden changes which occurred, particularly in the
South, in the social and economic position or rank of an individual . . . This
is because in Brazil, even where colonisation was at its most aristocratic as
in Pernambuco, patriarchalism was never absolute, nor could it be so, given
"the almost general practice of dividing property among several heirs"
referred to by Silvio Romero in a letter to Ed. Demolins.' (*Provocações e
Debates*, Pôrto, 1916; *Casa Grande & Senzala*, vol. I, note 34, pp. 171–2.)

The same author affirms: 'The fact that one meets so many Wanderleys
destroyed by alcohol and entirely lacking their former aristocratic prestige
is primarily due to social and economic causes which affected other illustrious families of the colonial era, today equally decadent: the instability
of rural wealth caused by the system of slavery and by monoculture; the
laws governing inheritance which favoured the dispersal of assets; the law
of abolition which did not offer any compensation to the slave-owners.'
(*Provocações e Debates*, vol. I, p. 448.)

Oliveira Viana observes that the abolition of the right of the firstborn
(1835) was in line with the proposal which sought to avoid the following

contingency: namely, that the concentration of economic power, favoured by the unified administration of entailed properties, would contribute towards consolidating in private hands a large measure of social and political power. In his own words: 'The real reason, the internal reason which justifies this measure, is simply the fear of the growth of a powerful hereditary aristocracy.' ('*Populações Meridionais do Brasil*', p. 295.) The author cited is supported by Armitage in whose work we read the following: 'The abolition of the law of entail, which liberal journalists affirmed as being so worthy of the efforts of a session but which was defeated in the Senate in the following year, has as its primary aim the prevention of the establishment of an hereditary aristocracy, rather than the remedying of any existing evil. Since 1824, when the Absolutists had received such protection, the public began to fear that the Senate might at some future date be replaced by an hereditary chamber; this suspicion had recently gained weight because of the frequent granting of titles to descendants of the existing aristocracy. The Chamber of Deputies, having little sympathy with the idea of the supremacy of a Senate whose members were appointed without any attention to the question of their talents or abilities, decided to annul completely the relevant laws, convinced that without them no hereditary institution could exist.' (*História do Brasil*, pp. 243—4.)

In the words of Pedro Calmon, the law of 6 October 1835 which abolished entails and pious bequests was 'a blow struck at the old landed nobility in the name of civil law.' (*História do Brasil*, vol. 4, p. 289, note 2.)

56   Referring to the areas of German settlement which present special features of an obvious kind, Professor Willems observes: 'In the political elite superimposed on the German—Brazilian population, it is possible to distinguish two factions: one which identifies itself completely with the national ethos, and another which maintains a marginal position defending an ethnic ideology. The discrepancy between the legal political position and the social status of German—Brazilians gave rise to the use of the political rights of those born as Brazilian citizens (i.e. the vote) in defence of the principles of a separate ethnic and cultural identity for them as Germans. (*Assimilação e Populações Marginais no Brasil*, p. 336.)

'The representatives of so-called "marginal politics" ', writes the same author, 'are chiefly state deputies, prefects, and municipal councillors . . . In German—Brazilian centres, the "politics of block-voting" functioned in the interest of the ethnically-defined minority. The political bosses and leaders of the districts, generally traders under the influence of the German pastors and press, would choose people who promised to defend the ethnic ideals of Germanism. No candidate who refused to make these pledges could count on any votes . . . The political compromise always involved agreements concerning *private schools and associated activities in the German—Brazilian areas*. The electorate ('led by the nose') never voted for candidates who were not indicated by the real manipulators of local opinion. The elected representatives never dared displease the German electorate. This machinery did not allow, for example, any measure which might envisage the incorporation of the private schools into the national system.' (*Op. cit.*, pp. 336, 325 and 326.)

In the particular case observed by Professor Willems, the 'system of block-voting' is not linked to land-ownership, as in almost the whole of the rest of the country. But even in his case the system of compromise functions perfectly.

2. Powers of the municipalities

1   '[T]itle of *vila*, condition of autonomy in municipal affairs.' (Capistrano de Abreu, *Capítulos de História Colonial*, p. 172.)
'As soon as hereditry captainships were created, the respective beneficiaries, in gratitude for the privileges conferred on them, gave the settlements designated as the seat of government the charter of a borough, setting up a pillory in each of them as an emblem of their jurisdiction and a symbol of municipal freedom; but such charters, to be considered definitive, had to be confirmed by the sovereign [by Letters Patent or Royal Charter] . . . Our history records the existence of three boroughs (two in the region of Rio de Janeiro, and one in the territory of the exploratory expeditions) founded by revolutionaries in the colonial period.' (Basílio de Magalhães, 'Algumas Notas sôbre o Municipalismo Brasileiro'.) The boroughs of revolutionary origin were Campos, Parati and Pindamonhangaba, whose creation is described by the author in minute detail in the same very informative work.
2   'In its deliberative function, the chamber was a body composed only of the judge and his councillors. Initially it was known as a *Vereacão* or a Council of Aldermen [*vereador* = alderman or councillor] ; later, the term *câmara* [chamber] was used to express the meeting of the councillors presided over by a judge.' (Max Fleiuss, *História Administrativa do Brasil*, p. 34.) Meetings of the chamber with other authorities with 'honourable men' ('nobility, military and ecclesiastical') were known as general assemblies. (*Juntas gerais*, see note 22, below.)
3   'In all cities and towns the number of these judges did not exceed two, and in a few cases only one was elected.' (Cândido Mendes, *Código Filipino*, note 1 to bk. I, t. 65, para. 1.) 'The ordinary judges were always two in number, exercising their function in alternate months of the year for which they had been elected.' (Caio Prado Jr, *Formação do Brasil Contemporâneo*, p. 313.) Yet we read in the Ordinances: 'And when there are two ordinary judges, each one will have hearings for a week, and the week during which he officiates, he shall do so alone.' (Bk. I, t. 65, para. 4.)
4   'An outside judge [*juiz de Fora*] or a "judge from elsewhere" [*juiz de fora-aparte*] as he was initially known . . . was the magistrate appointed by the king to any locality, under the pretext that he would be better able to administer justice to the people than the ordinary judges or those from the district, who would be swayed by their personal likes and dislikes . . . These visiting judges were delegated and nominated for periods of three years, and it appears that they were never nominated more than once. They usually presided over the chambers of the cities and towns in which they functioned'. (Cândido Mendes, *Código Filipino*, note 1 to bk. I, t. 65.) The ordinary judges only served when there was no visiting judge. (*Op. cit.*, note 1 to bk. I, t. 66; Caio Prado Jr, *Formação do Brasil Contemporâneo*, p. 60; Carvalho Mourão, 'Os Municípios', p. 308.)

5   Ordinances, bk. I, t. 58, para. 17; João Francisco Lisboa, *Obras*, vol.
II, p. 164; Enéias Galvão, 'Juízes e Tribunais no Período Colonial', p. 330.
6   Ordinances, bk. I, t. 58, para. 43; Orlando M. Carvalho, *Política do*
Município, p. 163.
7   Ordinances, bk. I, t. 66.
8   See below ch. IV, section I.
9   The Phillipine Ordinances greatly emphasised the administrative character of the chambers, and reduced their judicial functions 'to the least possible'. (Basílio de Magalhães, 'Algumas Notas'; Carvalho Mourão, 'Os Municípios', p. 308.)
10   See Caio Prado Jr, *Formação do Brasil Contemporâneo*, pp. 297 and
298, where the matter is clarified. The same author says (p. 316): 'In short,
there is no break in colonial administration, no clear division between local
and general government. It is added proof of this fact that all acts of the
chamber are subject to review by some superior authority: magistrate,
governor, Court of Appeal, even the Royal Court itself. On the other hand,
the chambers act as genuine local bodies for the over-all administrative
authority.' (Cf. also Salomão de Vasconcelos, quoted by Orlando M. Carvalho, *Política do Município*, p. 35.)
11   There must be some ambiguity in referring to the chief *alcaide* as the
assistant of the inspectors. (See Cândido Mendes, *Código Filipino*, note 1
to bk. I, t. 74, and note 1 to bk. I, t. 75.)
12   Carvalho Mourão, 'Os Municípios', p. 309.
13   See below, ch. V, section I.
14   Carvalho Mourão, *op. cit.*, pp. 309 and 310.
15   The government of territories conquered by the Dutch West India
Company, according to its first Statutes of 13 October 1629 (*Revista do*
Instituto Arquedogico e Geographico de Pernambuco, vol. V, No. 31, pp.
289–310), was shared between a Governor whose powers were essentially
military, and a Council of nine members, also known as an Assembly or
College of Councillors. This was the supreme administrative body and functioned under a presidency which rotated on a monthly basis, being held by
each member in turn. They were elected by the constituent chambers of
the Company, subject to approval by the Assembly of the Nineteen, the
controlling body of that privileged organisation. While the Council com-
municated directly with this Assembly, the Governor had direct access to
the States General, and from this frequent clashes of authority resulted
between the Governor and the Council whose multiple powers were political, administrative and judicial. (F.A. Pereira da Costa, in the review cited,
vol. IX, no. 51, p. 3.) Other minor authorities – judicial, police, fiscal, etc.
– completed the picture of the administration (Statues of 1629). In the
beginning the pattern of municipal organisation which the Dutch found in
Brazil, was not abolished.
     With the new Statutes, decreed by Maurice of Nassau on 23 August
1686, the leadership of the government was transferred to a Secret Supreme
Council and to the Governor, its President, who according to Handelmann
(*História do Brasil*, p. 193) had two votes, the second of which was certainly a casting one. (Cf. Pereira da Costa, 'Govêrno holandês', p. 5.)
Various authors say that there were three members of the Secret Supreme

Council (Handelmann, Pereira da Costa . . .), but in the records of the
General Assembly of 1640 four persons appear with this qualification.
(Review quoted, vol. V, no. 31, p. 173.) With the setting up of the Secret
Supreme Council, the old Council of nine members referred to in the
sources as the Political Council, began to play a lesser role. It retained certain functions, judicial ones in particular, but also administrative ones,
superintending the functionaries and authorities of the various districts as
a court of appeal. (Handelmann, *op. cit.*)

The municipal chambers set up by the Portuguese lasted from the
invasion (1630) until 1637 (Herckman, in the review quoted, vol. V, No.
31, p. 247; Varnhagen; *História das Lutas*, vol. I, p. 177; *História Geral do
Brasil*, vol. III, p. 358.) when, following the pattern that existed in the
United Provinces of the Netherlands, the *camara dos escabinos*, or municipal council, was set up with local administrative and judicial functions, un-
hampered by interference from any superior body in routine local affairs.
(José Higino, in the review quoted, vol. V. No. 30, p. 33, note and p. 29.)
When Herckman alludes to 'the justice tribunal of the whole captainship'
(Paraíba), he refers, without doubt, to the municipal council, since he says
that its powers were formerly exercised by 'two judges and by two or three
councillors' an institution which had existed here 'in the time of the King
of Spain'. ('Descriçao Geral', pp. 246–7.)

The municipal councils were set up 'in all the territories' and 'in all the
towns'. (H. Varnhagen, *História das Lutas*, vol. I, p. 385, and *História
Geral*, vol. III, p. 177.) In these were representatives of Dutch and Portuguese nationality; in equal numbers, according to Calado and Varnhagen,
the latter adding that the president (*esculteto*) was usually Dutch, thus
guaranteeing a majority to the 'rulers' (*op. cit.*, and *loc. cit.*, and Rodolfo
Garcia's note); Herckman's detailed work, however, leaves an element of
doubt in this area, since he mentions *five* municipal councillors, later
clarifying: 'there is, in addition, a president'. (Descrição Geral, p. 248.)
Friar Manuel Caladao declares that the chamber was composed of 'four
Portuguese and four Flemish judges' (Rodolfo Garcia's note quoted above),
but according to Varnhagen's suppositions (*ibid.*) the number of municipal
councillors varied from three to nine including the president (*esculteto*).

The selection of the municipal council, as it was practised in Paraíba
from 1637 to 1639, was done in three stages: (a) the Political Council (the
old Council of nine members of the regulations of 1629) selected 'from
among the best qualified inhabitants, Portuguese as well as Netherlanders,
a certain number of persons who would serve as electors'; (b) these selected,
'from among themselves and the other inhabitants . . . the most religious,
most capable and best qualified individuals', forming a list containing three
times the number of municipal councillors to be elected; (c) finally, the
Secret Supreme Council, under the presidency of the Governor, nominated
the municipal councillors, from among the persons on the list compiled by
the electors. (Herckman, *op. cit.*, pp. 247–8.)

Duarte Pereira José Higino (who examined the records of the Secret
Supreme Council up to 1654) affirms that the choice of electors was made
by 'council of justice' (Relatório', p. 27), but it is quite likely that he is
referring to the Political Council, since this functioned as a second Court

of Appeal; with this proviso, his description confirms (not in all the minor details, because it omits many of them) that the process of selection of the municipal councillors of Paraíba, just described, was the one employed in the whole area ruled by the Dutch.

José Higino adds that 'the terror of the Portuguese inhabitants' were the presidents (*escultetos*): 'The Colonial Governor himself took the initiative in the severest measures to restrain the insubordination of these "village tyrants". (*Op. cit.*, p. 36.) In the records of the General Assembly of 1640 summoned by Nassau, there are various observations and proposals on this issue. This meeting resolved that the municipal council in each chamber could register, in a book set aside for this purpose, the 'evil deeds and crimes' of the presidents and officials of the militia, to be brought to the attention of the Supreme Council at an appropriate time, there being a severe penalty for frivolous or untruthful entries. (In *Relatório*, No. 31.)

The president of the chamber was, as Varnhagen interprets it, 'the executive authority, or delegate of the administration and public prosecutor of the locality, as well as tax-collector'. It was his duty 'to enter complaints against malefactors and delinquents, to put sentences into effect, as well as the orders and dictates of the government . . . and undertake the other functions proper to the office of *esculteto*, according to the ordinances of Holland, Zeeland and West Friesia'. (Herckman, 'Descrição Geral', pp. 248–9.) The sources used in the compiling of this note were indicated to the author by Sr José Honório Rodrigues.

16   On the transformation of the settlements (villages) into towns organised into districts, cf. J. Capistrano de Abreu, *Capítulos de História Colonial*, pp. 188 ff.

17   Carvalho Mourão, 'Os Municípios', pp. 301 and 302. See below, note 26.

18   Gilberto Freire alludes to the 'slave-owning landlords, who, as Senates [*sic*] always lorded it over the representatives of the king, and by the liberal voice of their sons who were priests or doctors clamoured against all kinds of abuses in the Mother Country and in Mother Church herself'. Referring to our colonial aristocracy, he adds: 'Over it the King of Portugal reigns but does not rule. The Senates very early on limited the power of the kings and later of imperialism itself or, rather, of the economic parasitism which was seeking to extend its grasping tentacles from the kingdom to the colonies.' (*Casa Grande & Senzala*, vol. I, pp. 86 and 107–8.)

On the exuberant growth of private power in colonial Brazil, cf. also Nestor Duarte, *A Ordem Privada e a Organização Política Nacional*; Costa Pinto, 'Lutas de Famílias no Brasil'; Oliveira Viana, *Populações Meridionais*, etc.

19   Under the patriarchal colonial system the *protection* dispensed by the *paterfamilias* was a powerful factor in the family group, as Alcântara Machado observed: 'Of what worth is the single individual in a *milieu* in which misused force is the supreme law? . . . If he is not to succumb, he has to group himself with those who are close to him through common interest or by blood. It is the instinct of preservation which strengthens the kinship group. It is the need for self-defence which makes the colonial family a stable and homogeneous body. As a defensive organisation, the family group requires a head who leads and governs it in the Roman fashion, with military strictness.' (*Vida e Morte do Bandeirante*, cited by Costa Pinto, 'Lutas de Famílias', p. 33.)

On the peculiarities of the cattle-rearing regions of the Northeast and Rio Grande do Sul, and on other areas where the characteristic system of latifundia 'was not established or maintained', cf. Caio Prado Jr, *Formação do Brasil Contemporâneo*, pp. 267 ff.; Djacir Meneses, *O Outro Nordeste*. To the extent to which it developed, business was practically monopolised by the Portuguese, and represented an obstacle to the power of the rural landlords. This was sharply illustrated in the struggle between Recife and Olinda.

20   Caio Prado Jr, *Evolução Política do Brasil*, p. 52. Oliveira Viana underlines emphatically the dependence of the colonial chambers which, in the words of José Elói Otôni, 'as they are renewed annually, scheme during their term of office to remain in perfect harmony with the planters of the area, who are all either relations, friends or neighbours'. (*Populações Meridionais do Brasil*, p. 188.) His observations on local, elective justice are identical. (*Op. cit.*, pp. 183 ff.)

21   The title 'Senate' was a 'high honour' but did not signify any structural difference. (Basílio do Magalhães, 'Algumas Notas'; Caio Prado Jr, *Formação do Brasil Contemporâneo*, p. 312, note 23.)

22   João Francisco Lisboa, *Obras*, vol. II, p. 46. The same author says that in the deliberations of the general assemblies 'the governors, chief captains, legal and tax officials were usually present, either of their own volition or in answer to a summons from the chamber' (pp. 46 and 47). Later, he explains that the Phillipine Ordinances, denying any 'political function' to the chambers, only authorised assemblies of 'honest men' for the purpose of making laws within 'the strictly economic and administrative jurisdiction' of the districts (a clear allusion to para. 28 of t. 66 of bk. I); 'laws decreed by the colonies in the beginning' placed on the governors the obligation of convening assemblies, either of certain authorities or of 'principal citizens', for the purpose of studying predetermined matters, but having merely an advisory function with the governor having the final say, not to mention the personal right, to convene them in the first place. Nevertheless, later on, the power of the assemblies was implicitly recognised in relation to those 'accomplished facts which, with the passing of time, were being reproduced and perpetuated', but the Crown was careful, in a number of Royal Decrees, to limit the consequences of such 'facts' and to suppress 'usurpations on the part of the chambers'. 'It was the case that abuses and usurpations multiplied, and by being so commonplace, came in the end to constitute a sort of right, sometimes disputed, sometimes tolerated and sometimes formally recognised by the governors and by the Court.' (p. 4 and p. 50)

23   It is very instructive to read the account which is given in vol. II, p. 50 of the *Obras* of J.F. Lisboa. On the colonial chambers see also Pedro Calmon, *História Social do Brasil*, t. 1, pp. 242 ff.

24   Mini-factories (*engenhocas*): Royal Decrees of 10 September 1706; 13 October 1707 (J.F. Lisboa, op. cit., vol. II, pp. 191–2); debts: Provision of 21 April 1688; 27 October 1673; 6 February 1674; 26 February 1681; 15 January 1683 (*ibid.*, p. 190); election of *merchants*: Letter Patent of 29 July 1643; Royal Decree of 16 February 1671; 10 December 1689; 10 November 1700; 14 June 1710; Provision of 23 July 1745; 4 March 1747; Provision of 8 May 1705 (*ibid.*, pp. 169 and 171). Cf. as well Caio Prado Jr, *Evolução Política do Brasil*, pp. 31, 32 and 74. Here, the author focuses on the change in the Crown's attitude, at first forbidding, and later permitting, the election of merchants, a fact which meant a marked reduction in the influence of the rural landlords. See also the passage from the Marquis of Lavradio cited below, ch. III, note 14.

25   Caio Prado Jr, *Formação do Brasil Contemporâneo*, pp. 113 ff. and 226 ff.; *História Econômica do Brasil*, ch. 2 and pp. 122 ff.

Gilberto Freire writes: 'The plantation house, complete with slave-quarters, represented an entire economic, social and political system: of production [monocultural latifundia]; of labour [slavery]; of transport [ox-cart, hand-barrow, system of driveways and paths, the horse]; of religion [Catholicism of the family, with the chaplain subordinate to the *paterfamilias*, cult of the dead, etc.]; of sexual life and family life [polygamous patriarchalism]; of personal and household hygiene [the *tiger* – large barrel for the collection of faeces, the banana-clump, bathing in the river, wooden bath-tub, the hip-bath, the receptacle for washing the feet]; of politics [compaternity]. It was, in addition, fortress, bank, cemetery, hostelry, school, almshouse which received the old, widowed and orphaned.' (*Casa Grande & Senzala*, vol. I, p. 24.)

26   'Organizacão Administrativa do Brasil', p. 23. The reliable Capistrano de Abreu had already written in the same connection: 'The chambers of the interior did not differ from those of the sea-board, that is, they possessed the right of petition, could tax goods produced locally, supplied the ordinary judges, but were, above all, strictly administrative bodies . . . There is nothing to confirm the omnipotence of the municipal chambers discovered by João Francisco Lisboa and repeated in discussion by those who could not take the trouble of referring to the sources.' (Capistrano de Abreu, *Capítulos de História Colonial*, p. 151.) It is to be noted that more recent authors – Gilberto Freire and Caio Prado Jr amongst others – have not failed to go to the primary sources.

27   Cf. others in the same vein, quoted in J.F. Lisboa, *op. cit.*, vol. II, p. 169.

28   *Evolução Política do Brasil*, pp. 67 ff.; *Formação do Brasil Contemporâneo*, p. 314; *História Econômica do Brasil*, pp. 59 and 60.

29   In legal language, if the inhabitants of the state of Brazil, which already constituted 'an extensive and lucrative business and shipping interest', took part in industrial activities themselves, they would become 'completely independent of the controlling capital'. Because of this it was 'indispensably necessary to abolish from the state of Brazil the said factories and industries'. (Circular of 7 January 1785; cf. J.F. Lisboa, *op. cit.*, vol. II, p. 194.)

The confiscation of Antonil's book, published in 1711, is very symptomatic. The pretext was that it revealed 'the secret of Brazil to foreigners';

Capistrano de Abreu asserts, however: 'the truth is otherwise: the book taught the secret of Brazil to Brazilians, showing all that they possessed, justifying all their claims, revealing all their grandeur'. (*Capitulos*, p. 183.)

30   Cf. Costa Pinto, 'Lutas de Famílias no Brasil', esp. pp. 66 and 73.

31   'In each captainship in which there was extraction of gold, an intendancy was organised with powers completely independent of any other colonial body: it was accountable only to the metropolitan government . . . It was an administrative body as well, which controlled mining policy; also judicial, as a court of first and final appeal in suits relating to its own prerogatives; fiscal, as collector of the fifth. It was also, or was intended to be, technically responsible for the direction and growth of production . . . The intendancy was composed of a superintendent, popularly known as an intendant whose duty was the general direction of the service, and of an inspector general who distributed data and supervised the observance of regulations in the mines themselves. The inspector general could be substituted in "distant" areas by wardens – the law provided for this although it left the way clear for many abuses – nominated by himself. There were in addition clerks and other minor officials.' (Caio Prado Jr, *Formação do Brasil Contemporâneo*, pp. 170 and 171.)

32   Oliveira Viana, *Populações Meridionais*, pp. 259 and 260; and his *Evolução do Povo Brasileiro*, p. 188, note 2.

33   In his famous book, Felício dos Santos summarises the various sets of regulations concerning the government of the Diamantine District. From 1734 on, the highest authority was the intendant, to whom Article 11 of the Letter Patent of 23 May 1772 assigned 'all the disputed jurisdiction of the district'. He was answerable directly to the king and had practically unlimited powers. Suffice it to say that he could reach a judgement with secret evidence 'without the presence of any judge', and for this reason the practice of legal advocacy was prohibited in Tijuco. By the workings of this odious process, a person could be expelled from the district, have his goods confiscated or suffer the gravest penalty. Those who had denounced him obtained a third of his confiscated assets, and, in the case of slaves denouncing their owners, their freedom. The denunciations, received in complete secrecy, were formalised by the competent authority, without saying who the denouncer was, into a single paper, which afterwards would serve as the bearer's claim for receiving the reward. No one could enter or remain in the district without the written authority of the intendant, business premises were subject to strict vigilance and their number could be arbitrarily reduced, homes could be searched without the least formality. These and other evils, consolidated and exaggerated by the regulation of 12 July 1771 – the famous and terrifying *Livro da Capa Verde* – kept the inhabitants in permanent upheaval and complete insecurity. The abuses increased under the regime of the 'contracts', since a simple denunciation by the contractors was enough to secure the expulsion of an inhabitant from the area in question. All these tyrannical precautions were designed to avoid or restrict contraband trade in diamonds, which nevertheless managed to continue. The camp of Tijuco, in spite of its growth, was not elevated to the status of *vila* until 1831, in order to avoid the limitations to the intendant's absolute power which municipal status would bring. Yet, before that date the intendancy had lost some of its powers, as for example some of the licence already referred to (1821). Felício dos Santos gives full rein to his revulsion when he describes in strong terms the regime in force in Tijuco, this 'isolated colony, segregated from the rest of Brazil'. (*Memórias do Distrito Diamantino.*)

34   Cf. Carneiro Maia, *O Município*, bk. III, sections I and II. It should be noted as symptomatic of the period in question that the municipal chambers were generally in favour of the proposal, which was changed in the Constitution of 1824. The wide and general formula adopted in the constitutional text gave no hint of the puny offspring which the law of municipal organisation of 1828 was to be.

35   Articles 24 and 65.

36   Article 78 of the law of 1828: 'Moreover, it is forbidden to hold meetings to discuss or decide upon matters not contained in this regulation, such as propositions, deliberations or decisions made in the name of the people, and because of this, null, void and contrary to Article 167 of the Constitution, and much less to renounce prerogatives, it being understood that these are the jurisdiction of the presidents of the provinces, who are their primary administrators.'

37   On the doctrine of *tutelage*, cf. Visconde do Uruguai, *Direito Administrativo*, preface, p. 21; Carneiro Maia, *O Município*, bk. II, sections VII, VIII, X, XI and XII; bk. III, sections V and IX; Castro Nunes, *Do Estado Federado e Sua Organização Municipal*, pt. III, ch. VI; Orlando M. Carvalho, *Política do Município*, pp. 55 ff. Also the examples of the exercise of tutelage cited by Cortines Laxe, *Regimento*, p. XXVII.

38   Carneiro Maia. *O Município*, p. 206.

39   Articles 20 and 32.

40   Cf. ch. III, no. II.

41   Law of 12 August 1834, especially Article 10, Nos. IV–VII; Article 11, No. III.

42   'The Additional Act fettered our chambers to an iron post; to free them we required a bold cut, right in the link of the chain . . . The Additional Act was a sombre legacy of the revolution. Not for the first time administrative despotism rises from deep within a democracy which vanishes with the splendour of its conquests. By investing municipal tutelage with a legal form more extensive and repressive than under the previous regime, it is true, beyond doubt, that the Additional Act not only worsened the lot of the municipalities but was a tangible controversion of the very principles of administrative freedom which had led to the reforms of 1834'. (Carneiro Maia, *O Município*, p. XV and p. 229.)

'It is not fair to say as the Visconde do Uruguai and Cortines Laxe have said . . . and most of the conservative school of imperial times, that the depressed condition of subordination and atrophy found in the municipalities in imperial times was the work of the Additional Act. We have already seen that nothing remained of the independent life of Brazilian municipalities under the law of 1828. It is true, however, if strange, that the Assembly of 1834, for all its liberal and progressive ideas and instincts, instead of loosening the bonds which were strangling municipal freedom, drew them tighter.' (Carvalhos Mourão, 'Os Municípios', pp. 315–16.)

43 'The spirit of the constitutional reform was certainly to invest the assemblies with powers to superintend the chambers; but as far as the considerable powers relating to the municipalities were concerned, legislating on their economy, politics, officials, revenue and expenditure, it was the duty of the assemblies to apply to the localities of each province the most beneficial form of government . . . But . . . then came the law of 12 May 1840. The Additional Act was struck off.' (Aureliano Cândido Tavares Bastos, *A Província*, pp. 147 and 148.) See also Visconde de Ouro Prêto, *Reforma Administrativa e Municipal*, p. 77; Barbalho, *Constituição Federal Brasileira*, p. 281 (passage in which he cites a speech of Alvaro Barbalho Uchoa Cavalcânti).

44 The Assembly of São Paulo, when it instituted the system of the free nomination of prefects of which we shall speak later (cf. ch. III, section III; ch V, section II) at the same time (April 1835) conferred on the provincial government the right to appoint and dismiss, *freely*, certain functionaries employed in the municipal sphere. This provoked some reaction in the districts. The Chamber of São Sebastião was encouraged by that of Ubatuba in the session of 13 January 1838 to form a joint movement of various municipalities to petition the provincial legislature for the revocation not only of the law of the prefects (see ch. V, note 41) but also 'Of the Assembly's resolution of 11 April 1835, No. 19, which authorises the government to appoint and dismiss employees independently of the proposals of the municipal chambers, when it is well known that these bodies can and do have the necessary information as to which of the citizens of their respective municipalities are fit for the posts in question.' In the words of the Chamber of Ubatuba, this 'resolution has helped to raise to social eminence individuals whom it should not have, and on the other hand it has dismissed others whose services and consistently sober conduct do honour to their character; because of this we must ask the government that nomination and dismissal of these said employees be carried out only according to the proposals and information offered by the chambers concerned.' (The original of the document quoted belongs to Professor Hélio Viana, who kindly provided a copy.) The validity of Resolution No. 19 of 1835, at first limited to a year was later extended by Resolution No. 17 of 27 February 1836.

45 The Additional Act, Article 10, No. XI. Article 3 of the law of 12 May 1840, gave a restrictive interpretation to this provision.

46 '[T]he presidents', wrote Dom Pedro II in 1870, 'serve principally to win elections.' (Document transcribed in Joaquim Nabuco, *Um Estadista do Império*; vol. II, pp. 439–40.)

Tavares Bastos: 'In Brazil the president is an electoral instrument. It is through him that we periodically elect the chancery of dissembled absolutism. To set up, direct, perfect the electoral machine, this is his real mission, his care by day and by night.' (*A Província*, p. 135.)

47 The Council of State (Articles 137 and 144 of the Constitution) was suppressed by Article 32 of the Additional Act and re-established, with modifications, by Law No. 234, of 23 November 1841.

48 Consult the works already quoted of Carneiro Maia, Tavares Bastos and Ouro Prêto, especially this last.

49 'It was in this way that the centralised monarchy represented, on the
political level, one of the points of support and defence for slave labour. In
a country as extensive as ours, with a diversity of zones and climates, development was destined to take place in an irregular fashion, more in some
regions, less in others, here swifter and more pronounced, there slow and
difficult. For this reason, the independence of the provinces could have
gradually opened breaches in the wall of slavery, which to survive would
have had to defend itself as a whole. While the provinces enjoyed rights
and privileges which allowed them to regulate their own affairs and matters
of special interest, the possibilities of breaking down the system of slave
labour would have multiplied and thus become more favourable to the
forces seeking to renew the socioeconomic structure. In a centralised state,
on the contrary, the system of slave labour was better able to defend itself,
was not open to attack at weak points, but sought always to offer a
massive, united resistance to the enemy. In order to survive as the basis of
the national economy for such a long time, slavery was forced to find
support in a centralised system, whose commanding posts, influence,
wealth and interests based on slave labour were better placed either for
defence or for attack.' (Hermes Lima: preface to Rui Barbosa's *Queda do
Império*, pp. XIV and XV, reproduced in *Notas à Vida Brasileira*.) In
another study included in Lima's work we find the same thought, though
not as fully expressed: 'The conservative reaction aimed, among other
things, to curb the efforts of the abolitionists, and firmly advocated the
centralisation of power, since this assured it greater control over the
country than did the federal system' (p. 8). In the essay: 'O Destino do
Feijó' the author observes, *à propos* of the political struggles which followed independence and reached their critical point in the Regency, that
'the monarchic option was important for those who wanted to preserve
the society inherited from colonial times, chiefly in its most characteristic
feature — slavery'. For this reason the moderates, by 'incorporating into
their political programme the principle of a centralised system revolving
round the Crown', prepared 'the way for the monarchical centrepiece,
which could thus be reinstated: the throne, centralisation, slavery.' (*Op.
cit.*, p. 137.)

   To Dr J. Fernando Carneiro, who conducted lengthy research on the
history of immigration into our country, we owe the information concerning certain laws which clearly reflect the incompatibility of the slave system with one of free labour: Law No. 226 of 30 May 1840, of Rio Grande
do Sul, prevented the importation of slaves into new settlements, and Law
No. 304 of 30 November 1854 of the same province, prohibited the
exploitation of any area of settlement by means of slaves. (*Digesto Econômico*, no. 45, pp. 129 and 130.)

   'All things considered', writes Sr Otávio Tarquínio de Sousa, 'the
Regency period, by annulling certain principles which, in the time of Dom
Pedro I, counterbalanced the dominating influence of the agrarian interests,
gave an opportunity, in the form of a reaction to the more extreme of the
liberals' counterclaims, to what initially was called a policy of "regression",
but was properly speaking the conservatives' revenge. With the Regency,
government was completely focused at the national centre and was

naturally placed at the service of the major economic force in the country – large-scale cultivation.' (*Digesto Econômico*, No. 43, p. 107.)

50   A. de Roure, *A Constituinte Republicana*, vol. II, p. 209; *Anais* of the Constituent Assembly of 1933–4, *passim*.

51   'Os Municípios', p. 318. Apart from the powers relating to local administration, principally of the local government urban centre, in respect of which there has been little variation in the history of Brazilian municipalism, some states gave their municipalities functions of another nature. Many, for example, associated the municipalities (by their initiative) with the process of reforming the Constitution. (Felisbelo Freire, *As Constituições dos Estados e a Constituição Federal*, pp. 250–2.) In Rio Grande do Sul, the vote of a majority of municipal councils could nullify the nominations of the vice-president, the president having the power to nominate in the first instance, and revoke legislative decrees handed down by the president himself (Castro Nunes, *Do Estado Federado*, pp. 192–3), etc. We find frequent interferences by the municipal chambers in the electoral process, as we shall see in the relevant chapter.

52   Quoted by Castro Nunes, *Do Estado Federado*, p. 183, note 17. See also Carlos Maximiliano, *Comentários a Constituição Brasileira*, No. 416, p. 710.

53   Castro Nunes, *Do Estado Federado*, pp. 221 and 222; Felisbelo Freire, *As Constituições dos Estados*, pp. 68–70 and 222–4. The latter condemned, as inimical to municipal autonomy, the power, usually of the state legislature but sometimes of the state executive, to annul municipal acts and resolutions contrary to the laws and Constitutions of the state and of the Republic. The granting of this prerogative jointly to the executive, the legislature and the judiciary affected the harmonious working together of these three powers, in his opinion, since they had to decide which of them should take the initiative in the annulment. He maintained that only the judiciary should have this prerogative.

54   See its action of 28 July 1920, in José Afonso Mendonça de Avezedo, *A Constituição Federal Interpretada pelo Supremo Tribunal Federal*, p. 320. The Supreme Court examined the extension of the powers of the state in relation to the municipality almost exclusively *à propos* of the nomination of prefects and the examination of the powers of elected municipal authorities. We deal with this subject in chapter III.

55   The Constituent Assembly, by rejecting the amendment of Meira De Vasconcelos (which sought to define municipal autonomy) and preferring the general and imprecise formula which came to be Article 68 of the Constitution, clearly revealed a disposition to leave the matter within the competence of the state governments. (See ch. III, section IV; cf. A. de Roure, *A Constituinte Republicana*, vol. II, pp. 204 ff.; judgement of the Supreme Court in Mendonça de Avezedo, *A Constituição Federal*, p. 314, No. 1086.)

56   *Do Estado Federado, passim.* The nomination of prefects was included among the proposed measures.

57   *A propos* of an incidental remark of his, recorded in the *Anais* of the Constituent Assembly of 1933—4 (vol. XX, pp. 41 and 456), Sr Levi Carneiro thus clarifies his ideas: 'In reality, I ought not to have said − I shall not argue that I did not say − that the federal state is a unitary one. I should have said, and meant to say, if I did not do so − that the federal state can be a unitary one. It was this which I maintained in my book, *Problemas Municipais* . . . My brilliant colleague [Daniel de Carvalho], in a declaration published at the time, set out to show the contradiction with which he reproved me, citing passages from my book. From these same passages it is clear that I disputed the opinion − in some ways very valid − of the famous publicist Sr Castro Nunes who considers municipal autonomy as peculiar to the unitary system. This is the thesis which I ought to have advanced in my comments . . . This was not the opinion which I adopted in my book − as I have already said − but, in fact, I have always reconciled certain restrictions of municipal autonomy with the federal system.' (*Anais*, referred to above, vol. XXI, p. 9.)

58   'The desirable modification, in my opinion, would be . . . to lay down explicitly, in these cases [examination of the powers of elected municipal governments], that the prerogative should be exclusively one of the judiciary, and extend it in others. For the legislative bodies of the states have been so reduced, to the point where they are mere chanceries of their respective executives, that to allow recourse to the former would be the equivalent of giving this power to the latter . . . In spite of everything, it has not been possible to charge the judiciary with the same passive obedience to the will of the government.' (*Problemas Municipais*, p. 166.)

59   *Antecipações à Reforma Política*, pp. 30—146: 'the truth is that there are no interests which are exclusively those of any municipality, for the simple reason that interests, especially economic ones, depend on natural factors, subject to the influence of the general situation in the state, and, as natural factors, obey natural laws of attraction and combination, irrespective of artificial laws of locality by which the territorial boundaries of the municipalities are fixed. Those interests which, originally, because they were largely undeveloped, were of a strictly municipal character, come, through economic intensification or through being extended spatially, to involve the state, requiring its protection and its concern.' (pp. 34—5)

60   João Pandiá, *Estudos Históricos e Políticos*, pp. 463 and 490—1.

61   In the opinion of Levi Carneiro (*Problemas Municipais*), the elective nature of the office of prefect, which we will deal with in chapter III, was not the vital point of municipal autonomy, because the states had many more effective means of dominating them at their disposal, namely: electoral legislation (p. 99), fixing of terms for the elective mandates (p. 99), nomination of provisional intendants (p. 100), state intervention (p. 100), suppression of municipalities and the annulment of acts passed by their ruling bodies (pp. 100–5), creation of districts whose administration was entrusted to freely nominated bodies. (p. 105)

In the opinion of Deputy Alde Sampaio, 'the myth of autonomy' prevented the establishment in Brazil of an 'over-all political organisation', in which the municipality would have had, 'in effect, an important role'. And he exclaimed: 'To use the word municipality in Brazil is to talk of the defenceless victim of the centre's monopoly of power.' (*Anais* of the Constituent Assembly of 1933–4, vol. XVIII, p. 349.)

62   '[M]any municipalities did not possess a written form of organisation'. (Gabriel Passos, *Anais*, 1934, vol. VI, p. 392.) On the financial management of the regime of 1891, cf. Orlando M. Carvalho, *Problemas Fundamentais do Município*, pp. 119 ff.

63   Declaration No. 19,398 of 11 November 1930: 'The interventor will nominate a prefect for each municipality to exercise there full executive and legislative functions, the interventor having the power to dismiss him when he deems it convenient, to revoke or modify any of his acts or resolutions, and to give him instructions for the efficient discharge of his duties, and for the regularisation and efficiency of municipal services.' (Article II, para. 4.) 'The head of the provisional government shall have the right to review acts of the interventors.' (Article quoted, para. 8.) The second article confirmed the dissolution of all the state legislative assemblies and municipal chambers, declaring dissolved even those which had not existed.

Declaration No. 20,348 of 29 August 1931: 'A Consultative Council is to be instituted in each state and in the Federal District.' (Article 1) 'Consultative Councils are to be set up in all or certain municipalities of each state.' (Article quoted, para. 2.) 'The poorer municipalities can be grouped, according to the judgement of the Federal Interventors, into zones for which regional councils will be set up.' (Article 3, para. 3.) 'In the case of the municipality of the capital and others which do not have a council . . . the relevant functions will be exercised by the Consultative Council of the state.' (Article 3, para. 4.) This decree regulated in detail the mechanism of reviewing powers.

64   *Anais*, 1934, vol. XII, p. 526.

65   *Anais*, vol. XX, pp. 375 and 402.

66   *Anais*, vol. XIV, pp. 513–14, vol. XX, p. 394.

67   *Anais*, vol. IV, pp. 441 ff., vol. VI, pp. 387 ff. The text of the amendment, also supported by Deputy Negrão de Lima, was as follows: 'The municipalities shall be autonomous within the limitations laid down by the state constitutions and dictated by the interest of society.'

68   'The municipalities being organised under the banner of absolute "autonomy", it was obvious that the area in which this autonomy should have been least restricted and strongest, that is to say, as the source of political and civic life, was precisely where the municipality was often absorbed by the state or, more correctly, by the political machines which held power, to the point where, in the field of local administration, free, untrammelled despotism reigned – this is the greatest "autonomy" . . . Thus, between friends and allies, bound by party compromises, by affection and common interests, municipal administration was directed without the appeal or constraint of any other authority because the "chamber" was governed by an "autonomous" unit and its extravagances and irregularities could be corrected by its own membership, the power of the state being "extraneous" to it . . . The municipality had, in fact, the maximum administrative power through a minimum of political freedom. Now it is the converse of this formula which it is necessary to render possible.' (*Anais* quoted, vol. IV, pp. 442–3.)

Already, in 1923, Professor Basílio de Magalhães had made similar observations: 'There is, however, no one who does not know that in Minas, as in all Brazil, municipal life is characterised by centripetal politics in contrast to a centrifugal administration.' (*O Municipalismo em Minas Gerais*, p. 9.)

69   Gabriel Passos commented: 'On the other hand, a link of common interest has been established between municipal political organisations and the controlling party in the state government, and this prevents the municipality from becoming a nucleus of civic and political life.' (*Anais* quoted, vol. IV, p. 443.)

70   See ch. III, section V.

71   See ch. IV, section IX.

72   Constitution of 1934, Article 13, para. 3: 'The state is empowered to create a body to provide technical assistance to the municipal administration and to supervise its finances.'

73   *Anais* respectively, vol. IV, p. 449; vol. X, pp. 415 and 591.

74   *Anais* respectively, vol. XVII, p. 317; vol. XVIII, p. 362, Amendment No. 1478.

75   *Anais*, vol. XX, p. 409.

76   *Anais* respectively, vol. XVIII, p. 303, and vol. XX, p. 409. There is reference in this to the suppressive Amendments, No. 306 of Lino do Morais Leme (*Anais*, vol. XVIII, p. 345) and No. 1088 of Augusto Viegas and Mário Marques (*Anais*, vol. XVIII, p. 355).

77   *Anais*, vol. XX, pp. 414 and 415.

78   *Anais*, vol. XX, p. 411.

79   *Anais*, vol. XX, p. 395 (Fernando de Abreu, Vieira Marques); p. 371 (João Vilasboas); p. 405 (Acúrcio Tôrres); p. 409 (Cunha Melo), and again pp. 415 ff. and p. 455.

80   *Anais*, vol. XX, pp. 373 and 375.

81   Orlando M. Carvalho: 'In reality, these departments were transformed into political weapons placed within the reach of those who held power.' ('Política Constitucional do Município'; in the same vein, *Política do Município*, p. 121.)

82   Articles 19, Nos. 4 and 13, para. 4.

83   Article 17, letter a, with the exceptions of Article 6, No. 5.

84   Article 13. The governor of Minas was made practically the equal of the interventors.

85   Articles 32, 33, No. 14, 13, and 35.

86   The Commission was organised into a ministry, authorised by Article 54 of the Decree–Law No. 1202 of 1939.

87   Article 17, d, e, f; on the review powers, cf. Decree No. 2083 of 12 June 1939 of the Ministry of Justice.

88   Nevertheless during the *Estado Novo* many books and numerous articles in magazines and newspapers maintained that the Charter of 10 November had given new life to the municipality.

89   With the restrictions examined in chapter III.

90   Constitution of 18 September, Article 28.

91   See the résumé of the debates in José Duarte, *A Constituição Brasileira de 1946*, vol. I, pp. 525 and 528.

92   'When the municipality enjoys a wide freedom in the organisation of its services and in its administrative acts, in short, in everything which relates to its special interest, it is said that it has administrative autonomy. When it possesses and fully exercises the right to elect local rulers it may be said to have political autonomy. The co-existence of these two factors is what constitutes municipal autonomy in the full sense of the term.' (Geraldo Campos Moreira, 'O Municipalismo', p. 89.)

93   Article 24.

94   Article K.

95   Articles 146, 141 and 144.

96   Article 22. Cf. José Duarte, *op. cit.*, pp. 482 and 489. The present Constitution also permits state intervention in the municipalities for reasons of unpunctuality (Article 23) and requires authorisation of the Senate for their external loans. (Article 63, II.)

97   On the supplements to the municipal revenue referred to, cf. chapter IV, section XI. The allocation of the revenue derived from the taxes on lubricating and combustible fluids (Constitution, Article 14, para. 2), which was the original objective of Law No. 22 of 1947, is laid down in Law No. 302 of 13 July 1948. Articles 5 and 7 define the respective obligations of the states, Federal District and the municipalities, instituting a system of supervision of the municipal bodies responsible for state roads, the states in turn being responsible in this respect to the National Department of Roads and Transport. Article 8 foresees the solemnisation of an agreement in which other obligations will be laid down. The main objective of the system adopted is to incorporate municipal and state roads into the National Road Plan. Failure to observe legal prescriptions will result in the suppression of the quota of the guilty party. (Articles 11 and 12.)

As to the percentage of tax revenue set aside for the municipalities (Constitution, Article 15, section 4), Law No. 305 of 18 July 1948 was promulgated. However, this law does not define what 'benefits of a rural nature' are, but limits itself to imposing on each municipality the obligation to send a report to the National Congress and to the Ministry of Finance on the allocation of this revenue, 'as proof' that the constitutional requirements 'have been observed'. *A propos* of the precept of the current Constitution to which we have referred, President Dutra declared in his message of 1948: 'As a restriction – of a constitutional nature – has been established limiting the free allocation of funds handed over by the Union to each municipality, it seems to me that the Congress has authority to carry out some supervision of its contribution. I recall the possibility of using for this purpose . . . delegations of the Court of Audit, together with the Fiscal Delegacies of the National Treasury, and the system of the Brazilian Institute of Geography and Statistics.' (*Diário do Congresso* of 15 March 1948, p. 1701.)

98   When the present Constitution was being introduced, 'a famous representative from São Paulo' told the journalist Murila Marroquim that some of the municipalities would perhaps become 'maddened that fortune was continually knocking at their doors'. And the journalist commented: 'It is incumbent on the Union to be in a position to offer these municipalities its technical support and its constant supervisory assistance, so that the new revenue would not be dissipated without achieving any salutary result.' (*O Jornal* of 15 August 1946.) Cf. Also Oto Gil, interview in *O Jornal* of 7 June 1946 and Afonso Almiro, *A Constituição e o Código Tributário Nacional*. The latter pleads for a 'single fiscal code' for Brazil, given the difficulties which will emerge from the system of the sharing of taxes established by the present Constitution. We must add that the Constitution of 1946, in Article 5, XV, b, gives the Union legislative power to establish 'general rules of financial rights'.

99   Constitution of 1937, Article 29. Cf. Frederico Herrmann Jr, *Funções Específicas dos Municípios*, ch. IV; Arquibaldo Severo, *O Moderno Município Brasileiro*, ch. II, section 13. The silence of the present Constitution is no hindrance to foresight.

100   Orlando M. Carvalho, 'A Vitalidade da Tradição Municipal'; *Política do Município*, p. 113; *Problemas Fundamentais do Município*, p. 52.

101   Several state Constitutions are already making provision for the grouping of municipalities for administrative purposes, like those of São Paulo, Minas, Bahia, Paraíba, Mato Grosso etc.

102   Orlando M. Carvalho, *Política do Município*, pp. 139 ff.

103   Explaining the Cabinet's programme of 7 June in the chamber the Visconde de Ouro Prêto said that it was that of his party. He set out his plans for decentralisation as follows: 'Full autonomy for the municipalities and provinces.' The basic essential of this reform is the election of municipal administrators and the nomination of provincial presidents and vice-presidents, using a list drawn up from the vote of registered citizens. Anticipating afterwards the order of priority of the problems, he considered 'indispensable and most urgent the extension of the vote and the autonomy of the provinces, conceding to the municipality a neutral government and representation of its own, as befits its population and its wealth.' (*Anais*, session of 11 June 1889.)

104   'The autonomy of the municipalities was the palliative which the Empire offered in its last gasps; and such was the conviction that it would serve the monarchist cause better than republican aspirations, that Ouro Prêto could reply to the charge that he was serving revolutionary ideals by saying that, on the contrary, he was saving the monarchy.' (Castro Nunes, *Do Estado Federado*, p. 68.)

105   'Federalism summarises the largest slice of our political history', says Levi Carneiro. 'It is the constant, inevitable objective of our total political evolution throughout four centuries. It is the dominant preoccupation of the country – delayed, dissembled, stifled – and, finally, satisfied.' ('O Federalismo', p. 197.)

106   Carvalho Mourão, arguing that the formulators of the Additional Act, if they had wanted to be coherent, should have widened the municipal franchise, suggests: 'The legislators of 1834 did not see it this way, motivated perhaps by the inclination to maintain in their provinces where they were politically dominant, the reins of control in the chambers which were manipulative machines at elections.' ('Os Municípios', p. 316.)

'In this whole absorbing tendency of the supporters of centralisation', Domingos Jaguaribe wrote in his work of 1897, 'one perceives the desire to reduce the municipalities to mere political agents, supporting the lists of candidates organised at the centre.' (*O Município e a República*, vol. III, p. 65.)

Nestor Duarte, after affirming that the centralising tendency of the Imperial Constitution adopted 'the autonomy of the municipality against the hegemony of the provinces', that the Additional Act operated in the opposite direction, granting 'greater autonomy to the provinces to the detriment of the municipality', and that the centralising reaction of 1840 restored the prestige of the municipality at the expense of the province, observes: 'In the Charter of 10 November 1937 the question is again raised, in the same terms and in the same dialectical spirit as the restrictions which it imposed on the federal regime with which the Republic endowed us, in order to dislocate, for this very reason, the original pivotal issue of political representation for the municipalities.' (*Op. cit.*, p. 214.)

These observations do not appear totally logical to us. If it is true that the Additional Act did not improve, and in some respects worsened, the position of the municipalities, it is not the case that the Constitution of 1824 and the reaction of 1840 favoured the districts. These remained the abandoned children of imperial policy: although tutelage oscillated between the centre and the provinces, in both cases the municipalities were suppressed. Ouro Prêto summarised the position of the chambers in 1882 in these words: 'without initiative, without resources and without authority', (*Reforma Administrativa*, p. 86.) In the expression of Levi Carneiro, the municipal policy of the Empire was 'deficient, timid, illogical. No secure principle directed or restrained it. No legal text enshrined it.' (*Problemas Municipais*, pp. 73–4.) On the other hand, we must not forget that under the regime of 1937 all prefects could be freely nominated by the governors. The fact that the municipalities participated as units in the composition of the Electoral College of the President of the Republic (a body which, alas, has never functioned) should not dislocate in any way 'the pivotal issue of political representation'. The influence which the prefects always exercised over the electors, in the system of direct election of the President, continued to be important in indirect elections. It is clear that state autonomy was reduced in the Constitution of 1937, but not in favour of the municipalities, whose position worsened, but exclusively to the advantage of the Union, with the consequence, already pointed out, that the governors were allowed the full right to nominate and dismiss prefects.

107   See ch. VI, section V.

3. The elective principle in municipal administration

1   On the *prefects* created by some provinces after the Additional Act,
see section III of this chapter and section II of chapter V.

2   See section VII of this chapter.

3   Enéias Galvão, following others, says that the general magistrate
(under the system set out by the Ordinances of King Manuel) initiated the
service of correction in São Vicente, reducing the posts of the district to
an ordinary judge and two councillors, one serving as purveyor and the
other as treasurer. ('Juízes e Tribunais no Período Colonial', p. 326.)

Among the officials elected by the 'worthy men', the Ordinances
alluded to 'judge and clerk of the orphans where it is customary to have
them by election', to the 'judges of the hospitals in the places where they
had judges *per se*', and again to 'whatever officials it is customary to appoint by election'.

The oldest councillor could stand in for the ordinary judges (Pedro
Calmon, 'Organização Judiciária', p. 83; Ordinance, bk. I, t. 65, para. 4;
Provision of 27 October 1819).

4   See Cortines Laxe, *Regimento*, pp. XV and XVI. Caio Prado Jr says
that, among others, the clerk and the syndic were nominated by the
chamber, further explaining that the governor usually nominated the clerk.
(*Formação do Brasil Contemporâneo*, pp. 315 and 316.) Also Cândido
Mendes declares that the clerk was originally nominated by the chamber,
a right which was continually being usurped by the Crown. (*Código
Filipino*, note 1 to bk. I, t. 71.) Here, as at other points, the divergences
can be explained by the fact that the Ordinances were not adhered to uniformly throughout the country. On the prerogatives of the officials and
functionaries alluded to, cf. chapter II, section II, and chapter V, section I.

5   *Código Filipino*, note 3 to bk. I, t. 66, para. 28.

6   *Código Filipino*, note 1 to bk. I, t. 67, para. 6.

'The worthy men and members of the ordinary people who could vote
were noted down on record sheets by the *corregidors* or the judges whose
duty it was to preside at the elections. Their names were written, together
with all the necessary information required by law, charter and custom to
establish their fitness.' (Letter Patent of 12 November 1611.) Mechanics,
workmen, deportees and Jews did not qualify, together with others who
belonged to the class of farm labourers. (Provision of 8 May 1705; Cortines
Laxe, *Regimento*, p. XIX, note 3.) On the question of merchants, see above
chapter II, note 24.

7   By letters of donation the lords of the province had to supervise 'either
in person, or through their magistrates, the election of the judges and other
officials, checking the votes and sending letters of confirmation to those
who had been elected and who would serve in their name'. (J.F. Lisboa, *op.
cit.*, vol. II, p. 135.) By the regulations of 1628, the chief magistrate, whenever he was 'in any captainship', had to inform himself 'about the chambers,
about how their elections were conducted, and about whatever else is
important for good government, providing for this, there and then, if he
judges it convenient and with the approval of the governor'. (J.F. Lisboa,
Obras, vol. II, 164.)

Enéias Galvão, after summarising the process of election of officials of the chambers according to the Ordinances, has this to say: 'The impossibility of a practice like this in the early years of the captainships is obvious, the first investiture of the elective posts was naturally carried out by means of direct selection on the part of the governors.' ('Juízes e Tribunais', p. 327.)

Cândido Mendes makes it clear that the electoral process described in the text was partially altered by the Letter Patent of 12 November 1611 and by the Provision of 8 January 1670. (*Código Filipino*, note 1 to bk. I, t. 67.) On the ballot-sheets (*pelouros*), see Cândido Mendes, *op. cit.*, note 2 to bk. I, t. 65, para. 15.

'Any member of the public', says Cortines Laxe, 'could attack the election by hindering or damaging it in some way, without this having the effect of suspending it.' (*Regimento*, p. XXI.)

8   Bk. I, t. 67, para. 6.

9   Bk. I, t. 67, para. 10. J.F. Lisboa cites the Letter Patent of 23 March 1688, which exempted the 'owners of factories from serving in the chambers, given the need for their presence in the said factories'. (*Obras*, vol. II, p. 190.)

10   Bk. I, t. 67, para. 9. At such elections the judge's presence was not necessary. (Provision of 27 October 1819.)

11   'And the judges shall have a Letter of Confirmation to be used by their offices by the *corregidors* of the Legal Districts . . . or by our appeal judges at Court.' (*Ordinances*, bk. II, t. 45, para. 2; cf. bk. I, t. 3, para. 4; t. 67, para. 8.) Caio Prado Jr tells us that the election of the attorney was also subject to confirmation. (*Formação do Brasil Contemporâneo*, pp. 313–14 and 315.)

12   One of the hardest blows struck at local independence was the introduction of *outside judges* in Brazil to replace *ordinary judges* elected by the people. Aside from their judicial function, these judges undertook the presidency of the chambers. It is in 1696 that the first outside judges, nominated by the king, are created: 'in Bahia, in Rio de Janeiro and in Pernambuco, that is to say, in the three principal towns of the colony'. (Caio Prado Jr, *História Econômica do Brasil*, p. 60.)

According to Rocha Pombo, the magistrates of the legal district and the outside judges 'were almost always tyrants of the most cruel and vindictive kind'. (*História do Brasil*, vol. V, p. 433.)

'The chief aim behind their [the outside judges] creation was the usurpation by the monarchy of the jurisdiction of the territorial judges: this was gradually accomplished, but at the expense of alienating the settlements to whom this institution always appeared, and was, obnoxious.' (Cândido Mendes, *Código Filipino*, note 1 to bk. I, t. 65.)

The same author tells us 'the substitutes for the outside judges in the chambers organised in this way, were the councillors, ranked, not according to votes received but according to age, and they were called *Judges of Ordinance* and not *ordinary* judges. They carried white staffs of office and not red ones as the ordinary judges did, and they had the same competence and received the same emoluments as the outside judges.' (Note 1 to bk. I, t. 67.) On the standing in for the outside judge by the oldest councillor, cf. Letter Patent of 17 November 1716 in J.F. Lisboa, *Obras*, vol. II, p. 166.

Speaking of Bahia, Vilhena tells us that the president of the Senate was always 'the outside judge at civil law, and in his absence the criminal judge or the judge of orphans'. (Brás do Amaral, *Cartas de Vilhena*, vol. II, p. 77.)

13 *Código Filipino*, note 1 to bk. I, t. 67. Sometimes magistrates and outside judges were ordered to preside at elections in certain municipalities, according to Cortines Laxe. (*Regimento*, p. VIII of the first edition.)

14 'In Bahia . . . in this period [the last years of the seventeenth century] the councillors ceased to be elected, and came to be nominated by the king.' (Caio Prado Jr, *História Econômica do Brasil*, p. 60.)

A curious example is the provision of the Count of Atouguia, Governor General of Brazil from 24 November 1655, with respect to the struggle between the Pires and the Camargos in São Paulo. Among other measures adopted to settle the dispute, we find in this document: 'For the best and in the service of His Majesty, I have [decreed] that from henceforth an equal number of officials from each band shall serve in the chamber of the said town, so that this equality may bring an end to the disturbances, since the people will be incensed if this does not happen and the election shall proceed in the following manner: the magistrate of the captainship together with the clerk of the town, according to the Ordinances, shall summon the worthy men and the people of the town to the Council, and shall ask them to name six men to be electors, three from the Pires band and three from the Camargos [not the leaders of the bands, but others more zealous and conscientious], and when all the votes have been taken there shall be chosen from each band, by the electors, the three who receive the most votes. These six will separate into three groups each composed of a Pires and a Camargo, and they shall be ordered to draw up their three lists, as is customary, namely: six for judges, three from one hand and three from the other, plus a neutral; and three for attorney to the council, a Pires and a Camargo, and a neutral; and thus they will proceed for whatever other officials the chamber has, etc.' (Costa Pinto, 'Lutas de Famílias', p. 86.)

In the report of the Marquis of Lavradio, of 19 June 1779, we read this passage: 'As the laws of His Majesty have taken note of the merchants, I have chosen some of them as councillors, always having them nominated by a friend who is one of the best in the land . . . This was my system . . . in the first place, to accept everything that could contribute to the happiness, peace and preservation of this people and of this state which was entrusted to me, which belonged to me, and where I held jurisdiction to function in all districts, and to make provision in the best way I could to achieve these aims. On the government of the chamber, I left the president and the councillors to govern as their prerogatives allow, but I was watchful in case disorders arose, and when they did I wrote to the chamber saying what seemed to me to be the best procedure, and what their obligations required; however, my own decisions sent to the same chamber, or intimated to it, were ordered to be executed by the chamber in its name.' (Armitage, *História do Brasil*, pp. 342 and 345.)

15 'Until now what we had in Brazil was the Portuguese municipality transplanted here.' (Castro Nunes, *Do Estado Federado*, p. 42. On this point, the author cites Carvalho Mourão's study.)

16   The *Lei Saraiva* of 1881 increased the number of councillors: in the municipality of the Court to 21; in the capitals of Bahia and Pernambuco to 17; in the capitals of Pará, Maranhão, Ceará, Rio de Janeiro, Minas Gerais, São Paulo and São Pedro do Rio Grande do Sul to 13; in the capitals of the other provinces to 11. (Article 22, para. 5.)

17   Parochial electors, or of the first ballot.

18   The electoral laws of 1855 and 1860 did not alter the process of the election of councillors, nor the requirements for registration and elegibility.

19   An *elector* was a citizen elected by the voters (*votantes*) in the primary elections to vote in the electoral colleges (secondary elections). The requirements for an elector were defined in Article 94 of the Constitution.

20   For other details of Brazilian electoral legislation, cf. ch. VI.

21   Carneiro Maia on this matter suggests: 'Although it had been agreed that they could be suspended by the presidents, according to the law of 3 October 1834 which in Article 5, para. 8 gave them this power in relation to any employee, we believe that this did not include councillors, just as it would have been unseemly to include the jury council, the electoral colleges and the parochial assemblies. The proof that the law underwent ingenious restrictions to its apparent latitude, lies in the Decree of 23 January 1844 which exempted from this suspension members of the Courts of Appeal and Higher Courts.' (*O Município*, p. 249.)

22   See Rui Barbosa (*Comentários à Constituição Brasileira*, vol. V, pp. 84 ff. and 131 ff.), who defended the constitutionality of the measure and its advantages as a factor in the assimilation of immigrants.

23   'In some states [Bahia, Mato Grosso, Goiás and Minas Gerais] non-naturalised foreigners were allowed to vote in municipal elections once the requirements, laid down by the Constitutions and the electoral laws respectively, were fulfilled. The constitutional problem is not free from doubt.' (*As Constituições Estaduais*, vol. I, p. 49.)

24   'The designation of a territory, not called a municipality, as a seat of government, therefore, contrary to the view defended by Article 68 [of the 1891 Constitution] is a genuinely constitutional measure', says Nélson Campos, in *O Município Autônomo e a Capital do Estado Federado*, p. 15.

25   *Problemas Município*, pp. 106–7. Cf. also Castro Nunes, *As Constituições Estaduais*, pp. 163–5.

26́   Articles 13, I; 26, a; 28, I, respectively.

27   Cf. ch. II, section II.

28   Article 211.

29   Articles 167 and 168. The *Lei Saraiva* of 1881, having increased the number of councillors in the chambers of the capitals, determined that they should have presidents and vice-presidents elected by the councillors. (Article 22, para. 5.) Castro Nunes, referring to the law of 1828, which in conformity with the Constitution required that the president should be the councillor who had received the most votes, wrote: 'Later the president of the chamber came to be drawn in the same way by election among the councillors, in violation of what the Constitution decreed.' (*Do Estado Federado*, p. 167.) It is probable that the author was referring to the

Saraiva Law, but we are unable to verify that his affirmation was a general practice.

30   Carneiro Maia, *O Município*, pp. 195 and 196.

31   'These were the bold reforms of Pernambuco which threw the timid conservatives of the General Assembly into consternation: already in 1836 the Chamber of Deputies was called to revoke these laws, legitimate offspring of the Additional Act, logical consequences of the system adopted.' (Tavares Bastos, *A Província*, p. 169.) This revocation was not general. Even in 1838 some chambers in São Paulo were voting for the suppression of the prefects, and the rebels of Maranhão were making the same demand in 1839. (Cf. chapter V, note 41.)

32   See the bills in Ouro Prêto, *Reforma Administrativa*; Carneira Maia, *O Município*, pp. 251 ff.

33   In the state of Rio (until the reform of 1920) and in Rio Grande do Norte, the executive functions were exercised by the president of the chamber. In the former, there were also prefects, directly nominated and dismissed, in certain municipalities. In Minas (law of 1891) the executive functions were exercised either by the president of the chamber, expressly elected by the people with a cumulative mandate, or by a citizen from outside that body, specially chosen for the post by direct election. It was the chamber itself which decided, in the final year of the legislature, on the methods to be employed in the following triennium. From 1903, the executive function was uniformly entrusted to the president of the chamber, elected by the candidates for a period of time equal to their own mandate. In some states there was also a district executive, with the title of *sub-prefect* (S. Paulo), *administrator* (Bahia), *sub-intendant* (R.G. do Sul), etc. For these details cf. the laws on municipal organisation reproduced in Castro Nunes, *Do Estado Federado*; cf. also Felisbelo Freire, *As Constituições dos Estados*, pp. 211 ff. and *passim*.

34   *A Constituinte Republicana*, vol. II, pp. 204 ff.

35   *Ibid.*, p. 207.

36   *Ibid.*, pp. 207 and 208.

37   *Ibid.*, p. 208. Another detail of the amendment of Meira de Vasconcelos was the power to set up their own systems which it conferred on the municipalities: 'The municipalities *shall set up their own systems* in accordance with the Constitutions of the states concerned, the following bases being observed.' (Cf. Barbalho, *Constituição Federal Brasileira*, p. 282.)

38   A. de Roure, *op. cit.*, vol. II, p. 211.

39   According to Castro Nunes, the law of the state of Ceará No. 764 of 12 August 1904, which revoked Law No. 588 of 4 June 1900, and re-established Article 7 of Law No. 264 of 26 September 1895, made all prefects (called *intendants* under Law No. 1190 of 5 August 1914) subject to nomination by the governor of the state. (*Do Estado Federado*, p. 350, note 3.) According to what we read in the same work (p. 369), all the prefects and sub-prefects of Paraíba were also subject 'to nomination and dismissal by the president of the state'. (Article 3, II, of Law No. 424 of 28 October 1915.) The Bahian Law No. 102 of 11 August 1915 decreed for the whole state: 'The intendant shall be nominated by the governor with the approval of the Senate.' Further in the text we give part of the verbal defence in which Rui Barbosa unsuccessfully maintained in the Supreme Court that this law was unconstitutional. Levi Carneiro refers to the nomination of provisional intendants in Rio Grande do Sul. (*Problemas Municipais*, p. 98.)

40   See chapter II, note 52 and the corresponding text.

41   *Comentários*, vol. V, p. 74.

42   Calógeras, *Estudos Históricos e Políticos*, p. 462. The proposal also regulated intervention in the municipalities because of irregularities in their finances.

43   Cf. Levi Carneiro, *Problemas Municipais*, pp. 70 ff., esp. the passage on p. 87; Castro Nunes, *Do Estado Federado*, pp. 173 ff., esp. pp. 187–90; Carlos Maximiliano, *Comentários à Constituição*, p. 711, note 11; Mendonça de Avezedo, *A Constituição*, pp. 313 ff.

44   See chapter II, note 63.

45   Article 13, I and para. 1.

46   *Anais*, 1934, vol. XX, p. 413.

47   Articles 87 to 90, esp. Article 88, second part.

48   *Anais*, vol. IV, p. 441. See the text of the amendment in note 67 of chapter II, above.

49   Amendment No. 701, *Anais*, vol. IV, p. 448.

50   Making the argument more concrete, Cunha Melo proposed the substitution as follows: 'In municipalities where the state governments are installed, as well as those which contain hydro-mineral establishments, and in those which have secured a guarantee of a loan or financial assistance from the state, it will be possible for the municipal executive to be chosen by the said state governments.' (*Anais*, vol. X, p. 415.) The Constitutional Commission reduced the cases in which nomination was possible: 'The government of the state shall be empowered to nominate the prefect in the municipality of the capital, as well as in those in which the state bears the expense of municipal services, guarantees public loans or constructs or administers hydro-mineral establishments.' (Substitute proposal of 8 March 1934, Article 127, para. 2, *Anais*, vol. X, p. 591; the process of the Commission's work is described in the same volume, p. 558, *in fine*.)

51   *Anais*, vol. XVIII, p. 301.

52   *Anais*, vol. XVIII, p. 301.

53   Decree of 1937, Article 27.

54   Article 28, I. In view of the wide terms of Article 134 ('Suffrage is universal and direct'), it would appear that the indirect election of prefects, permitted under the Constitution of 1934, is forbidden. Yet Pontes de Miranda, basing himself (presumably) on Article 28, I, only, maintains that the states could permit the election of prefects by the chambers. (*Comentários à Constituição de 1946*, vol. I, p. 479.)

55   Article 28, para. 1.

56   Article 28, para. 2. To put this Constitutional Decree into effect, Law No. 121 of 22 October 1947 declared the following municipalities to be bases or military ports of exceptional importance for the external defence of the country: Manaus (Amazonas), Belém (Pará), Natal (R.G. do Norte), Recife (Pernambuco), Salvador (Bahia), Niterói and Angra do Reis (state

of Rio), São Paulo, Santos and Guarulhos (S. Paulo), Florianópolis and São Francisco (Sta. Catarina), Pôrto Alegre, Rio Grande, Santa Maria, Gravataí and Canoas (R.G. do Sul) and Corumbá (M. Grosso).

The Constitutional Decree cited resulted originally from the amendment of Deputy Artur Bernardes. (José Duarte, *A Constituição*, vol. I, p. 529.) According to the current political belief at the time, it was motivated by the electoral strength which the Communists had shown themselves to possess in the election of 2 November in certain cities, notably Santos, Recife and Natal. In reality, it appears that the country's defence needs were not really the prime reason behind this constitutional innovation, because the influence of an elected prefect is practically nullified in time of war by the extended powers of the military authorities. Besides, had the declared reason been the main one, prefects of these cities would have been nominated not by the governors of the states but by the President of the Republic, or by some military body of high standing.

57   Original bill, Article 126, a single para.
58   From the point of view of the elective principle, it is not the case, as Geraldo Campos Moreira affirms, that the Constitution of 1946 defined municipal autonomy 'on much broader bases that we ever had in other Constitutions'. ('O Municipalismo', p. 92.)
59   Cf. José Duarte, *A Constituição*, vol. I, pp. 525 and 527.
60   Constitution of 1891, Article 65, No. 2; Article 34, No. 21.
61   Domingos Velasco (*Anais*, 1934, vol. II, p. 298) refers to the 'Brazilian phenomenon of fraudulent state and federal elections and bitterly fought and genuine municipal elections.'
62   *Do Estado Federado*, p. 156.
63   Act No. 600 of the Federal Supreme Court, cited in Castro Nunes, *Do Estado Federado*.
64   Minister João Mendes, Act of 27 September 1920, in Castro Nunes, *As Constituições Estaduais*, p. 160.
65   Castro Nunes, *Do Estado Federado*, p. 156, note 4-A; *As Constituições Estaduais*, p. 161.
66   Castro Nunes, *As Constituições Estaduais*, p. 161.
67   *Do Estado Federado*, p. 161.
68   *Problemas Municipais*, pp. 154–6.
69   Further information on the evolution of the Brazilian electoral system may be found in chapter VI.
70   'The interpretation of Article 68 of the Constitution of 1891 was intended principally to determine if the clause on the "electivity of the local administration" survived in it. This has been the issue of greatest interest among us on the question of municipal autonomy . . . Among us, as we have already said in another chapter, this [the appointment of the municipal executive] has been, since the setting up of the Republic, the most disputed aspect in the conceptualisation of municipal autonomy.' (Castro Nunes, *Do Estado Federado*, pp. 86 and 176.)
71   *Problemas Municipais*, pp. 99 ff. See chapter II, note 61 above.
72   'To emancipate the municipal executive from the political servitude to which he is subject is to create, next to an essentially political body like the municipal assembly, an administrative organ in which political pre-

occupations and political competence would yield pride of place to powers and preoccupations of a technical order . . . As a technical organ the executive must organise itself, independent of the criterion of political representation, since technical competence cannot be conceived of as being subject to the law of the majority, which is suitable for application only in the purely or specifically political field.' (*Antecipações*, p. 63.)

73   Levi Carneiro also describes the prefect as a *technician* (*Problemas Municipais*, p. 117); similarly Herrmann Jr (*Funções Específicas dos Municípios*, p. 40) and others, reflecting foreign tendencies.

74   'Yoked to the political situation not only locally, but also at state and federal level, this is invariably the case with nominated prefects. If the yoke "to local politics" impedes the elected prefects from imposing taxes fairly, the same hindrance will exist in the case of nominated prefects, given that the nominations always fall upon citizens with local party affiliations, or at any rate on individuals with whom it is hoped that such ties may be created.' (Pedro Aleixo, 'Autonomia Municipal'.)

75   Rui Barbosa was already saying in the Supreme Court, referring to the suppression of elected prefects: 'And for what purpose, my lords? To entrust these localities to honourable administrators? To distinguished citizens? To able men? To the worthy men of each district? No: to establish on the intendancies and prefectures the most servile instruments of the electoral machine, the local associates of the oligarchs and satraps, page-boys to serve our governors.' (*Comentários à Constituição*, vol. V, p. 74.)

Pedro Lessa also testified: 'But what is certain, and at every instance is crudely confirmed, is that the nominations made by the state, as those made by the Union, do not offer any better assurance of moral fitness or intellectual capacity than those made by the municipality.' (*Reforma Constitucional*, pp. 76 and 77.)

76   By virtue of their ascendancy over the chambers, Deputy Fábio Sodré describes the prefects, including the elected ones, as municipal dictators. (*Anais* of 1934, vol. XX, pp. 400 and 401.)

77   Decree–Law No. 8188 of 20 November 1945: 'Article 1 – All municipal prefects who were in October last members of local directories of political parties, are dismissed from the exercise of their duties from the date of this law until December of the current year. Article 2 – Judges for life shall be responsible for the running of the prefectures in the municipalities which are capitals of the legal districts or territories, and will appoint suitable persons to carry out these responsibilities, under their [the judges'] supervision, in other municipalities of the same districts and territories.'

78   Among the proposals of the new state Constitutions which were declared unconstitutional by the Supreme Court, was the requirement of the approval of the legislative assembly in the nomination of prefects (Ceará, São Paulo), and the right of the assembly to dismiss prefects already in office (Piauí). (Cf. Presidential Address in the *Diário do Congresso Nacional* of 16 March 1948, pp. 1702–3). In the states referred to, the Governor was in dispute with the majority of the assembly and the latter was trying to wrest from the enemy the important weapon of the nomination of prefects.

79   'We must therefore react against these two prejudices of the old republican idealism: *the belief in the power of written formulas and the belief that political reorganisation is only possible by political means.*' (*O Idealismo da Constituição*, p. 116.)

80   Article 24.

81   Article 72.

82   *Anais*, vol. XII, p. 240.

83   'All the prerogatives of the federated units, under the system, are subordinate to the rhythm of the national ideal. The concept of autonomy does not proceed from any notion of equipping the states to defend their individual interests in opposition to the supreme imperative of the good of the nation . . . The nation, above and before all, if only because without the nation we would not be conscious of the existence of the states.' (Francisco Campos, *O Estado Nacional*, pp. 96 and 97. Cf. also above ch. II, note 106.)

84   *Reforma Constitucional*, pp. 65–9.

85   The misconception that the law is more powerful than economic and social reality is so deep-rooted among us, especially among jurists, that even outstanding minds, like Castro Nunes and Levi Carneiro, have never ceased to pay a certain tribute to the idea.

Thus the former, in defending the case for the nomination of prefects, argued that their legal functions were much less extensive than those of the chamber, because his executive duties presupposed a line of action determined by the deliberative body. And he added: 'If the chambers have become powerless and subject to the will of the prefect, the fact, peculiar to Brazilian politics or not, has arisen from the nature of things . . . but the law must not bear any responsibility for it; because, according to law, the body which *administers* the municipality is not only the executive, but also, and chiefly, the Council, which deliberates.' (*Do Estado Federado*. p. 176.)

The latter, after referring to the pro-government postures of the local factions which quarrel between themselves but adhere to the same state or federal party, declares: 'Thus it is in reality – but it ought not to be so. It should be the opposite. It must be the opposite if we want to achieve a genuinely representative system.' (*Problemas Municipais*, p. 174.)

86   *Comentários à Constituição*, vol. V, p. 66.

87   'Politically speaking, the rural areas are nothing. The "rule of the *coronéis*" is a thing of the past', wrote Olímpio Guilherme in 1944. ('O Campo e a Cidade'.)

88   Aires de Mata Machado Filho, after saying that during the dictatorship 'the legitimate *coronel*, who maintains contact with the people, who is one of the people . . . disappeared', observes: 'Now, the *coronel* returns to his traditional function. As before, he commands gunmen, if need be attacks or defends himself as the social conditions of his own *milieu* permit. The progress of the region is in his hands through favours which meet the cost of votes.' ('O Coronel e a Democracia'.)

'Perhaps', writes Afonso Arinos de Melo Franco, 'the name of the *coronel* is disappearing from the rural areas; but his type and his social function survive. And they will only disappear with the transformation of living conditions in these same rural areas.' (*História e Teoria do Partido Político no Direito Constitucional Brasileiro*, p. 98.)

4. Municipal revenue

1   *Formação do Brasil Contemporâneo*, p. 315, note 29.
2   J.F. Lisboa, *Obras*, vol. II, pp. 193 and 179–80.
3   Ordinances, bk. I, t. 66, paras. 40, 41 and 43; t. 62, para. 76; t. 58, paras. 43, 44 and 45. The levying of *fintas* depended on authorisation from above, as can be seen in the texts cited; cf. also the regulations of governors cited by J.F. Lisboa, *Obras*, vol. II, pp. 148 and 153. Cândido Mendes tells us that the law of 1 October 1828 abolished the chambers' right to levy *fintas*. (*Código Filipino*, note 6 to bk. I, t. 66.)
4   According to the practice of the time, public revenues were contracted out to private individuals by auction. (Cf. Caio Prado Jr, *Formação do Brasil Contemporâneo*, p. 319.) The chambers presented accounts to the purveyors of the district and had to show their books to the Court Auditor on demand. (Cortines Laxe, *Regimento*, p. XV.)
5   Ordinances, bk. I, t. 62, para. 67; t. 70, para. 3; Cândido Mendes, *Código Filipino*, note 3 to the provision in question; M. Fleiuss, *História Administrativa do Brasil*, p. 36; Caio Prado Jr, *Formação do Brasil Contemporâneo*, p. 315. Referring to the levying of *fintas*, the Ordinance of bk. I, t. 66, para. 40 has this to say: 'And because the income of the district is often insufficient for the things which the officials of the chambers are obliged, by their regulations, to provide and do.'
6   J.F. Lisboa, *Obras*, vol. II, p. 180. In spite of this, in 1720 and 1731 the records of the same chamber reveal surpluses from interest. (*Op. cit.*, vol. II, p. 179.)
7   For the years 1808, 1809, 1812 and 1813, cf. *Revista do Arquivo Municipal*, vol. 24, p. 265; vol. 30, p. 199; vol. 42, p. 228; vol. 44, p. 323; vol. 52, p. 167.
8   Letter transcribed in the *História Administrativa do Brasil* of M. Fleiuss, p. XVI. J.F. Lisboa tells us that in 1649 the General Assembly of São Luís rejected the proposal for a duty on wine and *aguardente*, '*in order that it should not remain fixed for the future*, the citizens arguing that they would prefer *to give alms*, each according to his means'. (*Obras*, vol. II, p. 179.) Referring to this fact, Varnhagen points out that in 1654 'the chamber discussed what they should do with regard to those who, having promised *alms* for the maintenance of an attorney in the realm, had not paid them'. In his notes Rodolfo Garcia gives Lisboa himself as his source. (*História Geral do Brasil*, vol. III, p. 205.)
9   Letter quoted, pp. XVI and XVII.
10   A. de Roure, *A Constituinte Republicana*, vol. I, p. 99.
11   A. de Roure, *op. cit.*, vol. I, p. 101.
12   A. de Roure, *op. cit.*, vol. I, pp. 99–101.
13   Article 10, no. V, and Article 13.

14   Articles 42–5 and 72.

15   Articles 42 and 44.

16   Articles 72 and 73.

17   *Op. cit.*, pp. 190 and 191, note 3.

18   In the words of Carneiro Maia, 'if the system under which the chambers functioned had been organised with attention to progress and to increased needs in the future, giving the municipality its own means, independent of superior authorities, the municipality today would not be in the situation where it has to beg the province for ridiculous donations in order to have an underground stream of drinking water, a few metres of road, or to repair an insignificant, little bridge. Had they been given better resources at the time of the early reforms relating to them, the chambers would not have lost the things which time had already conferred on them; nor would the inconveniences of the Additional Act have weighed so heavily upon the municipalities, which with adequate means would have considered themselves compensated for the tutelage which vexes them doubly, functioning as it does in the midst of poverty.' (*O Município*, p. 192.)

19   Tavares Bastos, *A Província*, p. 148. The words of the Visconde de Uruguai are: 'Our municipal chambers are seriously hampered. With their revenue generally consisting of a few meagre taxes, the receipt from which in some places hardly covers the expense of essential personnel, they are unable to raise the smallest levy for any local improvement, unable to incur the smallest expense, even of an obligatory nature, without the reluctant authorisation of the provincial assemblies. These, absorbed in wider political and parliamentary matters, have little care for such small details.' (Quoted by Prado Kelly, *Anais*, 1934, vol. II, p. 401.)

20   Visconde de Paranaguá, *Relatório* of 1883, p. 14. A good study on provincial taxes was published in 1883, by Sobreira de Melo.

21   Tavares Bastos, *A Província*, p. 319.

22   M. Fleiuss, *op. cit.*, p. 351.

23   *Relatório* (quoted above), pp. 14–17.

24   *Ibid.*, p. 15. Tavares Bastos, *A Província*, p. 320.

25   The first edition of *A Província* was published in 1870.

26   Pp. 336, 316 and 336 respectively.

27   'In 1869', Tavares Bastos writes, 'the provinces collected a total of 18,000 *contos*, and the municipalities in 1865 a total of 2668, giving a grand total of 21,000 *contos*. Even with exemplary administration, one could not expect great results with resources manifestly inadequate to meet the services most necessary to the wellbeing of the people.' (*A Província*, p. 308.)

28   Paranaguá, *Relatório*, pp. 17 and 18. The bill can be found on p. 145 of the report, signed by the Visconde de Paranaguá and other members of the commission and published in 1883.

Serving notice of these provisions to the General Assembly, Paranaguá described, as follows, the restrictions imposed upon provincial autonomy as a consequence of the indispensable financial aid from the centre: 'The national government kept them in a continual state of dependence by virtue of the revenue supplements; they lived at the mercy of the central authority and the aid it gave. As a result, their dignity suffered, and this constant wardship was not compatible with local autonomy . . . for ever subordinate to the higher administration, waiting always for a meagre grant from the national budget, which was itself insufficient to sustain them, in financial disarray, struggling with a deficit which increased annually, and devoid of means to improve production – the provinces came to the sad pass of having to abandon some of the prerogatives which constituted their autonomy, yielding to the national government certain duties and services whose cost they could not meet because of lack of credit. These duties and services ceased to be provincial in character and came to be classified as national, being paid for by the National Treasury.' (*Relatório*, as cited, pp. 13 and 14.)

29   *Relatório* of the Ministry of Finance of 1884.

30   Ouro Prêto, *Reforma Administrativa*, p. 87. A detailed official survey, published as a book in 1877, revealed the immense variety of names which municipal taxes had, and also gave proof of how little they brought in: *Quadros des Impostos Provinciais organizados no Tesouro Nacional segundo as últimas Leis de Orçamento Conhecidas*. (Rio de Janeiro, Tipografia Nacional, 1877.) The second part of this is devoted to municipal taxes and rates. A record of the revenues of the chambers in Rio province can be found in Cortines Laxe, *Regimento*, pp. 349 ff.

31   A. de Roure, *op. cit.*, vol. I, p. 101. On the financial measures contained in the bills relating to the reform of municipal government, cf. Ouro Prêto, *Reforma Administrativa, passim*. By the law of 1828, Article 46, the chambers presented accounts to the general councils. With the Additional Act, the question was decided by the provincial assemblies. (Article 10, VI.)

32   A. de Roure, *A Constituinte*, vol. I, p. 26.

33   *Ibid.*, vol. I, p. 117.

34   *Ibid.*, vol. I, p. 139.

35   *Ibid.*, vol. I, pp. 120, 121 and 122 respectively.

36   J.J. Seabra's proposal, *Anais*, 1934, vol. V, p. 467.

37   A. de Roure, *op. cit.*, vol. II, pp. 146–7.

38   Quoted by Prado Kelly, *Anais*, 1934, vol. XVI, p. 337.

39   *Anais*, vol. VIII, p. 29; vol. XVI, p. 318; vol. X, p. 234; vol. XIII, pp. 137 and 428.

40   A. de Roure, *op. cit.*, vol. II, p. 218.

41   Castro Nunes, *Do Estado Federado*, pp. 193 and 194.

42   *Ibid.*, pp. 194–6.

43   *Ibid.*, p. 202

44   *Ibid.*, pp. 203 and 204.

45   *Ibid.*, p. 196, note 6.

46   *Finanças dos Estados do Brasil*, vol. I, 1932, pp. 6 and 234.

47   With reference to external loans Nuno Pinheiro wrote in 1924: 'In three decades, the states and the municipalities contracted debts equal to almost half of the external national debt of the Union.' ('Finanças Nacionais', p. 126.)

48   *Anais*, 1934, vol. V, p. 415: a report presented to the Constituent Assembly by Deputy Alcântara Machado bringing together, state by state, federal receipts for 1931 and state ones for 1932. In the opinion of Deputy Cincinato Braga, the political consequences of the financial weakness of the states were: 'We have seen the abuse of autocracy of the central government exulting throughout Brazil . . . The political autonomy of the states, essential to federal life, has become a joke. The civic and economic life of nearly all of them is withering, because two-thirds of the taxes they pay do not belong to them! There is no secret wish which can free them from this evil.' (*Anais*, 1934, vol. X, p. 237.)

49   *Anais*, vol. V, p. 419.

50   *Anais*, vol. V, p. 418.

51   *Anais*, vol. V, pp. 419 and 416.

52   *Anais*, vol. V, p. 416. This feature has persisted until now. In a suggestion to the relevant sub-committee of the Constituent Assembly of 1946, the U.D.N. delegation from the state of Rio de Janeiro declared that it was necessary 'to check the abuse, prevalent in several states, by which, in order to meet the cost of certain services for which they were responsible, they exacted contributions from the municipalities to the tune of 20% in certain areas.' (*O Jornal*, 28 March 1946.) In the same period, Valentim Bouças wrote: that 'the contributions of the Prefectures to meet the normal services of the states accounted for up to 20% of municipal expenditure in some budgets for 1945'. ('Os Impostos e a Constituição'.)

53   Report prepared by Deputy Cincinato Braga, based presumably on the exercise of 1932 (proposal of 16 February 1934, *Anais*, vol. X, p. 234). These data were referred to and defended by Deputy Rodrigues Alves in the session of 9 April (*Anais*, vol. XIII, p. 428); and in the session of 4 May by Deputies Alcântara Machado (*Anais*, vol. XVI, p. 318) and Prado Kelly (*Anais*, vol. XVI, p. 334). Other deputies also dealt with the question of the distribution of revenue, but there was a certain discrepancy in the data, which we will not go into here for reasons of space. (Cf. *Anais*, vol. VI, p. 285; vol. VIII, pp. 30 and 31; vol. XIII, p. 105; vol. V, pp. 417–18.) In a more recent work, Rafael Xavier, whose authority was invoked in the assembly, gives the following percentages of the total public revenue received for the fiscal year of 1932: the Union, 50%; the states, 33%; the municipalities, 11%, excluding the Federal District. ('A Organização Nacional e o Município') Despite the known discrepancies, which were probably due, among other factors, to differences of criteria, it clearly emerged on the eve of the second Republican Constitution that the allocation to the municipal treasury was ridiculous.

54   Cf. Articles 14 to 18; 33, No. 20; 69, Nos. 6 and 7; 89; 102, para. A. The detailed comparison made by Deputy Cincinato Braga between the draft and the system of 1891 can be found in *Anais*, vol. X, pp. 117 ff., esp. p. 118. It is useful to note that while the Constitution of 1891 left municipal taxes entirely to the judgement of the states, the draft expressly included the municipalities in the constitutional differentiation of revenues. Rates, municipal services, house taxes and licences, besides others which the states transferred to them, belonged exclusively to the municipalities.

55   Cf. the comparative report prepared by Cincinato Braga based on the exercise of 1932. (*Anais*, vol. X, p. 226.)

56   *Anais*, vol. IV, pp. 78, 79–80, 449. Amendment No. 652 gave the

Union exclusive right to tax foreign imports, consumption, income (except from real estate), and the entry, exit and stop-over periods of ships and aeroplanes. It also gave the Union the exclusive right to stamp duties (except those relating to deeds emanating from state governments, state affairs or state economy), and to rates on federal telegraph services and federal mail, and other services carried out by the Union. All tax powers not specified in this connection would belong exclusively to the states. In the event of Article 18 of the draft (dealing with relative areas of tax competence) being maintained, i.e. in the event of the failure of the proposed system, Amendment No. 654 ordered that the return from unallocated revenue sources be divided *equally*, in an operation carried out after the collection itself, between the Union and the state in which the source existed. Another amendment, No. 702, ordered the suppression of Article 89 of the draft which included, in the text of the Constitution, the granting of certain revenues exclusively to the municipalities.

57   *Anais*, vol. V, p. 466.
58   *Anais*, respectively, vol. VI, p. 279 and vol. V, p. 464.
59   *Anais*, vol. VI, p. 465.
60   *Anais*, vol. VI, p. 277. It is worth mentioning Amendment No. 650, which provided for federal help for states whose revenue was less than 50,000 *contos*, the Union being empowered 'to arrogate or supervise the execution of the services subsidised', and Amendment No. 783, which forbade the states to impose 'any levy on municipal revenues'. (*Anais*, vol. IV, pp. 78 and 82.)
61   *Anais*, vol. VI, p. 278. From among the São Paulo delegation, worthy of mention are the speeches of Deputies Alcântara Machado (*Anais*, vol. V, pp. 14 and 414; vol. XVI, p. 318), Cardosa de Melo Neto (*Anais*, vol. V, p. 457; vol. VI, p. 275; vol. XIII, p. 511; vol. XX, p. 249), José Carlos de Macedo Soares (*Anais*, vol. XI, p. 47) and Rodrigues Alves (*Anais*, vol. XIII, p. 428). Cincinato Braga put down his own substitute amendment (*Anais*, vol. X, p. 219; vol. XV, p. 255.)
62   *Anais*, vol. IV, p. 82.
63   *Anais*, vol. IV, p. 449.
64   *Anais*, vol. V, p. 420. Cardosa de Melo Neto predicted: 'For the municipalities of Brazil which are in a state of lamentable poverty, the system put forward will result in their being stronger in the future.' He went on to mention his delegation's other amendment, which was drafted as follows: 'The Union shall hand over to the Federal District, and the states to the municipalities, all services of a municipal nature, with the relevant monies and duties.' He also anticipated another, to be put forward at the second reading, forbidding 'the exchange of services between the state and the municipality', since 'this exchange is nothing other than a pretext to decrease municipal revenue'. (*Anais*, vol. VI, p. 285.)
65   It was 'to financial inequalities and injustices' that Juarez Távora attributed a large measure of the responsibility, immediate or ultimate, for the 'complaints against federal imbalance'. The criterion for the allocation of revenues, which seemed to him the right one, consisted of sharing out taxation powers according to the administrative duties of the unit levying the taxes. Where this criterion was not applied, the results would be these:

'on the one hand, the abuse of creating or aggravating anti-economic taxes, and, on the other, that disastrous phenomenon, which has occurred among us, the excessive growth of the state to the detriment of the municipality'. (*Anais*, vol. II, pp. 368 and 369.) In this speech, Juarez Távora referred to the report which he had previously made to the Commission for the Economic and Financial Study of the States and the Municipalities, in which he said that the Brazilian state was like 'a limb financially and politically over-developed, within the body politic, disputing with the Union even the right of sovereignty and snatching from the municipalities their own means of material existence'. Hence his suggestion to 'give greater financial powers to the municipality', returning to it 'the prerogatives and responsibilities which have been arrogated by the state, and of whose execution the states in this half century of republicanism have proved themselves to be totally incapable'. (*Anais*, vol. IV, p. 49.)

It is as well to recall that the greater part of the criticisms voiced in the assembly lamented the excessive tax powers of the Union: 'Under the tax system which has been in force, the Union has the lion's share. All the important taxes, the really lucrative and promising ones, are appropriated by the Union.' (Cincinato Braga, *Anais*, vol. X, p. 234.) Juarez Távora wanted to weaken the states even more from the point of view of taxation.

66   *Anais*, vol. II, pp. 370–1; Juarez Távora was seeking, in this way, to reduce the state to the status of 'an intermediate and *cheap* body, with the function specified'. (*Anais*, vol. IV, p. 49.) In the opinion of Deputy Raul Fernandes, Juarez Távora's plan was excellent, but it would bring down the Federation. (*Anais*, vol. XII, p. 241.)

67   Amendment No. 262, *Anais*, vol. IV, p. 44.

68   *Anais*, vol. IV, p. 44., our italics. The proposed measure, more of a tactical than a juridical character, would make the matter dependent on a subsequent examination and, contrary to the proposals of its author, referred the question back to the ordinary legislator, who would be the judge of the appropriateness of the innovation and also of the 'equitable' percentages to be allocated to the Union, the states and the municipalities in the distribution of the national tax receipt.

69   *Anais*, vol. VIII, p. 44.

70   In the justification of Amendment No. 431, *Anais*, vol. IV, p. 69.

71   *Anais*, vol. II, p. 403.

72   *Anais*, vol. II, p. 410. See the measures proposed in *Anais*, vol. VI, p. 68.

73   The new amendment of P. Kelly – No. 1847 of 11 April 1934 – was no longer supported by the other members of this delegation; supporting the author were Deputies Alberto Surek, of the class delegation of employees, Fernandes Távora and Silva Leal of Ceará, Manuel César de Góis Monteiro and Valente de Lima from Alagoas. (*Anais*, vol. XVII, p. 290.)

74   *Anais*, vol. XVII, p. 290; vol. XVI, pp. 329 ff.

75   On the second topic (collection), he proposed that all taxes should be collected by the state (except import duties) with the supervision of the Union and the municipalities. (*Anais*, vol. XVI, p. 337.)

76   *Anais*, vol. XVI, p. 333.

77   'It is necessary to distinguish', he observed, 'between the power to

legislate on fiscal matters and the *division* of revenues allocated to the federal, state and municipal treasuries.' (*Anais*, vol. XVI, p. 333.)
78   Cf. the amendment quoted, Article 13 para. 4, *Anais*, vol. XVII, p. 291.
79   In the first amendment, he argued that the states should receive 50% of federal import and export duties, and consumer and income tax, and that the municipalities should receive 50% of state taxes on commerce, industries and trades. (*Anais*, vol. IV, p. 69.) In the second, however, he declared that the income from import duties should belong exclusively to the Union, and that from export duties to the state in whose territory they were levied (although both duties fell within the legislative competence of the Union). Finally, he argued that the total receipt from other taxes collected in their respective territories should be distributed between the Union, the states and the municipalities, 'in relation to their administrative duties and prerogatives'. (*Anais*, vol. XVI, p. 333.) But to prevent this distribution from being arbitrarily carried out, it was determined that there should be a 'rational comparison of the duties and prerogatives of public authorities with the revenue required for the provision of these services'. After this balance had been established, 'a fundamental federal law' would establish 'proportional quotas' to increase the exclusive revenue of the Union, the states and the municipalities. (*Anais*, vol. XVI, p. 335.) Periodically, the Federal Council would revise the legislation relating to taxation in order to harmonise the interests of the three administrative spheres.
80   'The great and salutary innovation of this Constitution would have been to assign the exclusive revenue of the municipalities to them, as has been done; in carrying through this measure, however, I wanted, at the same time, to assign to the municipalities, specifically, the services which must fall to them, because the division of income is valueless if the states are able to saddle the municipalities with all the services which they [the states] do not want to carry out.' (*Anais*, vol. XX, p. 398.) Alas, the text of his amendment did not completely avoid this danger, since, after enumerating succinctly the duties of the states and the municipalities, it continued: 'The Federal Constitution shall divide the remaining public services between the state and the municipality.' (*Anais*, vol. XVIII, p. 353.)
81   The observations and proposals of Deputy Alde Sampaio, an exposition of which would require too much space, were very interesting. They suffered, however, from a certain lack of legal precision; some because of their overwhelmingly tactical nature, like this one: 'It is forbidden to create any duty or to increase the existing ones in cases where these represent arbitrary impositions or seignorial tributes without any economic basis.' Others were too complicated: 'The duty which falls directly on raw materials, subject naturally to exclusively local manufacturing processes,

and the duty on the local agents of these processes, should be within the competence of the municipality. The state is free to tax them both when the raw material, subject to industrial use, is a product of general commerce.' (*Anais*, vol. IV, pp. 15 and 17.)

82   Apart from one of the amendments of the São Paulo delegation already mentioned, an identical suggestion was made by Deputies Lino Leme and Antônio Covelo (in Amendment No. 479, *Anais*, vol. IV, p. 438), Gabriel Passos and Negrão de Lima (in Amendment No. 587, *Anais*, vol. IV, p. 441) and Daniel de Carvalho (in Amendment No. 884, *Anais*, vol. IV, p. 463). The last named declared that the division of municipal revenues in the Federal Constitution was 'utterly useless'.

83   *Anais*, vol. X, p. 557.

84   Articles 14, 15, 18 and 19.

85   Text in *Anais*, vol. XII, p. 312.

86   *Anais*, vol. XX, pp. 262 ff.

87   *Anais*, vol. XX, pp. 262 ff. esp. pp. 271, 276 and 283.

88   Constitution of 1934, Articles 8, para. 2; 10, single para.; 13, para. 2.

89   Articles 28 and 23.

90   'Os Municípios e a Constituição'.

91   The extreme variety of the tax rubrics of the states and the municipalities, if on the one hand it reflects local peculiarities, on the other hand, it conveys the need on the part of the fiscal legislator to stretch his imagination in order to increase revenue, while respecting the constitutional rules of fiscal differentiation or bending them cleverly. With the proposal to rationalise the incoherent financial legislation in our country, there took place in October 1939 a 'Conference of Experts in Accountancy and Treasury Matters'. Its conclusions were approved by Decree—Law No. 1804 of 24 November 1939, to which was added Decree—Law No. 2416 of 17 July 1940. According to these laws, which sought to introduce some order into the finances, budgets and accounts of the states and municipalities, 'all taxes of the same nature were grouped under standard rubrics'. Yet in the state budgets for 1946, according to Valentim Bouças no fewer than eight rubrics which he mentions were used to describe 'taxes not fixed by the division of revenues'. He cites as an example the 'duty on agricultural and industrial exploitation', which had 21 different rubrics in the state budgets and 48 in the municipal ones. ('Os Impostos e a Constituição'.) Afonso Almiro informs us as well with regard to the municipalities, that in 1946 there existed 'about 800 tax rubrics all with the characteristics of licence duty', while the 'traditional and simple house tax' was 'covered by twenty different names'. (*A Constituicão*, p. 33.) On the great variety of municipal taxes under the Empire, see the inquiry quoted in chapter IV, note 30.

92   'A Diminuição Progressiva das Rendas Municipais'. The author gives percentages in round figures from the population census, respectively, 22.5%, 9.0%, and 68.5%. Cf. chapter I, note 20.

93   'A Organização Nacional e o Município'. Gerson Augusto da Silva gives still smaller percentages, *which fell progressively from 1940 to 1946.* The following are the figures which he gives: 1940, 9.1%; 1941, 8.6%; 1942, 8.5%; 1943, 7.1%; 1944, 6.0%; 1945, 5.7%; 1946, 4.9%. In this last year, the Union took 60.8% and the states 34.3% 'of the total of taxes collected in the country'. (*Sistema Tributário Brasileiro*, p. 81.) The difference noted between the percentages can perhaps be explained by the fact that these figures refer to *taxes*, while those of Rafael Xavier refer to *collection*. Orlando M. Carvalho also paints a revealing picture, comparing the years from 1868–9, 1910, 1920, 1930, 1936 and 1940, including the revenue of the Federal District among the municipal total. (*Política do Município*, p. 165.) In the Constituent Assembly of 1933–4 Deputy Soares Filho rightly emphasised that the condition of the rural municipalities was the more precarious because municipal taxes are of a predominantly urban nature. (*Anais*, vol. II, p. 369.)

94   On the occasion Deputy Aliomar Baleeiro declared: 'I believe that we have just carried out a genuine, just and complete social revolution in this country, opening up the possibility for municipal public services to assume that consistency which will ensure that forty million Brazilians will live with human dignity . . . The vote for proposals and amendments favourable to the financial improvement of the municipalities has this significance'. (José Duarte, *A Constituição*, vol. I, p. 405.)

95   José Duarte, *ibid.*, vol. I, p. 483.

96   The federal and state taxes were listed in Articles 15 and 19 respectively. In the tax division of 1946 the Union was still the chief beneficiary: 'In the sharing of taxes between the Union, the states and the municipalities, it is the first which gets the largest portion, more than half of the total collected'. (Prado Kelly, 'A Constituição Brasileira', p. 437.)

97   Articles 29 and 30.

98   Article 21.

99   Article 15, para. 2. Law No. 302 of 13 July 1948, which replaced No. 22 of 15 February 1947, controls the putting into effect of the constitutional principle relating to the taxing of lubricants and liquid fuels. The income from this is put into the National Road Fund, 40% of which belongs to the Union (National Highways Department), 48% to the states and the Federal District and 12% to the municipalities. The quota of the states and the Federal District will be allocated as follows: one-fifth in proportion to the area of each unit; one-fifth, proportionate to its population; three-fifths in proportion to respective levels of consumption of lubricants and liquid fuels. The same criteria will govern the allocation of the municipal quota.

100   Article 20.

101   Only after 1949 will the municipalities receive the full amount provided for in the quota; in 1947 they received nothing and in 1948 they will receive only half. (Article 13, para. 2, I of the measure indicated.) Law No. 305 of 18 July 1948 requires that the basis for allocation should be 'the

number of municipalities existing on 31 December of the previous year'.
(Article 4, single para.)

102   The index of yield from income tax in recent years was as follows,
1939 being taken as 100: 1941, 166; 1942, 305; 1943, 463; 1944, 630;
1945, 726. (*Anuário Estatístico*, 1946, p. 488.)

103   We can have some idea of how much each municipality will receive,
by doing a few calculations. In 1945 the collection from income tax
reached a total of 2,349,784,000 *cruzeiros*. (*Anuário Estatístico*, 1946, p.
488.) Ten per cent of this total divided between the 1642 municipalities of
the interior (excluding those of the capitals) gives 143,105 *cruzeiros* for
each one. In order to estimate the importance of this contribution to
municipal revenues, it is enough to consider that, according to the budgets
for 1945, 385 municipalities had an income of up to 100,000 *cruzeiros*
and another 677 were between 100,000 and 300,000. The position of the
poorest municipalities was as follows: up to 20,000 *cruzeiros*, 10; from
20,000–40,000, 56; from 40,000–60,000, 96; from 60,000–80,000, 110;
from 80,000–100,000, 103. (Cf. the report published by Valentim Bouças,
'Os Impostos e a Constituição'.)

The federal budget for 1948 reserves 160,500,000 *cruzeiros* for the
municipalities, a sum which corresponds to half of the quota provided for
in the Constitution, since the full amount will only be due from 1949 onwards. (In fact this grant is slightly less than 5% of the estimated total of
income tax for 1948.)

We do not know the exact number of municipalities *in existence* on 31
December 1947 (Law No. 305 of 1948), so that we are unable to calculate
how much each will receive in 1948; moreover, some of them created in
1947 were only given full status in 1948, hence it is a moot point as to
whether they are included in the division. Pedro Calmon warns against the
abuse of establishing new municipalities (a matter within the competence
of the states) for the sole purpose of increasing some states' share of the
revenue derived from income tax. (*Curso*, already quoted, p. 122.)

104   Article A, para. 3.

105   Article 127, III, and Article 21 respectively.

106   Summary of the debates in José Duarte, *A Constituição*, vol. I, pp.
476–9.

107   Articles B and 128, para. 2, respectively.

108   To establish the principles of sharing, the legislator, as laid down by
the Constitution, will have to take into account for each product taxed,
the area and population of the unit concerned and the relative production
or consumption of the product in each, with preference being given to one
or other of these criteria, or by combining them in some way according to
which method seems the more convenient. The units receiving these
revenue supplements must use them for purposes defined by federal law.
(See chapter IV, note 99.)

109   Summary of the debates in José Duarte, *A Constituição*, vol. I, pp.
387–93.

110   Article D, single para., and 127, VIII, respectively.

111   Summary in J. Duarte, *op. cit.*, vol. I, pp. 472–5.

112   Article 13, para. 2, III.

113   Article 128, para. 4.

114   Summary of the debates in J. Duarte, *op. cit.*, vol. I, pp. 402–9. On the tax division of 1946, see also Pedro Calmon, *Curso de Direito Constitucional Brasileiro*, ch. XV, pp. 121 ff.

115   In an interview with *O Jornal* of 23 July 1946, Rafael Xavier said: 'We are engaged in a campaign which at the moment is absorbing everyone. And the proof is that it has caused greater repercussions in the Constituent Assembly than any other problem. In the press there is no newspaper which has failed to support enthusiastically the national theme of the strengthening of the municipalities.' Nevertheless, in another work, 'A Diminuição Progressiva das Rendas Municipais', referring to the pro-municipal campaign undertaken at an earlier date by Juarez Távora himself, and his colleagues in the Society of the Friends of Alberto Tôrres, he observes: 'We were crying in the wilderness.'

116   The 1947 number of the *Anuário Comércial e Industrial de Minas Gerais*, which gives the federal, state and municipal receipts of almost all the municipalities in that state, is an eloquent document.

117   Referring to the Bank of Brazil, Deputy Cincinato Braga declared in the Constituent Assembly of 1934: 'This establishment has in its vaults more resources in ready money than the National Treasury itself. The business of the Bank of Brasil annually is more than three times that of the National Treasury. In addition, the agencies of the Bank, *throughout Brazil*, deal with nearly one-quarter or one-fifth of the capital invested in concerns in Rio de Janeiro . . . In federal terms, this situation should be reversed in favour of the National Bank . . . The concentration of colossal sums of public money in the hands of a central government is always, in itself, a misfortune for the generality of the population scattered throughout the country . . . This concentration of money leads, as we have seen, to a concentration of bank business, and these two lead to the centralisation, in the capital and its environs, of all the best experts in all branches of manufacturing industry. The interior of the country is deprived of technical skills. It will not develop without the capital that banks can supply and without skilled manpower.' (*Anais*, vol. X, p. 236.)

118   'A Organização Nacional e o Município'. The following passages are taken from the same work: 'The Union and the states took over the control and the execution of all the duties which, by nature and by definition, should have been the function of local governments. They created a centralised, bureaucratic machine to carry out agreed programmes and, by so doing, reduced the potential of the municipalities for development to a minimum. The slow process of draining away not only resources but human potential began . . . The provinces grew, to the delight of the pro-state faction . . . Industries designed to maintain a life of pleasure and luxury, and which are normally the most lucrative, increased and multiplied in the large urban centres. Some of them merged in the search for better consumer markets. Secondary and higher education, also concentrated in the capitals, attracted the young people. Moreover other factors worked in favour of concentration: large buildings; easy and effective bureaucracy; property speculation; the natural attractions of large centres; and even, with its train of spiritual misery, the national lottery.'

119   '[T] he percentage of the population living in rural areas is high –
almost 70% of the total. But in practical terms they can expect hardly any
services from the local'administration, since 6% of the tax collected in the
municipalities, hardly covers the cost of minor improvements in the municipal capital.' (Rafael Xavier, 'A Diminuição Progressiva das Rendas Municipais'.)
120   'Algumas Notas', already quoted.
121   We should not forget that the richest and most powerful landowners
had links with commerce and industry or, in other words, investments of
an urban nature.
122   Caio Prado Jr, *História Econômica do Brasil*, pp. 268 ff.
123   In the 'Carta Econômico' of Teresópolis of 1945 the *producing
classes* 'suggest that the public authorities should carry out an objective
inventory and classification of industries created during the war, with the
purpose of ensuring that only the necessary ones, and those presenting conditions of viability, were supported.' (Ch. IV, para. 14.)
124   Industrial statistics for Brazil are very defective, as is shown in the
critical introduction to the voluminous document prepared by Rômulo de
Almeida on our 'industrial production', and presented to the Constituent
Assembly of 1946 by the Committee for Social and Economic Research.
The most exact data, it appears, are those calculated indirectly from statistics on the consumption tax. These data, however, refer to the *value* of
industrial production, and through comparison of production levels in
various periods, this demands difficult calculations based on changes in the
purchasing power of money. We are not qualified to do this. In addition,
statistics on the manpower employed in industry can only be interpreted
with difficulty. It seems clear, however, that our industry has developed,
at least quantitatively, through periods of expansion, stagnation and
retrenchment, described by Caio Prado Júnior in his *História Econômica
do Brasil* (pp. 268 ff.). Already in 1932, according to official data referred
to by Cincinato Braga in the Constituent Assembly of the Second Republic, in this 'essentially agricultural country' 'industrial production' reached
5,050,000 *contos*, as compared with the value of 'agricultural crops' calculated at 5,105,000. (*Anais*, vol. XV, p. 129.) A study of Roberto
Simonsen's authoritative work, *A Evolução do Brasil*, is indispensable for
a concise exposition of the facts. The regional study done by Limeira Tejo
on the industries of Rio Grande do Sul is also very interesting. Recent
statistics on the industrial output of Brazil can be found in Rafael Xavier,
Síntese Econômico-Financeira do Brasil and in the reply of the São Paulo
Federation of Industries to the *Inquérito Continental sôbre Fomento e
Coordenação de Indústrias promovido pelo Conselho Interamericano de
Comércio e Produção* (1946). This document repeats and endorses the
following passages from the publication of the 'Itamarati' – *Brasil 1943/
1944* – 'The industrial expansion of Brazil is the most significant feature
of its economy during the last decade. The value of industrial output in
the country which was 8 billion *cruzeiros* in 1937, reached 12 billion in
1940, and exceeded 37 billion in 1943. These are figures which reveal the
development of an industrial sector and the potential of regional raw
materials. Between 1938 and 1942, about 15,000 factories were set up in

Brazil, and since then many of the existing ones have been enlarged and more new ones built. At the moment there is no state in the Federation which does not possess more than 100 industrial establishments, excepting the Federal Territories . . . A revealing index of industrial expansion is its relationship with external trade. In 1913 Brazil depended on external markets for the greater part of its manufactured products, importing, on average, 30% of its consumption of cotton fabrics, 60% of woollen ones and 85% of silk. Purchases of iron, coal and cement were equivalent to almost its entire requirements. Today the greater part of these and other products is produced in the country itself.' (p. 5).

125 *Anais*, 1934, vol. VIII, pp. 44, 50 and 51. See also his observations on protective tariffs. (*Anais*, vol. II, p. 328.)

126 *Anais*, vol. XI, p. 47.

127 *Anais*, vol. XI, p. 53.

128 *Anais*, vol. XI, p. 54.

129 *Anais*, vol. XI, p. 54 and p. 55.

130 Immediately afterwards, the author declared that the two areas in question were destined by their wealth and technical progress 'to supply the rest of Brazil with the necessary personnel to rationalise its production, to increase its value and to allow other states the economic progress which depends to such a large extent on technical expertise', but when he came to cite the scientific institutions of São Paulo capable of carrying out this task, he named particularly the Institute of Agronomy at Campinas and the Colleges of Agriculture, thus revealing that, subconsciously perhaps, his idea was that the other federal units should develop in the agricultural field, this development to include mechanisation in cultivation. Another São Paulo deputy, Cincinato Braga, referring to the fall in Brazilian exports which was sharper in the North than in the South, and to the increase in public expenditure especially in southern states, said: 'I would say that the northern states have to resort to agriculture and stockraising as the bases of the possible, probable, and, God willing, the certain renewal of their economies.' (*Anais*, vol. XV, p. 141.)

131 In the conference of 1945, the 'producing classes' affirmed 'their conviction of the need for the setting up of an organic and rational system to defend [national] industries'. 'This protective system', they continued, 'should provide not only a customs policy capable of allowing our industries, when necessary, to face normal competition from better established and better endowed foreign industries, but also legislation which would enable the country to face situations arising out of unfair competition, caused by such methods as "squeezing" and "dumping" on the part of foreign countries.' (*Carta Econômica de Teresópolis*, ch. IV, para. 7.)

132 'A Organização Nacional e o Município'. The same author does not disguise his disapproval of the technical deficiencies of our industry. ('A Diminuição Progressiva das Rendas Municipais'.)

133 'The São Paulo delegation, through the voices of the leaders of all parties, initiated the movement in the direction of strengthening municipal revenues.' (Rafael Xavier, interview with *O Jornal* of 23 July 1946.)

134 Items II, VII, and VIII; cf. *O Jornal* of 27 September 1947. As early as 1939 Getúlio Vargas understood that 'the strengthening of the domestic market would be achieved by reforming the tax system'. (Cited in Afonso Almiro, *A Constituição*, p. 33.) The First Brazilian Industrial Congress, opened in São Paulo on 8 December 1944, included in its programme an item which read: 'the strengthening of the domestic market and the winning of new markets abroad'. (*O Jornal*, 9 December 1944.)

135   Caio Prado Jr, *História Econômica do Brasil*, pp. 297 ff.

136   If in diagnosing the phenomenon we have tended to emphasise some factors, this does not signify that we deny the existence of others. It is quite likely, for example, that the raising of the standard of living of our people is related to two other projects: creating a market for foreign industry as well, and preventing the spread of communism especially among the rural masses. On the first point, 'an economics observer' published a piece in *O Jornal* of 27 December 1944 from which we have taken the following passages: 'As has already been observed many times, the industrial economy of big countries demands large and stable markets to guarantee continuity of production . . . It is clear that such markets are not to be found in "backward regions", but in countries of greater economic density, of high national income fairly well distributed, with a higher standard of living and a purchasing power of some importance'. On the second point, Associated Press, in a telegram from Washington, revealed that the Assistant Secretary of State, Spruile Braden, had declared 'that one of the best ways of combating communism in Latin America is to offer to the people the real hope of improving their way of life'. (*O Jornal*, 14 March 1947.) Even among ourselves, those who repudiate the idea of fighting communism by violent methods, never tire of insisting on the effectiveness, to this end, of administrative and economic measures designed to create better living conditions for our people. And the fear of the expansion of communism in the countryside is justified by many facts. The following thoughts on the subject belong to Artur Tôrres Filho: 'Brazil has more than two million rural properties and about eight million rural workers, according to the last economic census. This great economic force in the country, the real producer of the country's wealth, must be cautious about the infiltration of subversive ideas.' (*O Jornal*, 24 November 1946.)

137   See the observations of Deputy Cincinato Braga on the public debt of Brazil (Union, states and municipalities) put before the Constituent Assembly of 1934, in *Anais*, vol. X, pp. 245–7. 'The fact that in Brazil we have already suffered the shame of three refundings in the space of only a few years, amply justifies the need to apply a constitutional brake to the abuse of the Nation's credit . . . The state finances are as disorganised as those of the Union . . . The liabilities of the municipalities reach a figure of around two million *contos* (external and internal debt).

138   Gabrial Passos commented: 'We know that economic autonomy is the basis of political autonomy.' (*Anais*, 1934, vol. VI, p. 391.) 'In Paraná', said deputy Antônio Jorge in 1934, referring to the regime of 1891, 'it was enough for the municipality to contract a loan for the state to nominate its prefect.' (*Anais*, vol. VI, p. 393.)

139   The regulations (Decree No. 2977 of 15 October 1910) made it clear that the state should collect taxes only on the transferring of property *inter vivos* and from the rates on electricity, main drainage and water

supply, excluding market taxes, the fines and contingent payments. When
the sum required for the municipality's commitments had been deducted,
the remainder was handed over to the president of the municipal chamber.
The dates and conditions of the handing over of surpluses were laid down
in the contract for the loan.

140   See, among others, Decree No. 19,593 of 24 August 1945, which
regulated the process whereby federal help was given for the development
of primary education, and the agreement signed in 1942 between the
Union and the states. The supervision, 'in all senses of the term', of the
agreements provided for, remained the prerogative of the Union, the states
which were party to the agreements being obliged to obtain from their
municipalities, by means of a compact, the obligatory allocation of a fixed
percentage of their monies for the carrying out of the plan. (Cf. *Correio da
Manhã*, 26 August 1945.)

141   This law was so absurd that it appears that no one ever attempted
to put it into effect.

142   Referring to the increase in municipal revenue in the Constituent
Assembly of 1946, Deputy Aliomar Baleeiro declared in an interview for
Correio da Manhã (reprinted in the *Revista Forense*): 'This is being called
the "municipal revolution", and in fact this innovation will have the political consequence of shaking the unlimited power which the governors
exercise over the rural population, so completely dependent upon them.
At last, the Constitution has ratified it on paper. Now it remains to engrave
it on all hearts and consciences.' (*Revista Forense*, vol. 110, p. 10.)

5. Organisation of the police and the judiciary

1   Only after the law of 1871 were serious attempts made to entrust these
powers to separate authorities. However, the line of distinction between
police and judicial functions is sometimes so blurred that the separation is
very difficult in practice. (Cf. João Mendes, *O Processo Criminal Brasileiro*,
pp. 249–50.) This difficulty has produced results which are still apparent
today, as can be seen in the inquiry carried out by the police and which
serves as a basis for penal action. (Decree–Law No. 3689 of 1941 – Penal
Code, Articles 4 ff.)

In the present chapter we are concerned solely with the police in the
narrow sense of the term, in other words with the security police (concerned with the prevention and suppression of crimes and misdemeanours).
The other aspects of police work, which in administrative law could be
known as police power, are outside the scope of this study.

2   Ordinances, bk. I, t. 65: 'The ordinary judges and others whom we
shall send from outside, must work to ensure that in the districts and their
boundaries misdeeds and wrongdoings do not take place. And should they
take place, they should attend to them and proceed against the guilty with
diligence.'

We must mention, in particular, the *judge of the people*, created in
Bahia on the initiative of the populace and later confirmed by a Letter
Patent of 28 May 1644 which replied to petitions addressed to the king
from the individual elected to be judge, the councillors and the inhabitants

of the city. (Varnhagen, *História Geral do Brasil*, vol. III, p. 171; Rodolfo Garcia's note to the text cited.) The post was abolished by an edict of 25 February 1713, at the request of the chamber and because of the disturbances in which the office had become involved especially the serious riot which took place there in 1711. (Acióli, *Memórias Históricas e Políticas*, vol. I, p. 260.)

Basílio de Magalhães considers the people's judges to be a 'survival . . . of the ancient tribunes of the plebs of the Romans' (*O Municipalismo em Minas Gerais*, p. 5), and Acióli declared that they were 'more dangerous' than the latter. (Loc. cit.) For João Ribeiro (*História do Brasil*, p. 204), this office of judge was a 'revolutionary tribuneship', and Handelmann (*História do Brasil*, p. 446) has an identical description although he mistakenly calls it a 'revolutionary tribunal'.

With the people's judge there had also been elected guild-masters (known as *mesteres*) and their position was confirmed by the same Letter Patent of 1644 which confirmed the office of the judge. They continued to exist in Bahia 'in the form in which they have existed in other cities of this kingdom, and with the same sanctions and privileges as they ask for in their petition'. (Andrade e Silva, *Coleção*, pp. 237—8 of the corresponding volume.)

The *mesteres* or *misteres*, according to Pereira de Sousa, 'are twenty-four skilled artisans who have their proxies in the House of Twenty-Four, and these work together with the chamber to regulate trades and crafts, and to fix the level of wages and the prices of goods.' (*Dicionário Jurídico*, vol. II.) The same author adds that in the House of Twenty-Four, the creation of Dom João I, no one younger than 40 was allowed. (Letter Patent of 27 September 1647.) The regulating of trades and crafts and the selection of those who annually sent representatives to the House, were contained in the Letter Patent of 3 December 1771. (*Op. cit.*, vol. I.) Only 'after' the election of the people's judge, regulated by Letters Patent of 10 December 1641 and 7 October 1644, 'had been made public' could the *mesteres* be elected. The people's judge and his scribe received a salary paid by the chamber (Letter Patent of 20 April 1624), the insignia (the staff) of the office of magistrate (Decree of 13 January 1641 and Letter Patent of 7 February 1641), and reviewed the accounts not only of their predecessors but also those of the House of Twenty-Four, in all expenses 'relating to the people'. (Letter Patent of 7 June 1526; *op. cit.*, vol. II.)

Although we have been unable to find the legislation quoted in the most accessible compilations, the importance of the office of the people's judge can be imagined — an institution linked to manual workers — when we consider that (according to Cortines Laxe, chapter II, note 6, above), 'mechanics, workers, deportees, Jews and others who belonged to the class of peons' were not allowed to vote for posts within the chamber. Their representative before the authorities — with the power to 'bring before the monarchy the representations of the people' independently of the chamber (Cândido Mendes, *Auxiliar Jurídico*, p. 556) — was precisely the people's judge. Hence the constant presence of this official in popular rebellions, this being the reason for the abolition in 1661 of the House of Twenty-Four in the city of Pôrto. It was re-established in 1795. (Pereira de Sousa, *Esbôço.*)

In the case of Bahia, it should be noted that the riot of October 1711 was occasioned by the levying of an import duty and an increase in the price of salt, matters which directly affected the lives of poor people. In addition, it is not strange that the chamber, the political voice of the well-to-do, should use the occasion to ask for (and obtain) the abolition of this tribuneship of protest and extreme action.

3   Bk. I, t. 67; Enéias Galvão, 'Juízes e Tribunais', p. 329. 'The judges of the orphans, who served for three years and were separate from the ordinary judges, were created in Brazil by Letter Patent of 2 May 1731.' (Cortines Laxe, *Regimento*, p. XIX, note 4.)

4   In relation to Bahia, for example, Vilhena tells us that 'the office of the criminal judge was created by Dom João V in the year 1742'. (Brás do Amaral, *Cartas de Vilhena*, vol. II, pp. 311 and 337.)

5   The councillors continued to hear cases (together with the judges) of verbal insults, certain thefts and, as an appeal court, questions relating to weights and measures. (Ordinances, bk. I, t. 65, paras. 23–5; Carvalho Mourão, 'Os Municípios', p. 308.)

6   Two served each month. In the first three months, according to the order established by law, the judges and the members of the chamber of the preceding year served. For the other nine months 'nine pairs of worthy men from among the best citizens', were elected. (Bk. I, t. 67, paras. 13 and 14; Enéias Galvão, *op. cit.*, p. 328.) Cândido Mendes tells us that the Letter Patent of 15 April 1618 provided a new regulation for the election of inspectors of weights and measures, who were abolished by a decree of 26 August 1830. (*Código Filipino*, note 1 to the Ordinance quoted.) According to Varnhagen there was an inspector of weights and measures in every district. (*História Geral*, vol. I, p. 186.)

7   Bk. I, t. 65, paras. 73 and 74; Cândido Mendes, note to the text cited; Enéias Galvão, *op. cit.*, pp. 328–9.

'We believe that pedestrian judges were the same as parish judges . . . They were called pedestrian at first, because they heard cases *on foot* (so to speak) with little formality and without a set procedure.' (Rocha Pombo, *História do Brazil*, vol. III, p. 60, note 6.)

8   Bk. I, t. 75. On the election of the junior *alcaids*, cf. M. Fleiuss, *História Administrativa*, p. 38. According to João Mendes, as the institution of the junior *alcaids* fell into disuse they were replaced 'in many of their duties not only by the guards but also by the neighbourhood judges', at the same time as the ordinary judges were acquiring police functions. (*O Processo Criminal*, p. 250.)

9   Bk. I, t. 73. According to Cândido Mendes, as time went by the guards *quaddrilheiros* were replaced by others, 'pedestrian guards', 'municipal' guards and policemen, etc.' and fell into oblivion to such an extent that in spite of the Letter Patent of 31 March 1742 almost no subsequent legislation mentions them. (*Código Filipino*, note 2 to bk. I, t. 73.)

10   The most accessible authors frequently affirm the existence, on Brazilian soil, not only of magistrates (*ouvidores*) but also of divisional *corregidors* (*corregidores de comarca*). 'In each division', says Rocha Pombo, 'the highest judicial authority was the *corregidor*, who exercised jurisdiction

over the magistrates and the other judges functioning in the legal district. (*História do Brasil*, vol. V, p. 417.)

In reality, the Ordinances gave a long title to that magistrate (t. 58 of bk. I). Cândido Mendes says, however, that since the lands of Brazil belonged to the Order of Christ, for this reason we had not *corregidors* but magistrates (*ouvidores*) to whom the king granted the powers of the former. The reason given by Mendes is that the *corregidor* represented royal justice and that the *ouvidor* personified seigneurial justice. (*Op. cit.*, note 2 to bk. I, t. 7, para. 22.) João Mendes confirms the seigneurial nature of a system of *ouvidores* to the point — he observes — where the legislation is at great pains to make out that Brazilian *ouvidores* were judges of the Crown. (Letter Patent of 24 March 1708) and did not belong to the lords of the provinces (Royal Charter of 4 March 1802). In his opinion, however, the presence of *ouvidores* in Brazil can be explained by the fact that the lords of the provinces were the first administrators of the colony. (*O Processo Criminal*, vol. I, p. 138.)

This illustrious legal expert alludes repeatedly, nevertheless, to the *corregidors* of the legal divisions, and Cândido Mendes himself by a strange contradiction recognises their existence when he says that they were abolished by Article 18 of the law of 29 November 1932. (*Op. cit.*, note 1 to bk. I, t. 58.) This law, however, does not refer to the *corregidors* of the legal divisions but to those of the Court of Appeal.

In the many regulations concerning the appeal courts of Brazil which we have had occasion to examine, we have never found the name *corregidor* given to any of their judges, and all the courts entrust the duties of the *corregidor* either to a general, civil or criminal magistrate, or to general magistrates specialising in each of these branches of the law. Nevertheless in the Brazilian House of Entreaty (a remodelling of the appeal court of Rio de Janeiro by a Letter Patent of 10 May 1808) two *corregidors* had been known to sit: one 'Criminal Judge of the Court and the House', the other 'Civil Judge of the Court'. It would have to be these two judges to whom the law of 1832, cited by Cândido Mendes, refers.

From what we have been able to find out with the few sources at our disposal, it seems likely, in spite of the widespread opinion to the contrary, that there were no *corregidors* of the legal divisions as distinct from the magistrates (*ouvidores*). This hypothesis is confirmed by Cândido Mendes in the first of the passages mentioned above. In the House of Entreaty, created in 1808, magistrates called *corregidors* functioned. An important fact corroborates this theory: the criminal code of 1832, when it listed in Article 8 former judicial authorities which would be abolished and not feature in the new legal system, mentioned the magistrate (*ouvidor*) and did not specifically refer to the *corregidor* of the legal divisions.

Vilhena declares, nevertheless, that in 1696 the office of *Corregidor* in the legal division of Bahia was created, and that the first person nominated to the post was Melchior de Sousa Vilas Boas. (*Cartas*, vol. II, p. 311.) In another place, however (*op. cit.*, vol. II, p. 331), he tells us that the same Melchior, in the same year of 1696, was named general magistrate of the division (*ouvidor geral da comprea*), and his name heads the list of *de capa e espada* magistrates (*lay* magistrates, according to Rocha Pombo, *História do Brasil*, vol. V, p. 418).

It is possible that in the absence of more detailed research ancient authors like Vilhena are referring to *corregidors* of the divisions to denote not judges superior to the *ouvidores* but the *ouvidores* themselves who *took the place of corregidors*. (*Op. cit.*, vol. II, p. 307.) They would thereby be describing an occasional function by the name of the office. We could also explain in this way the express references to *corregidors* of the divisions which occur in some laws, like those of 20 October 1823 (Article 24 para. 11) and 1 October 1828 (Article 65?).

11   'The magistrates were of two kinds: magistrates of the division and general magistrates, the former of lower rank and a more limited territorial jurisdiction than the latter. There was the same distinction between the general magistrate, with authority in various captainships, and the general magistrate for all Brazil.' (Enéias Galvão, 'Juízes e Tribunais', p. 330.) It was also customary to have one magistrate for each captainship; and, on the other hand, he could receive the title of general magistrate for a single division. (Cf. Vilhena, *Cartas*, vol. II, p. 311.) 'Each division could be subdivided into two or more areas each with its own magistrate, and sometimes a single town had its own magistrate.' (Rocha Pombo, *História do Brasil*, vol. V, p. 417.)

12   Enéias Galvão, *op. cit.*, pp. 330–1. Caio Prado Júnior tells us that 'by the Royal Charter of 22 July 1766, the magistrate also exercised the function of intendant of police.' (*Formação do Brasil Contemporâneo*, p. 318, note 31.)

13   J.F. Lisboa, *Obras*, vol. II, p. 135; Tavares de Lira. *Organização Política e Administrativa do Brasil*, p. 20.

14   Tavares de Lira, *op. cit.*, p. 31; Caio Prado Jr, *Formação do Brasil Contemporâneo*, pp. 303 and 304. On the title of *Viceroy*, cf. M. Fleuiss, *História Administrativa*, p. 47.

15   Caio Prado Jr, *op. cit.*, pp. 299 and 307.

16   When the Royal Court was transferred to Brazil we had two Courts of Appeal: that of Bahia, created in 1626 and re-established in 1652, and that of Rio de Janeiro, created in 1751. (M. Fleiuss, *op. cit.*, p. 40; Pedro Calmon, 'Organização Judiciária', pp. 87 and 88.) The latter tells us that the Letter Patent of 1751 set up, in the Court of Appeal of Rio, 'a new organ for the execution of justice, a copy of the Board of Appeal of the Royal Court', 'with the same name as the one in Lisbon'. (*Op. cit.*, p. 89.) The Court of Appeal of Rio had jurisdiction over the captainships from Espírito Santo southwards, including the inland ones; about the Court of Appeal of Bahia there is conflicting information. (Cf. Caio Prado Jr, *Formação do Brasil Contemporâneo*, pp. 302 and 318; M. Fleiuss, *op. cit.*, p. 40; Vilhena, *Cartas*, vol. II, p. 308.)

17   J.F. Lisboa, *Obras*, vol. II, pp. 154–5. The same author tells us of the existence, in certain captainships, of *assemblies of justice* presided over by the governor and sometimes composed of members nominated by him. (*Op. cit.*, pp. 154, 166, 167; see also Pedro Calmon, 'Organização Judiciária', p. 89.)

18   Caio Prado Jr, *Formação do Brasil Contemporâneo*, p. 306.

19   Tavares de Lira, *Organização Política e Administrativa*, pp. 27 and 28. On the suppression of the Council of India and the setting up of the Overseas Council, cf. Varnhagen, *História Geral*, vol. II, pp. 76 and 77; vol. III, p. 264.

20   *Obras*, vol. II, p. 75; cf. the passage from an unpublished work of Salamão de Vasconcelos, quoted by Orlando M. Carvalho, *Política de Município*, p. 35.

21   'This elective nature of the ordinary judges and the parish judges makes them, logically, the train-bearers to the local chiefs . . . Thus the colonial magistrature, by the partisanship and corruption of its local judges, becomes one of the most powerful agents in the formation of rural cliques, one of the most effective forces contributing to the tendency to political herding among the lower classes in the country.' (Oliveira Viana, *Populações Meridionais do Brasil*, pp. 183 and 185.) Interesting information on corruption and defects in the colonial judicial system are to be found in an article by Otávio Tarquínio de Sousa, entitled 'Vara Branca e Vara Vermelha'.
The Letter Patent of 4 October 1819 justified the creation of the office of the outside civil judge, criminal judge and judge of the orphans in the city of Oeiras (Piauí), arguing that the ordinary judges were not capable of seeing that the laws were carried out 'through lack of knowledge of them, without the help of zealous and intelligent advisers, and by ties of kinship and friendship they were of necessity constrained in their place of residence and origin'. (Antônio Delgado da Silva, *Coleção da Legislação Portuguêsa*, 1811–1820, p. 701.)

22   See ch. III, note 1 above.

23   Referring to the causes of mismanagement in affairs dependent on the Senate of Bahia, Vilhena tells us that 'many had themselves elected as councillors, undeservedly, with the set intention of securing from their colleagues many unjust things, as far as their usefulness was concerned, for relations, friends and patrons, in spite of the opposition of the president, who was immediately voted down'. (*Cartas*, vol. I, p. 77.)

24   'The outside judge was usually a man of learning, or at least, instructed in Roman Law, a legal code much copied by monarchs by reason of the predominance which it accorded to them in the state.' (Cândido Mendes, *Código Filipino*, note 2 to bk. I, t. 65.)

25   Ordinances, bk. I, t. 65, para. 39.

26   Bk. I, t. 65, para. 69.

27   Bk. I, t. 65, para. 70. The outside judges, nominated by the king, were not subject to inquiry on the part of their successor. (Cândido Mendes, *Código Filipino*, note 3 to the regulation quoted above.)

28   According to Carpenter the inquiries, quarrels and denunciations 'were some of the worst scourges and calamities of that time'. ('O Direito Processual', p. 192.) The general inquiries, the most frightening, were brought to an end with the law of 20 October 1823, which ordered that the law of 12 November 1821 be implemented. This had been approved by the Portuguese Constituent Assembly. (Cândido Mendes, *Código Filipino*, note 3 to bk. I, t. 65, para. 31; João Mendes, *Processo Criminal*, pp. 144–8; Astolfo Resende, 'Polícia Administrativa', p. 405.)

29   'When the accused is tortured and totally denies the crime with which he is charged, the torture will be repeated in three cases.' (Bk. and t. quoted, para. 1; cf. J. Mendes, *O Processo Criminal*, p. 130.)

30   Bk. V, t. 133, para. 3.

31   J. Mendes, *O Processo Criminal*, p. 139. The Courts of Appeal of Maranhão and Pernambuco were created in 1812 and 1821, respectively. (J. Mendes, *ibid.*; M. Fleiuss, *História Administrativa*, p. 40.)

32   J. Mendes, *op. cit.*, p. 140.

33   Letter Patent of 10 May 1808. On the commissioners of police, cf. directive of 25 May 1810 and Decree of 4 November 1825.

34   J. Mendes, *op. cit.*, p. 250.; C.A. de Gouveia, 'A Reforma da Polícia Civil do Distrito Federal', pp. 320–1.

35   Articles 153, 155 and 154. From the time of the Additional Act until the interpretative law and even after that date, many provinces legislated on the judicial system, even to the extent of declaring that qualified judges should be nominated by the provincial presidents. (Cf. Uruguai, *Estudos Práticos*, vol. I, pp. 431 ff.) Articles 2 and 3 of the interpretative law, in the words of the same writer, 'constructed a dike against the torrent of excesses and usurpations which marked the period from 1835 to 1840'. (p. 443)

36   The national government, through the regulation of 30 March 1854, set up in each municipality where it was necessary, a judge–commissioner nominated by the provincial presidents and forcibly imposed upon local authorities. His duty was to 'carry out the measuring and demarcation of land grants or concessions of the national or provincial governments, subject to revaluation, and possessions subject to legal confirmation'. (Articles 30 and 34.) According to a directive of November of the same year 'only if there were no suitably qualified person and an emergency arose, could the nomination of the judge–commissioner fall upon the municipal judges'. (J. Mendes, op. cit., p. 1093, note 3.) The judges–commissioners did not receive regular salaries but emoluments from the parties involved. (*Op. cit.*, p. 1105, note 3.)

37   The office of the *conserving* judge (*juiz conservador*) is of no interest in the present study. He was nominated by the government on the recommendation of British merchants, and matters involving both British and Brazilian citizens were brought before him. According to Enéias Galvão, this private judge for the English was created by a Letter Patent of 4 May 1808 and confirmed by the treaty of 1810. Abolished by the treaty of 1825, which the English never ratified, it was confirmed by another of 1827. It was only suppressed in a directive of 22 November 1832 under protest from Great Britain, as a result of the Criminal Code ('Juízes e Tribunais', p. 334; cf. also Calogéras, *Formação Histórica do Brasil*, pp. 83 and 177; Armitage, *História do Brasil*, p. 54; Eugênio Egas, note; Rio Branco, *Efemérides*, 19 March 1645, p. 167). (Note to second edition: After this work first appeared in 1949, Professor Hans Klinghoffer was kind enough to point out to the author that, contrary to the usual opinion, as a result of this diplomatic exchange the abolition of the *juiz conservador* of the English was only made effective in 1844. See his later study, 'British Jurisdictional Privileges in Spain, Portugal and Brazil: A Historical Reminiscence', in *Österr Zeitschrift für Offentliches Recht*, Vienna 1953.)

Another privilege of the English that was slow to be abolished was concerned with the collection of abeyant inheritances. (Calogéras, *História do Brasil*, p. 178; cf. also Sobreira de Melo, *Comentários à Legislação Brasileira sôbre Bens de Defuntos e Ausentes, Vagos e do Evento*.)

38   The justices of the peace, instituted by Article 162 of the Constitution of 1824, were created by the law of 15 January 1827. On their powers, cf. J. Mendes, *O Processo Criminal*, p. 156; Astolfo Resende, *op. cit.*, p. 407. On the details incompatible with the exercise of functions, cf. Cortines Laxe, *Regimento*, pp. 131 ff. of the first edition.

The law of 6 June 1831 had already extended the competence of the justices of the peace, permitting them to nominate 'their own delegates in the districts, and abolishing the neighbourhood officials'. (J. Mendes, *O Processo Criminal*, p. 162.) On the powers of the justice of the peace in the Code of 32, cf. Carpenter, 'O Direito Processual', pp. 190–1. Later we shall refer to the police guards under the command of the justices of the peace.

39   Carpenter, *op. cit.*, p. 200; J. Mendes, *O Processo Criminal*, pp. 170 ff. Armitage refers to the links between the justices of the peace and the political parties as follows: 'The municipalities and the justices of the peace were, by virtue of the electoral system, representatives of a party. In cases where this party was in agreement with the government all went well, although the administration was always obliged to treat these authorities with the greatest tact and care, otherwise it could not be expected that any individual would perform any job disinterestedly; and in the contrary cases, when the opposition party was stronger the government's authority became little more than nominal: it promulgated its edicts in vain, they were not obeyed.' (*História do Brasil*, p. 291.)

40   'Here, the government doubtless has in mind, as a model, the *prefects* and *sub-prefects* created by the Legislative Assembly of the province of São Paulo, having been convinced that they meet the administrative needs of the province.'

41   See ch. III, note 31, above. Tavares Bastos underlines the contradiction of centralising politicians in these terms: 'In fact, if it is anarchy that they fear, the provincial laws of the time are not anarchic in any way. They all approximate to the type which later was amplified into the law of 1841; all tend to strengthen the executive authority, giving it its own agents in small places.' (*A Província*, pp. 169–70.)

The *presidential* nature of the law of the state of Maranhão was clearly shown in the provision which forbade the vice-president of the province to dismiss prefects or sub-prefects. The Senate Committee for provincial assemblies, according to the evidence of the Visconde do Uruguai, described this prohibition as 'unjust and odious', since 'by national law the vice-presidents exercise all the prerogatives of, and enjoy the same powers as, the presidents'. (*Estudos Práticos*, vol. I, p. 397.)

Carneiro Maia, referring to the prefects of that period, describes them as 'officials antipathetic to the presidency, installed by the provinces in the midst of the chambers, with help from inside the latter, creating voting pressures, and carrying out acts of arbitrary supervision which became so many more curbs on the activity of the municipal bodies'. And he adds 'the institution of the prefects [was] so unpopular that it served as a reason for revolt in Maranhão, and in 1839 when the president was hearing the views of the leaders of both parties in the light of the capitulation terms proposed by the insurgents, the party leaders were both of the opinion that the law of the prefects should be revoked'. (Pp. 240 and 241, note 8.) The author bases himself on Pereira da Silva, whose work (*História do Brasil de 1831 a 1840*, pp. 279 and 280–1), with an imprecise and incomplete reference, sends us back to the source. This is the 'Memória Histórica e Documental da Revolução desde 1839 até 1840', by Domingos José Gonçalves de Magalhães, published in volume X of the *Revista* of The Historical and Geographical Institute of Brazil (I.H.G.B.).

In the words of Pereira da Silva, with the president meeting the leaders of the two parties in the capital at the presidential palace, 'the leader of the *bentevi* party, Dr Joaquim Franco de Sá, said that it seemed to him right that the provincial assembly should be called to revoke the law setting up the office of prefect and to adopt certain other measures by which they could eliminate the serious political pretext for the revolt, reducing it thereby to a simple uprising of rogues and brigands who could be exterminated with vigour'. Gonçalves de Magalhães tells us that the calling of the assembly at the suggestion of the *bentevi* leader was done 'on the pretext' of concluding the vote on the budget, and he quotes the rebels' proposals, where we read: 'Article 2 – The military council declares that the people and the troops, united and armed, have no other objective than to ask His Worship the President of the Province to abrogate the provincial laws which created the prefects and offended against national law on the organisation of a National Guard, apart from the following articles.' (p. 282)

On the unpopularity of the prefects in the same province where they were created in the first place, we refer to the document kindly made available to us by Professor Hélio Viana, and to which we have already alluded. (Ch. II, note 44.) Addressing itself in an official letter of 13 January 1838 to the Chamber of São Sebastião, the Chamber of Ubatuba declares: 'we have recognised from experience how unproductive has been the creation of prefects in our respective municipalities, since, instead of carrying out the aims envisaged by the law of co-operating with the chambers to the advantage of the municipalities and putting their decisions into effect with despatch, the opposite has occurred, and these employees are seizing immense power for themselves. If this power is not checked, it will constitute at the very least a threat to the sovereignty of the chambers. And since this major disadvantage has also been recognised by various other chambers in the province, they are, at the invitation of the chamber of the capital and that of Sorocaba, uniting to present a petition to the legislative body of the province asking for the revocation of the law which created the prefects. It is for this reason that this chamber is asking you to join with us in making representation when the Legislative Assembly of the province meets.'

42   See above, ch. II, note 49.

43   Regulated, as far as the criminal section was concerned by Decree–Law No. 120 of 31 January 1842.

44   The powers of the chief of police were defined in a decree of 29
March 1833. (Cf. C.A. de Gouveia, 'A Reforma da Polícia', p. 321.)
45   Experience has shown that these gatherings, for easily understood
reasons, almost never took place.
46   J. Mendes, *O Processo Criminal*, pp. 168–9.
47   On the investiture of the police authorities under the law of 1841,
see Pimenta Bueno, *Apontamentos sôbre o Processo Criminal Brasileiro*,
pp. 6 ff.
48   J. Mendes, *O Processo Criminal*, pp. 186–7. The justices of the peace
also had police functions. (Cf. Pimenta Bueno, *O Processo Criminal*, p. 17.)
    Defining the principal features of the law of 1841, Professor Carpenter
said: 'The police in Brazil were, so to speak, created by the law of 3
December.' This law 'committed two serious errors in creating the police
authorities: the first error was to give the police the power to conduct court
cases and pronounce sentence . . . The law of 3 December gave the police
the power to take individuals to law, i.e. to formulate the criminal's crime,
and the power to pass judgement, i.e. to determine innocence or guilt . . .
The second error was the failure to give to police sheriffs and their deputies, dispersed throughout the country, any tenure in their posts or any
independence. They were therefore obliged to accept any nominated
official, did not receive any salary and could be dismissed summarily. This
legion of sheriffs and deputies, during elections and at other times, could
be a powerful instrument of compulsion in the hands of the government.'
('O Direito Processual', pp. 202 and 208.) The sheriffs and deputies were
substituted for by regular proxies. (Pimenta Bueno, *O Processo Criminal*,
pp. 8 and 9.)
    Judgements as to guilt or innocence by sheriffs or deputies were subject
to confirmation, modification or revocation by the municipal judge, against
whose decision there was the right of appeal. (Cf. Pimenta Bueno, *op. cit.*,
p. 15.) It is well known, however, that the provision for appeal does not
redeem all the harm done in the first place, especially in criminal matters.
    'One of the functions of the police consisted in submitting to the com-
petent judges, *when they considered it appropriate*, all the facts, evidence
and clarifications which they had obtained about an offence, together with
an exposition of the case and its circumstances, with a view to formulating
the charge. But . . . [the law adds] if more than one competent authority
begins a process of litigation, *it is the chief of police or the sheriff who will
be the one to prosecute*. The police, therefore, remained in the position of
an investigating tribunal with marked superiority.' (Astolfo Resende,
'Polícia Administrativa', pp. 411–12.)
49   Otávio Tarquínio de Sousa, *Bernardo Pereira de Vasconcelos*, pp. 234
and 235.
50   'The law of 3 December 1841 served to accelerate the imminent
explosion.' It was 'one of the determining factors in the revolution of 1842'.
(Carpenter, *op. cit.*, pp. 205 and 207.) 'The country', says Joaquim
Nabuco, 'saw the Liberal government of 1844–8 fail to carry out any of
its promises; fail to touch even one of the laws of 1841, against which the
party had launched the two rebellions of Minas Gerais and São Paulo.' (*Um
Estadista do Império*, vol. I, p. 72.)

51   Speech in the session of 23 August 1870, in J. Mendes, *O Processo Criminal*, p. 202. Otávio Tarquínio de Sousa writes: 'It was the same Liberal Party, which in 1842 rose up in arms against the law of 3 December 1841, which charged itself with demonstrating that it was not so evil after all. From 1844 to 1848, for more than four years, when the Liberal Party held power in the majority of chambers, there was not the least pressure to repeal it. Moreover, the Liberal Party used it, finding it excellent. Vasconcelos could not have had better confirmation of his political genius than this sanction by the Liberal Party.' Referring to the elections of 1844, the same author writes that they 'proceeded with fraud, violence and oppression, in which the Liberals had specialised in 1840; and the principal weapon was the notorious law of 3 December, the same one which had caused them to take up arms in 1842. Moral and political Phariseeism exists at all times.' (Otávio Tarquínio de Sousa, *Bernardo Pereira de Vasconcelos*, pp. 236 and 245.) Cf. quotation from Nabuco in the preceding note.

52   'This august chamber knows that in Pará the president of the province and the sergeant at arms were assassinated and the province given over to the horrors of rebellion and anarchy; that the president of Bahia was assassinated as well, and there the celebrated *Sabinada* [a revolution which took place in Bahia during the Regency period] took place; in Paraíba, an attempt was made on the president's life; in many other provinces revolutionary fury raged in a most terrifying manner! The province of Maranhão had to struggle against the Balaiadar [the revolution of the so-called *Babaios* in Maranhão, 1838–40]. Pernambuco and Alagoas with the war of the *Cabanos* [a political faction in Pernambuco c. 1830], in Panelas de Miranda and Juaripe; the regular detachments of troops of the line became so undisciplined that twice they rebelled in the important city of Recife. The criminal statistics were dreadful! In all provinces federalist societies were created; and as if the country were not sufficiently afflicted and dismantled by all this, the provincial assemblies, each interpreting the Additional Act in its own fashion, sought to render themselves all powerful, arrogating the prerogatives of national bodies. There was disorder, anarchy and chaos everywhere!' (Deputy Mateus Casado in J. Mendes, *O Processo Criminal*, pp. 201–2.)

53   Cf. Caio Prado Jr, *Evolução Política do Brasil*, pp. 135–64; Djacir Meneses, *O Outro Nordeste*, pp. 14, 79, 122, 167, etc. On the revolt of the *Cabanos*, see the revealing comments of Basílio de Magalhães in *Estudos de História do Brasil*, pp. 241 ff.

'I believe', said Deputy Alencar Araripe in the session of 10 September 1870, 'that it was not the Criminal Code which produced the state of anarchy referred to, nor the state of social disorder which has been alleged. The revolutions or movements which took place in the country at that time did not arise out of the fact that common crimes were going unpunished but out of the raising of political consciousness and expectation; moreover, even after the law of 3 December was passed, revolutions and disturbances continued to take place.' (J. Mendes, *O Processo Criminal*, p. 203.)

The following passage from Gilberto Freire on the theft of slaves in the cities of the North in the first decades of the nineteenth century, also shows that it is an exaggeration to attribute the lawlessness of this period to the Criminal Code: 'Agrarian interests still dominated the provincial presidencies, the judicial system and the police. One can understand then how kindly disposed they would be towards bands of slave thieves.' (*Sobrados e Mucambos*, p. 80.)

54   Tavares Bastos wrote: 'Is it by chance that this tyrannical law has fulfilled its ostensible purpose — to prevent crime going unpunished? Contemporaries give their answer; the news received every day from the interior provides an answer.' And in another passage: 'the Criminal Code imagined a country in which there was an equal level of civilisation, morality, respect for the law, and aversion to crime throughout: this generous conviction created the free police, the police of the justices of the peace. The law of 3 December imagined a corrupt country, an anarchic population: this sad hopelessness created the police of the janissaries with which the executive dreamed of, and won, dictatorial power.' (*A Província*, pp. 210 and 163.)

55   Regulated by Decree No. 4824, of 22 November 1871.

56   Carpenter, 'O Direito Processual', p. 211; see résumé in J. Mendes, *O Processo Criminal*, pp. 274—5.

57   Carpenter, *op. cit.*, p. 208.

58   J. Mendes refers to various official documents of different periods, denouncing violence and arbitrary acts relating to arrests. (*O Processo Criminal*, pp. 142, 160, 164, 165, 194, 197, 201.)

59   Nabuco de Araujo, judge and politician, decried the setting up of political magistrates with vehemence. This is his deposition: 'The magistrature is despondent as to its vocation, as to its future, because of the political magistrates, because it is only they who will enjoy any advantage.' (J. Nabuco, *Um Estadista do Império*, vol. I, p. 88.)

   'It is the government', said Pimenta Bueno, 'which gives the financial advantages, promotions, honours and distinctions; the government which confirms in office or removes, the government which issues writs not only to the magistrates but to their children, relations and friends.' (*O Processo Criminal*, p. 39.)

   In the burning words of Tavares Bastos, the centralising politicians of the Empire 'fettered and degraded the principle of the lifelong magistrature': the institution of the 'debunked judge' removed the notion of perpetuity; that of immovability disappeared in the face of removals, promotions from one area to another and the obligatory despatches of the chief of police; finally, the commissions undermined its independence. The legal judge, in such conditions, became 'an assiduous solicitor for audiences with the provincial president and the Minister of Justice'. (*A Província*, pp. 196—7.)

   According to Carlos Maximiliano, in a single day — 4 July 1843 — 52 judges were removed for political reasons. (*Comentários à Constituição*, p. 50, note 3.)

60   Jobs for relations, removals and promotions are the principal factors.

61   Several state constitutions under the regime of 1891 authorised the creation of municipal guards or local police. (Cf. Felisbelo Freire, *As Constituições Estados*, pp. 209 and 216.)

62   According to Castro Nunes (1920), in some states, 'like Paraíba and

Ceará, the prefect (nominated by the governor) is the local police chief'. (*Do Estado Federado*, p. 210.) In Alagoas, the municipal council, on the recommendation of the intendant, nominated a police commissioner for the municipality, and assistant commissioners for the districts. (*Op. cit.*, p. 395.) In Rio Grande do Sul, the sub-intendant, nominated by the intendant, exercised 'the functions of police authority' in the district concerned (*op. cit.*, p. 521), etc. It should be noted that when there was a municipal police force, the general rule was that it remained under the control of the executive.

63 To cite only one example, let us remember that the Interventor Nisio Batista de Oliveira, in the period of 'government by the judges', instituted in Minas the career police force, with the intention of giving the police officers independence and impartiality. (Decree–Law No. 1591 of 28 December 1945.) But this reform, whose merit we failed to appreciate, was very quickly rescinded when the partisan government of the Interventor João Beraldo took power in the state. (Decree–Law No. 1684 of 23 February 1946.) Pedro Aleixo wrote, with reference to this law: 'We have therefore reverted to the system of factional police and *ad hoc* officers. With the exception of the capital and the municipalities where Regional Delegacies exist, the police officers will be laymen, nominated on the recommendation of local political leaders.' ('Polícia de Fâccao e Delegados *ad-hoc*'.)

64 In Minas Gerais, Decree–Law No. 2105 of 25 April 1947 included among the requirements for the exercise of the functions of police sheriff and deputy, that the candidate be morally suitable; he should never have been 'charged and tried' for any of a number of specific crimes. This law also allows any citizen to contest the nomination within a period of fifteen days from the publication of the document of nomination. The objection should be examined by the Secretary for the Interior or by a committee 'composed of men of well-known and blameless public reputation', under the presidency of the chief of police.

65 C.A. de Gouveia, 'A Reforma', p. 322.

66 The Constitution of 1946 (Article 5, XV, f), which reproduced measures analogous to those of the Constitutions of 1934 (Article 5, XIX, 1) and 1937 (Article 16, XXVI), gives exclusive competence to the Union to legislate on 'the organisation, instruction, legal powers and privileges of the military police, and the general conditions governing their use by the federal government, in case of general mobilisation or in time of war'. The constitutional authorisation was converted into Federal Law No. 192 of 17 January 1936, which established, with regard to military justice in the states, the same principle currently enshrined in Article 124, XII, of the Constitution: 'Military Justice in the states, established in observance of the general concepts of federal law, will have as courts of the first instance, councils of justice, and as a court of the second instance, a special tribunal or a Tribunal of Justice.' Moreover, the problem of punishing crimes of a military nature, and errors of discipline committed by officers and other ranks of the military police of the states, provoked much controversy. For the regime of 1891, see the legislation and legal comments quoted by Castro Nunes in *As Constituições Estaduais*, paras. 55, 56 and 75. On the compatibility of Law No. 192 with the Constitution of 1937, see the interview granted by the Minister Costa Manso to *O Jornal* of 12 December 1937. In an agreement of the Federal Supreme Court of 11 October 1944, mentioned by the Minister Filadelfo Azevedo, various judgements of that court on the subject are referred to, and all the relevant federal legislation is carefully indicated. (*Revista de Direito Administrativo*, vol. VI, pp. 131 ff.)

67   Decree–Law No. 20,348 of 20 August 1931 (code of the interventors) laid down that the states could not devote more than 10% of ordinary expenditure to the military police except in special circumstances, and then on the authorisation of the provisional government; the state police was forbidden to use or own artillery or planes, and the allocation of automatic weapons and ammunition to each body of infantry or cavalry could not exceed the regular allocation of similar army units, the excess had to be handed over to the Minister of Defence by the interventors. (Article 24) These measures are a clear reflection of the fear that the military police might become superior to the army in arms and ammunition.

In spite of this, state expenditure for 'public safety and defence' for 1932 reached 176,425 *contos*, representing 14.86% of the total budgeted for that year. The allocations for 'public education' (15.62%), 'the external debt' (16.81%), and 'public works and transport' (21.63%), were higher than this. Expenditure for 'health and medical services' was a mere 4.8%, with 'the legal system' even lower at 3.07%. In some states (Paraíba, Pernambuco, E. Santo, Paraná, Rio Grande do Sul and Mato Grosso) the expenditure for 'public safety and defence' exceeded that envisaged for 'education'. (*Finanças dos Estados*, vol. I, table of p. 232.)

Domingos Velasco, arguing against the excessive autonomy of the states under the regime of 1891, said in the Constituent Assembly of 1934: 'In 1917 state forces reached a figure of 29,797 men, while the army had 24,070. In 1919 expenditure on the public forces of the states reached the figure of 58,778,327,000 *cruzeiros*, and for education the amount was 44,138,144,000 *cruzeiros*.' He chose the earliest available figures because, he said, 'from 1922 until now there has been an excess which can be explained by the state of revolution in which we have been living'. And he concluded: 'the allocation for the upkeep of the military police forces is exceeded only by that assigned to the payment of public debts, another ill effect of an excess of autonomy'. (*Anais*, vol. II, p. 295.)

68   Referring in 1935 to the problem of the presidential succession, Hermes Lima wrote as follows in an article entitled 'Que Federação é Esta?': 'Three large states at least desire it. Three large states which symbolise all our economic power oppose it. Three large states are armed to the teeth to defend their autonomy. What sort of Federation is it in which the basis on which it functions – the autonomy of the states – has to be defended by force?'

69   Constitution of 1946, Article 183: 'The military police forces, established for reasons of internal security and the maintenance of order in the states, the territories and in the Federal District, are regarded as auxiliary forces – reserves of the army. When mobilised in the service of the Union, in times of foreign or civil war, their personnel will enjoy the same advantages given to personnel of the army.' The Constitution of 1934 contained similar provisions. (Article 167) That of 1937 left to ordinary federal law the decision as to how military police were to be used 'as reserve forces of the army'. (Article 16, XXVI.)

70　Decree–Law No. 6378 of 23 March 1944, altered by Decree–Law No. 9353 of 13 June 1946. Decree–Law No. 5839 of 21 September 1943 'decides on the setting up of a guard of a civil nature for the policing of the Federal Territories'. (C.A. de Gouveia, 'A Reforma', p. 322.)

71　The local legal system in the Federal District and that of the Territory of Acre were the subject of laws emanating from the Union. On juridical division under the regime of 1891, which was not the same in all states, see J. Mendes, *Direito Judiciário Brasiliero*, pp. 83–4. Decree–Law No. 311 of 2 March 1938, among the various rules which it adopted to make the territorial division of Brazil more systematic, made the names of the various divisions more uniform, and made administrative boundaries coincide with juridical ones, laying down that the states and the Union could only alter the territorial divisions of the units of the Federation every five years. Throughout the country, the juridical divisions were known as *comarcas*, *têrmos* and *distritos*. The administrative districts (*distritos*) and the juridical ones were made to coincide, and the *têrmos* and *comarcas* continued to embrace one or more municipalities, with the limits of these being always respected. (Cf. the study of the I.B.G.E. (Brazilian Institute of Geography & Statistics) which gave rise to the legal decree cited in the *Revista Forense*, vol. 73, p. 651; this document describes, in the form of a summary, the defects of the system until then in force in the territorial division of the country.)

72　The federal legal system was created by Decree–Law No. 848 of 1890, and its organisation and procedure were consolidated by Decree–Law No. 3084 of 5 November 1898. (Cf. José Tavares Bastos, *Organização Judiciária Federal*.) Outside the chief centres of the sections, subsidiary, substitute centres were created by federal decree, on the representation of the sectional judge; nominations were made every four years and could theoretically fall upon laymen. (Law No. 221 of 1894, Article 3.) The electoral law of 1904 decreed the nomination of three subsidiary centres in every municipality, and this provision was reinforced by the electoral law of 1916. Before the setting up of the subsidiary centres in all the municipalities, the federal legal system had often asked the local authorities to deal with routine legal matters. (Cf. C. Maximiliano, *Comentários*, pp. 682–3.)

73　According to Law No. 224 in all areas where there were deputies of the sectional judge, there was also an assistant to the attorney general; the electoral laws of 1904 and 1916 established assistant attorneys in all municipalities, with laymen being eligible for nomination.

74　Article 60.

75　The name varied: High Court of Justice, Court of Appeal, or just Appeal (*Relação*), Court of Justice, High Court, High Court of Justice.

76　In Rio Grande do Sul they were known as divisional judges (i.e. *de comarca*).

77   The name of the body varied from state to state. In the Federal District immediately below the district judges came the praetors and their assistants.

78   Castro Nunes, *As Constituições Estaduais*, pp. 142, 149–50; Felisbelo Freire, *As Constituições dos Estades*, ch. X. João Mendes also mentions the correctional assemblies or tribunals which existed in many states. (*Direito Judiciário Brasileiro*, p. 85.)

79   J. Mendes, *op. cit.*

80   See ch. V, note 85 and the corresponding text.

81   An interesting summary of the main arguments can be found in the judgement quoted by Mendonça de Azevedo, *A Constituição*, p. 133, No. 352. In the same work on pp. 129 ff. a number of other decisions taken at different times are listed.

82   Article 6, i.

83   Cf. the judgement of the Supreme Court of 4 January 1908, in Mendonça de Azevedo, *op. cit.*, p. 130, No. 340.

84   Sebastião José de Sousa, opposing the granting of the power of final decision to lay judges, referred to their habit of giving themselves advisers, clandestinely, to hide their lack of competence ('Cômpetencia dos Juízes de Paz'). According to Cândido Mendes, lay judges in colonial and even in imperial times could have advisers, in conformity with a habit sanctioned by long use and by Letters Patent of 1785 and 1802 and by a decision of the Supreme Court of Justice in 1841. (*Código Filipino*, note 1 to Ordinance of bk. I, t. 65, para. 10.)

On the party affiliations of justices of the peace, Deputy Pedro Aleixo had this to say in 1934: 'The justices of the peace belong to political parties, to political factions, and many of them are wholly preoccupied with the factional interests of their group. Now, among the functions which are commonly attributes to the justice of the peace, is that of substituting for the municipal judge and at times the district judge himself. Police authorities of municipalities are often partisan, given that they are nominated on the suggestion of local political leaders. There is no opponent who can resist the collusive forces of the partisan judge and the factional police chief. On the eve of electoral contests the opposition supporters of remote districts will often find themselves arrested in the subdivisional or divisional headquarters.' (*Anais*, vol. XI, p. 403.)

85   Several of the numerous expedients used by the states to abolish or reduce the privileges of the magistrature are given in Amaro Cavalcânti, *Regime Federativo*, pp. 365–6 and note 22.

The then Deputy Raul Fernandes in the Constituent Assembly of 1934 referred to the legal systems operated in the states under the regime of 1891, as follows: 'Hence the clamour which reached the centre from the periphery: it was public opinion in the states complaining that the Judiciary in a general sense, save a few notable exceptions, did not have the support promised in the Constitution, since state magistrates lacked basic guarantees. The governments were free to dispense with them when they wished, by abolishing their divisions or by removing them in defiance of the law from one division to another, by means of a reform in their relevant laws, and when all of this was not enough some governments oppressed them to the point of sadism: they deprived the magistrates of their salaries.' (*Anais*, vol. XII, p. 237.)

86   Cf. Bilac Pinto, *Ministério Público*, pp. 26 ff. In the most backward areas, the attorney's assistants were usually laymen.
87   Articles 7, e; 12, No. V; and 104.
88   Articles 9, e, 3; 103, e and ff.
89   Articles 7, VII, g; e, 124.
90   Cf. Decree–Law No. 6 of 16 November 1937.
91   See Constitutional Laws No. 2 of 16 May 1938, and No. 8 of 12 October 1942, the second of which ordered that salaries should be related to length of service in cases where Article 177 was applied. As far as the states were concerned, the application of Article 177 was originally left to the discretion of the governor or interventor; but later prior authorisation by the President of the Republic was required. (Decree–Law No. 1202 of 8 April 1939, Article 33, No. 14.) This formality was later dispensed with at the time of the political campaign of 1945. (Decree–Law No. 7518, of 3 May 1945, Article 1, e.) Article 177 of the Charter of 10 November was revoked by the Constitutional Law of 7 November 1945 (No. 12), and Law No. 171 of 15 December 1947 made possible the return of those who had been compulsorily removed or retired in that exceptional way.
92   Constitution of 1934, Article 104, para. 4; Constitution of 1937, Article 104.
93   Decree–Law No. 536 of 5 July 1938.
94   Article 124, X.
95   The intention of the proposer of the amendment, according to José Duarte (*A Constituição*, vol. II, p. 450), was 'to avoid abuses which the states frequently commit in their judicial arrangements. By a misinterpretation of the law or by bad editing of the text, it is very often supposed that untrained, informal, elected or nominated justices of the peace can be given the power of passing sentences.'
96   Constitution of 1934, Article 104, para. 7; Constitution of 1937, Article 106; Constitution of 1946, Article 124, XI.
97   Articles 127 and 128. As for the Ministry of Justice under the regime of 1934, see Bilac Pinto, *Ministério Público*, pp. 31 ff.
98   A. de Roure, *Formação Constitucional do Brasil*, p. 137.
99   Articles 151 and 152. In the Constituent Assembly dissolved in 1823 the proposal relating to the jury was discussed and voted upon. A summary of the debates as well as a discussion of the bill relating to the jury of the press is to be found in A. de Roure, *Formação Constitucional do Brasil*, pp. 131–8 and 154–5. In the matter of civil questions 'the jury did not ever exercise the functions assigned to it' by the Constitution of 1824. (Cf. Cândido de Oliveira Filho, *A Reforma do Júri*, p. 9.)
100   According to Conselheiro Cândido de Oliveira, Decree–Law No. 562 of 1850 and Decree–Law No. 1090 of 1860, reduced the powers of the jury, but these were largely restored by Decree–Law No. 3163 of 7 July 1883. 'In the last stage of legislation of the Empire the jury was, consequently, the common type of court for the greater number of crimes listed in the Penal Code. Its authority was only not exercised: (a) over

those exempted by the Constitution; (b) in so-called police crimes; (c) in crimes involving the responsibility of public functionaries; (d) contraband offences, counterfeiting offences and others listed in the Decree of 2 July 1850.' ('A Justiça', p. 77.)

101   Summary of the debates in A. de Roure, *A Constituinte Republicana*, vol. II, pp. 122 ff.

102   '[N]o power constituted in this Republic, has the right to lay hands on the jury to diminish its powers. And if they do so all these reforms will be void . . . Guaranteeing the jury does not mean merely guaranteeing its name. The substance, the reality and the power of it must be guaranteed.' (*Comentários à Constituição*, vol. VI, p. 182.)

103   'The jury, therefore, is not a sort of *noli me tangere*. It must be maintained but its organisation must be changed in the interest of justice and liberty . . . Yet in reforming the institution, no innovation should be made which would cause it to be sacrificed . . . on the contrary . . . that would be to abolish a constitutional guarantee under disguise.' (Barbalho, *Constituição*, pp. 337–8.)

104   Cf. Law No. 515 of 3 November 1898. Before this and after Decree–Law No. 848, Law No. 224 of 1894 also discussed the idea of the Federal Jury.

105   Law No. 515 on the Federal Jury, Alfredo Pinto's bill on the legal system of the Federal District, and the law of Rio Grande do Sul, which we shall mention later, provided an opportunity for the important studies in which Rui Barbosa sought to define the characteristics of the institution of the jury.

106   Carlos Maximiliano tells us (*Comentários*, p. 811): 'The judge Alcides Lima rebelled against the law and, presiding over the popular tribunal, excluded citizens rejected by the parties from the council of judgement. He was brought before the Supreme Court which, taking into account a revised appeal, absolved him from punishment on other grounds and declared the law of Rio Grande do Sul to be constitutional.' (Judgement No. 406 of 7 October 1899.) Cf. also the judgement of 19 October 1904 summarized in Mendonça de Azevedo, *A Constituição*, p. 456, No. 1667. Pinto da Rocha refers to the case of Alcides Lima, giving more details. (*O Júri e Sua Evolução*, pp. 193–4, 206 ff.)

107   See the exposé of his reasons given by the author of the bill, High Court Judge Rafael Almeida Magalhães, in *Revista Forense*, vol. 47, pp. 190 ff.

108   Cf. exposition of reasons for the Decree–Law No. 167 of 1938. (*Revista Forense*, vol. 73, p. 220.)

109   J. Mendes, *Direito Judiciário Brasileiro*, p. 87; Cândido de Oliveira, 'A Justiça', pp. 87–9; Castro Nunes, *As Constituições Estaduais*, vol. I, pp. 152–3.

110   Article 72.

111   Article 5, XIX, a.

112   Subsequently incorporated, with slight alterations, in the Penal Code of 1941, Cf. Ari Franco, *O Juri no Estado Novo*.

113   Article 96 of Decree–Law No. 167.

114   Exposition of the reasons for the Penal Code of 1941, para. XIV.

115   On the formalities of the amendment arising from the precept cited, cf. J. Duarte, *A Constituição*, vol. III, pp. 68 ff.

116   Law No. 263 of 23 February 1948.

117   Cf. for example, Pimenta Bueno, *Processo Criminal*, p. 40.

118   After underlining the wide-ranging powers held by the jury in the last phase of the Empire, repeating almost literally the words of his father, already given in another note, Cândido de Oliveira Filho said: 'In the Republic, on the contrary, while the competence of the jury is generally recognised in theory, it is in fact a rare exception.' (*A Reforma do Júri*, p. 24.)

119   'The Imperial Law on penal procedure, generally maintained by the Republic, helped to assure the predominance of political despots, laying down that the clerk of accusation could not set aside the decisions of the jury when the Ministry of Justice agreed with them.' In acquittals obtained through political influence, 'the public prosecutor, with rare exceptions, did not appeal'. (Cândido de Oliveira Filho, *op. cit.*, p. 20.)

Pinto da Rocha, after emphasising the political dependence of divisional and even High Court Judges in Rio Grande do Sul, referred to the jury as follows: 'The dominant political group will get whatever it wants from a tribunal of this sort.' (*O Júri*, p. 219.)

Cândido de Oliveira Filho explained the mechanism of political influence on the jury as follows: 'The legislators of the Empire, generally followed in this by those of the Republic', surrendered 'the power to compile lists of jurors to the justices of the peace, judges of the lowest rank, elected by the parties, and devoid of all the conditions which ensure the independence of magistrates . . . In these lists were included, with rare exceptions, only the unconditional electors of political leaders, electors who were the justices of the peace themselves. The method was engineered to make the jury a homogeneous body prepared to condemn or acquit in agreement with the orders of the local leaders . . . Opposition to the exclusiveness of this list was rare, since jury service in Brazil had always been held to be a heavy burden . . . except for those who made a way of life of it, managing the vote . . . Through this system the jury, instead of being the conscience of the society, was simply the conscience of the political chiefs.' (*Op. cit.*, pp. 18–19.)

It should be said in passing that, at the present time, it is the magistrate himself who draws up the list of jurors.

120   'Ordinarily, the jury is excessively benign and morbidly sentimental . . . The sympathies of the jury are not with those who die but with those who kill.' (Viveiros de Castro, quoted by Pinto da Rocha, *op. cit.*, p. 170.)

121   *Formação do Brasil Contemporâneo*, p. 322. 'Type of National Guard' is how Capistrano de Abreu describes the citizens' militias. (*Capítulos*, p. 81.) 'The ancient citizens' militias, according to what we read in M. Fleiuss, were in existence as early as 1575 in several captainships; they were later regulated by laws of 18 October 1709, 21 April 1739, 30 April 1758, 24 February and 7 June 1765.' (*História Administrativa*, p. 158.) Caio Prado Júnior explains that they were created in Portugal by a law of December 1569, put into effect on 10 December of the following year, and reinforced by a regulation of 1758 which has various measures relating to Brazil. (*Op. cit.*, p. 311, note 22.)

According to Cortines Laxe, the Letters Patent of 18 October 1709 and 28 February 1816, made it the duty of the chambers, under the presidency of the divisional magistrate or the divisional supervisor, to undertake the election of the militia commanders, and also, under the presidency of the commander, the election of the sergeants. (*Regimento*, pp. XV–XVI.) This was the reason for the following observation made by Caio Prado Júnior: 'If we look again at the names to be found in the commanding posts of the corps of militia, we are going to discover in them the cream of the colonial population, its economic and social exponents.' (*Formação do Brasil Contemporâneo*, p. 325, note.)

122   Cf. the regulation of Tomé de Sousa. (Passages in J.F. Lisboa, *Obras*, vol. II, pp. 138–9.)

123   M. Fleiuss, *História Administrativa*, pp. 160 and 161.

124   'These guards had to help the judicial authorities, were obliged to obey and to appear already armed when summoned by judges or police sheriffs.' Cf. Visconde do Uruguai, *Estudos Práticos*, vo. II, p. 158, where he says that the law was very defective and was incompletely regulated on 14 June 1831. In the words of M. Fleiuss, the municipal guards were 'Composed of citizens who qualified to be registered as electors, excepting only the unfit and those prevented by public duties, armed at their own expense when they lacked a spear, but having the right to be subsequently indemnified for any expense, organised in companies under the orders of a general commander for each district, immediately subordinate to the justices of the peace.' (*Op. cit.*, pp. 157–8.)

125   M. Fleiuss, *op. cit.*, p. 160.

126   Regulation referring only to the Court, in a decree of 22 October 1831. (Cf. Uruguai, *op. cit.*, p. 159.)

127   Cf. Uruguai who summarises the controversy aroused by these laws in the light of the Additional Act. He says that the national government not only tolerated but also recognised the exercise of such prerogatives by the provinces. (*Op. cit.*, pp. 157–71.)

128   Uruguai, *op. cit.*, p. 160.

129   M. Fleiuss: 'The nomination of officers, subalterns and captains was done under the presidency of the justice of the peace; that of colonels and majors by the Government of the Regency, which also nominated instructors and quartermasters on the proposals of the chief of the legion. (*Op. cit.*, p. 161.) Tavares Bastos refers to this in some detail. (*A Província*, p. 180.)

130   Cf. A.C. Tavares Bastos, *A Província*, pp. 181 ff.; M. Fleiuss, *op. cit.*, pp. 212 ff., where the later legislation is quoted. Already, before the general law of 1850, some provinces had converted elective posts into nominative ones and made other alterations in the organisation of the National Guard. The Assembly of Minas Gerais even went so far, in a law of 1848, as to declare 'all the posts to be held in perpetuity and for life'. Cf. Tavares Bastos, *op. cit.*, pp. 181–2; Uruguai, *Estudos Práticos*, vol. I, pp. 404 ff. The latter, considering such laws to be in line with the dominant

views of the exorbitant organs of national government set up by the
Additional Act, refers to the political motives which in some states determined the reform of the National Guard.

131 'Commander in Chief of the police, the Minister of Justice also held
the same post in the National Guard. Here are two armies which march at
the sign of command. Conquest is certain; hence, unanimous chambers
since 1850!' (Tavares Bastos, *A Província*, p. 183.)

132 In the unfolding of 'military questions' which preceded the collapse
of the monarchy, it is well known that the decision of the government to
mobilise the police and the National Guard of the city of Rio de Janeiro
was interpreted as a manifestation of the proposal to dissolve the army. (C.
Maximiliano, *Comentários*, pp. 75 and 76.)

133 Decree–Law No. 13,040 of 29 May 1918 which regulated the organisation of the National Army of the second line, declared 'the units, commands and services which currently form the National Guard, to be dissolved'. (Article 22) At the same time it safeguarded the rights and
prerogatives of the officers of this body, and laid down the means by which
they could be accommodated in the army of the second line. This decree
was issued by means of the authority which Law No. 3446 of 1917 (Article
1, III, No. 32) had conferred on the Executive to 'reform the measures
which regulate the National Guard'.

134 The Union also benefited after 1930, especially during the *Estado
Novo*.

6. Electoral legislation

1 Ch. III.

2 For this chapter our main sources were the specialist studies of Francisco Belisário, Tavares de Lira, Colares Moreira, Barão de Paranapiacaba,
João Cabral, Domingos Velasco and Leão Vieira Starling. On many
occasions we also refer to legal texts and other sources which will be indicated at the relevant places.

3 Article 122 ff.

4 Article 90 ff.

5 'In the chamber of 1826 there was the first Committee of 5 which
came to have such great importance in our parliamentary tradition and
which was given the task of verifying the documents or titles assigned to
the elected deputies.' (O. Tarquínio de Sousa, *Bernardo Pereira de Vasconcelos*, p. 22.)

6 According to the instructions of 19 June 1822, the secretaries and
examiners were also chosen by acclamation.

7 In this summary of the legislation of the Empire up to but not including the Saraiva Law, we shall use the term *voter* for the electors of the first
ballot, reserving the term *electors* for those of the second ballot, in accordance with usage in the laws themselves.

8 Francisco Belisário, *O Sistema Eleitoral no Brasil*, pp. 46–8; Tavares
de Lira, 'Regime Eleitoral', pp. 334–6; M. Fleiuss, *História Administrativa*,
p. 245; Barão de Paranapiacaba, 'Eleições', p. 251. In the election of 1840,
nicknamed the election 'of the cudgel' (O. Tarquínio de Sousa, *op. cit.*, pp.

230 and 239), 'violence and things contrary to law and morality, which exceeded all previous examples', were committed. (Calógeras, *Formação Histórica do Brasil*, p. 202.)
9   Tavares de Lira, 'Regime Eleitoral', p. 337; O. Tarquínio de Sousa, *Bernardo Pereira de Vasconcelos*, p. 245. Basílio de Magalhães states that, by the law of 3 December 1841, 'the running of elections was put in the hands of the police, always the beneficiaries of the transitory confidence of the executive'. (*Estudos de História do Brasil*, p. 41.) Doubtless this observation has to be interpreted with the electoral decree of 1842 in mind.
10   Apart from the details specifically covered, the choice proceeded as follows: the electors who had obtained the most votes at the last election were summoned, up to the number agreed by the parish and the electoral college. They were divided into two groups, one containing those with the greater number of votes, the other containing those with the lesser number, the individual with the most votes of all being excluded if there were an odd number of electors. The member of the first group who had received least votes, and the member of the second group who had received most votes joined the board as representatives of the electors. The other members of the board represented the substitutes and were chosen from among these in the same way. Appeals against the board's actions were made to the board itself; in specific cases, appeals could be made to a municipal council generally composed in each municipality of the municipal judge, the president of the chamber and the elector of the most important parish who had received the most votes. In certain cases there could be appeals against this body to the District Court of Appeal.
11   Tavares de Lira tells us that the principal merit of the law of 1846 was to give relative stability to electoral registration, since the qualifying boards functioned well when they were properly constituted (cf. also Paranapiacaba, 'Eleições', p. 251); yet 'they could not extinguish from one day to another the *intruder*, the *bandit*, the *electoral "bosses"*, in a word, the party chiefs of every order who appeared whenever contests were being fought'. ('Regime Eleitoral', p. 337.)
12   Cf. Colares Moreira, 'A Câmara e o Regime Eleitoral no Império e na República', pp. 28 and 29.
13   Tavares de Lira, 'Regime Eleitoral', p. 338.
14   Instructions for the implementation of the law of 1855 were handed down with Decree No. 1812 of 23 August 1856.
15   Tavares de Lira, 'Regime Eleitoral', p. 339; Colares Moreira, 'A Câmara', p. 36.
16   Assis Brasil, *Democracia Representativa*, pp. 153 ff.; Colares Moreira, *op. cit.*, p. 40; Paranapiacaba, 'Eleições', p. 254.
17   As far as registration was concerned, the form of the composition of the parochial qualifying boards was altered. Four board members and four substitutes now had to be elected by the electors of the parish in conjunction with those who had come next in the voting, in proportions corresponding to a third of the former. The president of the board was now to be elected by the electors only. The lists drawn up by the qualifying board of the parish were reviewed by another board consisting, in each municipality, of two members elected by the chamber, under the presi-

dency of the municipal judge or a deputy of the district judge. Appeals against the decisions of the municipal board in cases of denunciations, complaints or representations relating to the work of the parishes, were directed to the chief judge of the legal district; and in cases of voters being excluded there was the further right of appeal from the district judge to the District Court of Appeal. The law defined what was admissible as proof of income, and listed the cases where such proof was not necessary. Thus variously organised, registration was relatively stable, the only cases of subsequent exclusion being those provided for in the contingency clauses.

As far as the electoral process itself was concerned, the same rules of composition were adopted for the parochial boards as for the qualifying ones. It was these boards which verified the identity of electors, decided incidental questions and checked the votes. The electoral colleges verified the powers of the respective members, and the records of counting in secondary elections, organised by the boards of the colleges, were examined in the final review, this being the duty of the municipal chamber of the capital of the province. In the province of Rio de Janeiro, this last operation was the duty of the municipal chamber of the Court.

18   Tavares de Lira, 'Regime Eleitoral', p. 342; Colares Moreira, 'A Câmara', p. 58.

19   Oliveira Viana, *O Ocaso do Império*, pp. 35 and 38; Carlos Maximiliano, *Comentários*, pp. 51 and 52; Calogéras, *Formação História do Brasil*, p. 329.

20   Quoted by Colares Moreira, 'A Câmara', p. 40.

21   Quoted by Oliveira Viana, *O Ocaso de Império*, p. 32. According to Calogéras, it was 'considered by everyone, without distinction, that the only immorality the party in power could commit was to lose the election. And to avoid this outcome any method, however fraudulent, was admissible.' (*Formação Histórica do Brasil*, p. 327.) The usual justification for the policy of rotation carried out by Dom Pedro II is based precisely on the unreliable nature of the elections of the period. (Cf. among others, Afonso Celso, *Poder Pessoal de D. Pedro II*.)

22   The decree in question widened the right of suffrage, in principle, to all men over twenty-one. Illiterates who could show an elector's certificate obtained under the Saraiva Law, according to Tavares de Lira, were also allowed to vote, by a ministerial injunction of 12 May 1890. ('Regime Eleitoral', p. 342.)

23   On the Alvim Regulation, see the views of the Barão of Paranapiacaba ('Eleiçoẽs, pp. 255 and 256) and of José Maria Belo. (*História da República*, p. 342.) Amara Cavalcânti, writing in 1900, emphasises the decisive nature of governmental influence on elections in our country, a situation which, in his opinion, was largely caused by the atrophy of municipal institutions. (*Regime Federativo*, pp. 374 ff.)

24   The law, it should be said in passing, excluded women. The Constitution also excluded beggars, illiterates, professional soldiers (excluding pupils receiving higher education in military schools) and members of religious orders who had taken a vow of obedience implying a renunciation of individual freedom.

25   Constitution of 1891, Article 34, No. 22. Castro Nunes summarised the chief characteristics of the electoral system adopted by the states. (*As Constituições Estaduais*, vol. I, pp. 49—57.) In those states which allowed foreigners to vote in municipal elections there was as a result a municipal register. The principle of the representation of minorities only became obligatory for the states after the constitutional reform of 1926.

26 On the law of 1892, see Paranapiacaba, 'Eleições', pp. 258 and 259, and Barbalho, *Constituição*, p. 85.

27 Law No. 246 of 15 December 1894, revoked by No. 543 of 23 December 1898. Cf. Barbalho, *Constituição*, pp. 85 and 86; Araújo Castro, *Manual da Constituição Brasileira*, p. 297.

28 In time, the registration committees in each municipality came to be composed of three citizens (elected by the effective members of the municipal chamber and by those closest to them in votes, in equal strength), and of the four largest contributors: two of urban property tax and two of tax on rural property; in the capitals, and in places where rural property was not taxed, these last two were replaced by the largest contributors from the duty on industries and trades. The president of these committees, who had only a casting vote, was the district judge, or, in municipalities which did not correspond to legal districts, the highest judicial authority, or even the Prosecutor of the Republic or his assistant, when there was no judicial authority. Appeals against the registration committee were heard by a state board, consisting of the Federal Judge, his deputy and the general prosecutor of the state. In the case of total withdrawal of a register, appeal could be made to the state board itself and from this to the Supreme Court.

The Supreme Court did not sanction the legal obligation to provide new registers for state and municipal elections, since this did not fall within the competence of the Union. (Tavares de Lira, 'Regime Eleitoral', p. 345.)

29 States which had seven deputies or less would form a single district. There were special rules for those cases in which the number of the state's deputies was not divisible by five.

30 The joining of the two principles did nothing to prevent sharp practices. (Assis Brasil, *Democracia Representativa*, p. 163.)

31 In the capitals of the states and in the Federal District the composition of the supervisory board had special features.

32 The organisation of the electoral board was changed. It came to have five serving members and five reserves. Each group of thirty electors of the section could choose a board member according to the established formalities. If no choice was made, or if, the choice having been made, vacancies still existed, these (or the whole board if necessary) would be filled by the choice of a special body made up of serving members of the registration committee and their substitutes, plus the first substitute replacement of the Federal Judge and the assistant to the Prosecutor of the Republic (these last two without voting rights). Each member of this body voted for two names; if the whole board was being elected, those voted in the 1st, 3rd, 5th, 7th and 9th places were considered serving members and the rest their substitutes. The same rules applied in the partial election of the board, following the voting order indicated and limited by the number of vacancies.

33   Cf. Tavares de Lira, 'Regime Eleitoral', p. 344; Alberto Torres, *O Problema Nacional Brasileiro*, p. 31; Carlos Pontes, 'Um Episódio Eleitoral'.
34   Especially Laws No. 4215 of 20 December 1920, and No. 4226 of 30 December 1920, and Decree No. 14,631 of 19 January 1921.
35   Cf. Carlos Maximiliano, *Comentários*, pp. 53 and 54.
36   In each district of peace or legal subdivision there would be only one electoral board, in the chief town of the municipality, where the notaries and officials of the civic register of the locality would also be. In the centre of the legal division one of the boards would consist of the district judge, the first substitute of the Federal Judge, and the president of the municipal chamber. In the centres of the subdivisions one of the boards would be made up of the same officials, but as there would be no district judge, the municipal judge would serve as president (or the prosecutor or his substitute depending on what title he had). In the chief towns of those municipalities which were neither legal divisions nor subdivisions, one of the boards was composed of the first substitute of the Federal Judge, as president, and as ordinary members, the president of the municipal chamber and an elector presented for the post by the electors of the section in the manner laid down by law. Obviously in the other sections of the municipal centres the boards could not have the same composition, nor could they in the sections of the districts of the peace. Here they were composed of three electors appointed by the electors of the section themselves. The law controlled the process of selection in some detail, in order to avoid fraud. A minor justice official was a member of each board in the capacity of secretary, and he was chosen by the district judge. The candidates could appoint fiscals.
37   See the observations of Cristóvão Barcelos and Soares Filho in the *Anais* of the Constituent Assembly of 1933–4, vol. II, p. 125 and vol. VI, p. 263, respectively. On the seeming opponents, approved by the government party itself and referred to by Deputy Cristóvão Barcelos, see also the article of Carlos Pontes already cited.
38   *Anais*, vol. II, p. 507. 'There have been', said Deputy Carlos Reis, 'three frauds perpetrated: in the election, in the count, and in the recognition.' (*Anais*, vol. II, p. 231.)
39   *Anais*, vol. II, p. 49. Raul Fernandes commented: 'the legislature has been corrupt from the beginning; it was not a representative power. The elections were a comedy and the recognition a tragedy.' (*Anais* of 1934, vol. XII, p. 235.)
40   See the platform of the candidate for the Liberal Alliance in Getúlio Vargas, *A Nova Política do Brasil*, vol. I, pp. 22–4, the passage referring to electoral legislation. Item 7 of the programme outlined in his inauguration speech (3 November 1930) by the new head of the government promised the 'reform of the electoral system, especially with regard to guaranteeing the vote'. (*Op. cit.*, p. 72.)
41   The draft bill was prepared by the 19th Legislative Sub-Committee composed of João Cabral (Chairman), Assis Brasil and Mario Pinto Serva. On the law of 1932, see João Cabral, *Código Eleitoral*; Otávio Kelly, *Código Eleitoral Anotado*; Tito Fulgêncio, *Anotações no Código Eleitoral*; Domingos Velasco, *Direito Eleitoral, passim*.

42   According to Alceu Amorosa Lima, universal female suffrage came as a result of a suggestion by the Catholic Confederation of Rio de Janeiro. (*Indicações Políticas*, p. 149.) In 1924, Basílio de Magalhães proposed, in the Chamber of Deputies, the adoption of the 'secret, obligatory vote, as well as the suffrage and eligibility of women'. (*Estudos de História do Brasil*, p. 85, note.)

43   The organisation of the electoral legal system underwent minor alterations through special decrees.

44   Decree No. 22,653 of 20 April 1933, and Decree No. 22,696 of 11 May 1933.

45   The intervention of Deputy Odilon Braga reporting on electoral matters for the Constituent Assembly, can be found in *Anais*, vol. X, pp. 276 ff. Because of an editorial error, the text of the Constitution did not refer specifically to the secrecy of the vote in the election of senators (Pontes de Miranda, *Comentários*, vol. II, p. 554), governors and prefects.

46   The High Court, with jurisdiction all over the country, was based on the Federal District. In each state, in the Federal District and in the Territory of Acre, a regional court functioned.

47   The electoral legal system had its own officials, headed by a general prosecutor who worked with the High Court, and twenty-two regional prosecutors, each of whom worked with a regional court. They were all nominated by the President of the Republic from among notable jurists who had to be registered electors; the supervisory boards functioned with the help of local officials from the regular justice department.

48   In spite of all the precautions, factional or negligent judges could favour one of the political groups, setting up partisan boards, or nominating to them precisely those individuals who were the most active among party opponents, in order to prevent them from being free to bring together, guide and help their electors on election day. Incidents of this kind, according to Domingos Velasco, were confirmed in the election of 1933. (*Direito Eleitoral*, p. 72.) It was also mainly through partisan boards that various irregularities, especially with regard to the secrecy of the ballot, took place in that election. A curious kind of fraud consisted of handing over the envelope to the elector, with all the legal requirements, but already containing the voting paper showing the board's choice: if the elector was of the same party the existence of two papers made no difference in the examination of the vote, but when he was of the other party, two conflicting papers would appear in the envelope and the vote would be invalidated. In a case submitted to it, the High Electoral Court concluded that 'the elector received envelopes already containing voting papers', because on these could be distinguished, in tracing, the stamp of the president of the board which indicated that the papers must have been already in the envelopes when the latter were stamped. (*Op. cit.*, p. 122.)

49   Domingos Velasco, *Direito Eleitoral*, pp. 108 ff.

50   The use of uniform opaque official envelopes became obligatory. After receiving it from the hands of the president of the board, already numbered and stamped, the elector retired to a secret booth, to place his vote inside it. It was then shown to the president to confirm that the number and the stamp were the same, but he did not touch it. Only then did the elector put it into the ballot-box. The numbering of the envelopes was done repeatedly from one to nine so that they could not be identified in the examination, and the box had to be sufficiently large for the votes not to pile up in the same order in which they were put in. The voting papers, apart from a printed or typed description saying what the vote was about, could not contain any other information or special marks of any kind. It was because of the use of transparent, or simply translucent envelopes, which allowed the shape of the voting papers to be seen, that the High Court annulled the elections held in May 1933 in the states of Santa Catarina and Espírito Santo. (Domingos Velasco *Direito Eleitoral*, pp. 110 and 113.)

51   The author knew for a fact that in some places it was possible for the ballot-boxes to be broken into, and for additional votes to be put into them without any trace of the disturbance being left to arouse the attention of the supervisory judges. After the opening and checking of votes, this clever addition was no longer possible.

52   See the discussion on this issue and the solution suggested in Domingos Velasco, *Direito Eleitoral*, pp. 37 ff.

53   J.J. Seabra, *Anais*, 1934, vol. VI, p. 58; Pedro Aleixo, 'Representação Proporcional'.

54   Cf. Domingos Velasco, *Direito Eleitoral*, p. 51.

55   For a complete understanding of the calculation of proportions adopted by the law of 1935, see Domingos Velasco, *Direito Eleitoral*, p. 52.

56   In the midst of vigorous contraditions by his opponents in the Constituent Assembly, Deputy Minuano de Moura accused the government of Rio Grande do Sul of having coerced electors in the contest of 3 May 1933. 'I ran through the plains of Rio Grande', he declared, 'persecuted and accompanied by the "provisionals" of General Flores da Cunha. Not even in the quietest houses where registration was to take place, did they dispense with this para-military guard.' (*Anais*, 1934, vol. XV, p. 212.)

57   Decisions quoted by Domingos Velasco, *Direito Eleitoral*, pp. 120–1. See the comment on this above, ch. I, note 37.

58   Referring to the work of João Cabral, *Sistemas Eleitorais*, Afonso Arinos de Melo Franco says: 'His book, published in 1929, can be considered a repository of progressive thinking, as was the study of Assis Brasil in 1893. The difference is that social and economic conditions were now favourable to reforms which were not to be granted immediately after the setting up of the Republic.' (*História e Teoria do Partido Político no Direito Constitucional Brasileiro*, p. 71.)

59   The interview given by José Américo to the *Correio de Manhã*, marked the official date of the opening of the campaign, because from that moment the papers of Rio de Janeiro regained their freedom. The interview was published on 22 February 1945.

60   Constitutional Law No. 9 of 28 February 1945.

61   The bill was drafted by a committee composed of José Linhares, Vicente Piragibe, Lafayette de Andrada, Miranda Valverde and Hahnemann Guimarães. It was published with a view to receiving further suggestions and became law, incorporating the recommendations made to the head of the government by the Minister of Justice, Agamemnon Magalhães.

62   However, the High Electoral Court interpreted the law in the sense of surrounding the exercise of electoral law with stronger guarantees. (Cf. Leão Vieira Starling, *A Nova Lei Eleitoral*, pp. 114 ff.)

63   Articles 94, Nos. IV, and 109 and 121.

64   Article 43.

65   See the interview of João Mangabeira in the *Diário Carioca* of 30 March 1947; reports of Temístocles Cavalcânti and Romão Côrtes de Lacerda in *O Jornal* on 25 March 1947 and 25 February 1947 respectively; and among others, the resolutions of the High Electoral Court, Nos. 1587, 1672, 1703, 1663, 1759, 1704, 1977, published in the *Diário da Justiça*, on 15 March, 16 and 18 April, 6, 20, 24 and 25 May 1947, respectively.

66   Pedro Calmon, *Curso*, pp. 17–18: 'Possibly, the elections of 2 December – disputed by re-organised parties – were the freest, or the most perfect in Brazilian history, or let us say that they were supervised by an impartial government, clarified by debate in the press, enlivened by intense propaganda and by competition at the ballot, to an unprecedented degree.'

The president elected on 2 December 1945 pardoned, by a general amnesty, possible electoral crimes committed in that conflict. (Article 44 of Decree–Law No. 9285 of 14 May 1946.)

67   Interesting from this point of view is the substitution of prefects decided on by the Linhared government. (Cf. ch. III, note 77.)

68   General Eurico Gaspar Dutra obtained 3,251,507 votes (55.38%) against 2,039,341 (34.74%) cast for Brigadier Eduardo Gomes. The two other candidates – Iedo Fiúza and Rolim Teles – obtained, respectively, 569,818 (9.70%) and 10,001 (0.17%). (*Anuário Estatístico*, 1946, p. 516.)

A propos of this result, a party colleague of Gomes' wrote: 'this election was genuine in form and false in content', attributing the fact to the 'automatic functioning of the machinery set up to elect Vargas'. (Afonso Arinos de Melo Franco, 'Democracia Eleitoral'.)

Another publicist wrote about elections in Brazil: 'We have found an honest method of carrying out and checking elections. This is the form: the content is lacking.' (José Maria Belo, 'Eleição Livre Não É Tudo'.)

69   Representation in the Constituent Assembly was as in table 3.

The voting according to parties corresponded almost exactly to the percentages of representation, as can be seen from the table of votes cast for deputies on 2 December 1945.

From tables 3 and 4 we have the numerical expression of the majority referred to by Nereu Ramos, although to facilitate calculation they have taken only the P.S.D. and P.T.B. delegations to be pro-government, and all the others to be anti-government.

70   As a result of the agreement two members of the National Democratic Union (U.D.N.) and one of the Republican Party (P.R.) entered the government. José Américo was later to comment during his party's Third Convention: 'Since the investiture of this president the U.D.N. has never been in opposition.' (*Diário de Notícias* of 12 August 1948.)

71   In the instructions of the High Electoral Court, sent in a circular to all interventors by the Minister of Justice, we read: 'the interventor shall recommend to all those who exercise public authority, especially to the

Table 3

Parties	Senators	Deputies	Party alignment totals		%
P.S.D.	26	151	177		
P.T.B.	2	22	24	201*	61.28
U.D.N.	10	77	87		
P.R.	–	7	7		
U.D.N.–P.R.	2	6	8		
P.C.B.	1	14	15		
Other parties	1	9	10	127	38.72
TOTAL	42	286		328	100.00

(*Senator Getúlio Vargas, elected simultaneously for São Paulo (P.T.B.) and for Rio Grande do Sul (P.S.D.), opted for the latter and the number was reduced to 200, since the vacancy was only filled in the election of 13 January 1947.)

Table 4

Parties	Valid votes cast	Party alignment total	%
P.S.D.	2,531,944		
P.T.B.	603,500	3,135,444	59.67
U.D.N.*	1,575,375		
P.R.*	219,562		
P.C.B.	511,302		
Other parties	482,933	2,789,172	40.33
TOTAL	5,924,616	5,924,616	100.00

(*The official tables showing deputies elected under the banner of the U.D.N.–P.R. alliance (Maranhão and Sergipe), do not specify the voting under this label. Source of the two tables: *Anuário Estatístico*, 1946, pp. 516–18.)

police, the complete absence of partiality and rigorous respect for the freedom of the vote'. (*Correio da Manhã* of 16 January 1947.) Nevertheless, Deputy José Augusto imposed serious restrictions on the conduct of the authorities in the state contest in Rio Grande do Norte. (*Diário do Notícias* of 30 March 1947.) Moreover, in his message of 1948 President Dutra called for a 'complete review of the electoral laws, removing the defects which make fraud possible and encourage chicanery'. And he added: 'The stamping out of electoral crimes has been hampered, since the promulgation of the Constitution, by defects in the law which regulate electoral procedure, as is confirmed by those bodies from inside the electoral legal system, who ought to know of such crimes.' (*Diário do Congresso* of 16 March 1948, p. 1700.)

Let us note in passing that the High Electoral Court, judging from what happened under the electoral codes of 1932 and 1935, adopted a restricted concept of coercion, as can be seen in Resolution No. 1956 referring to the state elections in Sergipe. The party lodging the appeal questioned the validity of the election, saying that 'religious associations and priests' had 'recommended and enjoined upon Catholic electors not to support candidates from the U.D.N. on pain of mortal sin', and the court rejected the appeal, going on to define what could be understood as electoral coercion. (*Diário da Justiça* of 23 June 1947, p. 3625.)

The *Diário da Justiça* of 15 March 1948 (section II, p. 71) published statistics from those sections whose elections in the contest of 19 January 1947 were annulled because of irregularities.

72   See the table published in *Diário da Justiça* of 15 March 1948, section II, p. 62.

73   Compare table 3 cited in note 69 with the second table given on p. 67 and with the constant ratio of pp. 73 ff. of *Anuário Estatístico*, 1947. In a speech given in Paraná, the President of the Republic alluded to the 'paradox of the same elections producing executives and legislatures of different parties', and expressed the hope of putting an end to this anomaly by 'a carefully thought out electoral law and a statute to regulate political parties'. (*O Globo* of 16 February 1948.)

74   The strong words used by João Francisco Lisboa are well known. He used them to describe the 'combined system of swindling, falsehood, betrayal, immorality, corruption and violence' which dominated the elections of his time. (*Obras*, vol. I, pp. 153 and 165.)

75   The writer Raquel de Queirós, who served as a board member in a constituency on the Ilha do Governador, noted the regularity of their work and continued: 'I do not know if the feeling will be one of regret; but the truth is that elections have changed a great deal. I recall previous elections — shooting galleries, food, clothing, all free for the electors, drink in abundance, it was a carnival. The living voted and the dead voted, the lunatic from the asylum voted, only our political enemies did not vote.' ('Recordações do Dia 19 de Janeiro'.)

76   The Constituent Assembly of 1933–4, according to Abelardo Marinho, was 'elected with the same essential vices, and by the same people who elected the Congress of the previous Republic'. (*Anais*, vol. IX, p. 54.) In the same assembly Domingos Velasco stressed the influence of *coronel-*

ismo in spite of the 'electoral code [of 1932] and the full effect of its efficient machinery' (*Anais*, vol. II, p. 298), and later called attention to the victory of the parties 'of the state governments' in the contest of 1934 through the work of the local leaders and the prefects. (*Direito Eleitoral*, p. 21.)

Commenting on the lucid deposition presented by a judge from Espírito Santo to the Federal Interventor of his state on the political reality of the interior (published in *Correia da Manhã* of 14 February 1932), Professor H. Sobral Pinto wrote: 'If Brazilian politics has limited horizons, and if public administration functions by means of disconnected and disjointed movements, it is because it is built on unstable and unreliable foundations, that is, the tribal spirit which reigns in the communities of the interior. When this is the case, it is folly to consider operating a representative system in Brazil, demanding as it does enlightened and alert public opinion, a folly all the more consummate as we do not, on the other hand, have a selection of outstanding men in public life who, recognising the undoubted reality of the political backwardness of our people, would attempt to conduct public business through a legal framework suited to the limited experience of our fellow citizens.' ('Crônica Política' of 18 January–17 February 1932.)

In a work of 1947 Pedro Calmon writes: 'Of what value is the careful mechanism protecting the right to vote, if, in the provinces and in the backlands, the old *coronelismo* is encamped, overriding power checks civic impulses, petty dictatorship subverts and smothers the conscience of the people, and elections are processed according to the will of the local leaders or, rather, according to the will of the centre, imposed on them as on the rest? How can pure water flow from a contaminated source?' (*Curso de Direito Constitucional Brasileiro*, p. 228.)

77   See above, ch. I, note 20.

78   'A Organização Nacional e o Município'.

79   '[E]ven considering that a larger percentage of literates is found in urban centres, it seems clear that the electorate of Brazil is, predominantly distributed in small nuclei and in rural and semi-rural areas'. (Afonso Arinos de Melo Franco, *História e Teoria*, p. 97.) See also above, ch. I, note 27.

The division of the electorate into the census categories 'rural', 'urban' and 'suburban' could be done, approximately, by the statistics of registration by district, which have not yet been drawn up.

A tentative result could be predicted by calculating the percentage of the electorate 'of the capitals' and 'of the interior' of the respective populations, and later using the first percentage in relation to the 'urban population' and the second in relation to the 'rural population', arriving at an approximate figure for the 'urban' electorate and the 'rural' electorate. Such calculations, however, would contain many errors. In the first place, the average rate of registration 'in the capitals' is not equal to the average of 'the urban population', since this last category includes the population of all the towns of the interior which are not capitals. In the second place, the average rate of registration of the 'interior' is not the same as the average for the 'rural population' because the first category includes the 'urban' electorate of the interior. On the other hand, the census category 'suburban population' presents special difficulties, because one could apply to it either of the two averages of registration ('of the capitals' and 'of the interior'). Another source of error lies in the fact that the existing statistics, which distinguish the electorate 'of the interior' and that 'of the capitals' (1945), do not include the Territories; apart from this, many registrations were later cancelled without any adjustment being made to take these cancellations into account. It has also to be observed that in the registration 'of the capitals' is included the rural and suburban electorate of the municipalities of the capitals. With so many possibilities of error, the calculation would become useless and we have therefore decided not to do it.

80   After the contest of 2 December 1945, the High Electoral Court of São Paulo cancelled 131,995 certificates that had been issued to illiterates. (*Diário da Justiça* of 15 March 1948, section II, p. 61.)

81   There is no room here for any didactic comment on the campaign in question.

82   In his message for 1948, the President of the Republic says the following: 'There are party labels to which it would be difficult to ascribe any other character, and whose value in political terms is the same as that attributed in commercial life to the trade marks and brand names used there.' (*Diário do Congresso* of 16 March 1948, p. 1700.) The precarious nature of parties in Brazil is mirrored in the inveterate tendency to personality cults in political life: during the Empire, Dario de Almaida Magalhães wrote: 'the theatricals, the ceremonial and the characters were the tie-beams of the political order; and the system, whatever it was, had to rely above all on men, in the absence of any other more consistent and reliable infra-structure . . . In the same way as the monarchy — all the more as the practice was already rooted in tradition and custom — the Republic imperiously called upon a moral and intellectual patrician class who would support it over uncertain ground until it put down roots and was itself able to resist opposition.' (*Digesto Econômico*, No. 38, p. 73.)

In this respect, the revelations of the archive of Américo Brasiliense has an enormous documentary value. There we see how men of the highest responsibility and stature quite naturally traded votes in spite of belonging to opposing parties. (J.M. de Camargo Aranha, *Revista do Arquivo Municipais*, May 1937.)

The observations of Professor Sobral Pinto on the 'personal power' of the Head of State in the Empire and the Republic, are very interesting. ('Crônica Política', *A Ordem*, 18 September—17 October 1931.)

83   Defending himself later against the accusations made against him, the ex-President declared that when he assumed office 'the principle of intervention was in the forefront of public opinion, had even come to be included in presidential addresses and to be given obvious importance in debates in the Legislative Congress. The bills which emerged then, with the apparent intention of regulating Article 6 of the Constitution, clearly envisaged a major modification in the text of the Constitution.' Reacting against this state of affairs, he says, he declared himself to be 'the intransigent and irreconcilable opponent of interventionist politics', since the federal government, according to the Constitution, had to be scrupulous in respecting the 'sovereignty' of the states. And he continues: 'So much for

principles, now for the facts. It was on the occasion of the confirmation of powers in the legislative session of 1900, that people began to speak of the "politics of the governors" . . . Two large party groupings, opposed to each other – the alliance groups and the republicans – intervened forcefully in the electoral contest, each wanting to have a majority in the new chamber with the resultant dominance in national politics . . . The primary objective was the charter to rule, even if it meant employing the most daring duplicity . . . The country therefore felt itself to be threatened by the possibility of two chambers, the logical result of fraud and duplicity . . . The head of the nation could not remain impassive and indifferent in the face of this great danger . . . I assumed my role. I appealed to the patriotism of the leaders of certain states which were most strongly represented in the Federal Congress, urging them to use their advice and good offices to ensure that a rigorously fair, legitimate and just system of the confirmation of powers, capable of saving the moral integrity and high prestige of the legislature, was adopted.' (Article in the *Jornal do Comércio* of 20 November 1911, quoted by Morais Andrade in the Constituent Assembly of 1933–4, *Anais*, vol. II, pp. 150–2.)

The understanding of Campos Sales with the governors of the larger states, and the agreements between the governors and the state delegations, produced the following concrete result, according to Alcindo Guanabara: 'the leader of the government in the chamber, Augusto Montenegro, secured the approval, almost in the last days of the session, of a change in the standing orders. By virtue of this change, it was established that the provisional president of the new chamber, who was usually the oldest of the qualified candidates present, should be the president then in office. In order to define what was meant by being qualified, it was established that for this the general record of validity of the election, signed by the majority of the municipal chamber competent by law to carry out the check, would be accepted. The "Committee of 5", nominated by the president, which had been named beforehand, now had nothing to do but to roll off the names of the candidates who presented certificates signed in this way, whatever representations came with them. It was from among these qualified candidates that the commission of inquiry, whose duty was to judge all elections, were to be chosen by lot.' (*A Presidência Campos Sales*, quoted by Odilon Braga, in the previous Constituent Assembly, *Anais*, vol. II, p. 237.)

It must be made clear that the electoral law in force at the time – Law No. 35 of 1892 – divided the country into electoral districts with three deputies, and the final check on the records of the electoral boards was carried out by a body composed of the five councillors who had received the most votes in the chamber of the municipality which was the centre of the constituency, and of the five who came next in voting strength, under the presidency of the head of the municipal government.

Continuing his narrative, Alcindo Guanabara declares: 'The majority of the supervisory body, demanded by the standing orders in order that the certificate be considered valid, was obtained from the opposition parties of the states by a variety of tricks. The amendment of Senhor Montenegro, however, was drafted with skill and good judgement and functioned with the rapidity and precision of a guillotine: state by state, the opposition, whether members of the Alliance or the Republican Party, were executed without prolonged suffering. It was obvious that they did not have the certificate signed by the majority of the legal body.' (*A Presidência Campos Sales*.)

84   'There are, at the root of the "politics of the governors", two facts which cannot be denied: on one hand, the presidential judgement in the recognition of powers; on the other, the unconditional support of the governors . . . to put it tersely, arbitrary recognition and unconditional support.' (Odilon Braga, *Anais*, vol. II, p. 232.)

85   *Anais*, vol. II, p. 163.

86   'In the face of the power of the President of the Republic', said Deputy Fábio Sodre in 1933, 'there were only two possible attitudes: either subservience – total docility, or revolution. And the revolution could not come from the small states but from the large ones, as it did in 1930.' (*Anais*, vol. II, p. 103.)

87   *Anais*, vol. V, p. 257.

88   It is certain that after setting up the system of electoral law, one cannot *de rigeur* speak of the 'politics of the governors', because this expression defines a concrete system of political compromise from which an important element, namely the recognition of power carried out by political influence, cannot be omitted. Yet, *a propos* of the state elections of 1947, some of our electoral tribunals were severely criticised, whether justly or not we do not know.

A propos of the legal system devised for elections by the Code of 1932, Professor Sobral Pinto observed: 'Apparently, the new electoral system reflects an unequivocal improvement in what it says with regard to the guarantees in checking the elector's vote . . . But let us not be fooled by these guarantees . . . The government, which intervened openly and unrestrainedly in the recognition of powers when this fell within the competence of the legislative chambers, can continue to intervene with the same effrontery in recognitions carried out by the Electoral Courts.' ('Crônica Política', *A Ordem*, 18 January–17 February 1933.)

89   'The whole problem consists in replacing the electoral chief, as the defender of the man of the people, by another person or group who would serve the people as a duty and not as an *interested* benefactor.' (Abelardo Marinho, *Anais*, vol. IX, p. 61; on the 'professional suffrage' proposed by this deputy cf. *Anais*, vol. III, pp. 343 ff., vol. IX, pp. 57–8, 309 ff.) Intervening, Deputy Odilon Braga declared: 'All is very clear: professional representation is desired not for the advantages which its fervent apologists assert – linked as they are with practical returns to the state; professional representation is to be desired because with it we shall be able, if not to eradicate political representation at once, at least to prepare the way for its eradication. The charge against the latter is direct and open.' (*Anais*, vol. X, pp. 282–3.)

90   *Anais*, vol. VII, p. 324; 'if we maintain the economic deficiencies which we have at present, it is useless to think in terms of modifying our political customs. For good or evil Brazil will continue to be dominated by caciquism: municipal, state and federal.' (Vol. quoted, p. 326.)

Bibliography

With reference to the proceedings of the three Constituent Assemblies of the Republic, we do not repeat here the indication of the sources given in the notes.

Abreu, J. Capistrano de. *Capítulos de História Colonial* (1500–1800). Rio, 1934.

Acióli de Cerqueira e Silva, Inácio. *Memórias Históricas e Politicas da Província da Bahia*. Vol. I, 2nd ed., Bahia, 1892.

Aleixo, Pedro. 'Autonomia Municipal', *O Jornal*, 18 April 1946.

'Polícia de Facção e Delegados *ad hoc*', *O Jornal*.

'Representação Proporcional', *O Jornal*, 28 April 1946.

Almeida, José Américo de. Speech in the 3rd Convention of the U.D.N. *Diário de Notícias*, 12 August 1948.

Almeida, Rômulo de. *Produção Industrial*. Work compiled with the help of the technical staff of the Seção de Estudos of D.N.I.C., and presented to the Constituent Assembly of 1946 by the Comissão de Investigação Econômica e Social. Typescript copy made available to the author by Dr Américo Barbosa de Oliveira.

Almiro, Afonso. *A Constituição e o Código Tributário Nacional*. Rio, 1947. Offprint of *Boletim Estatístico*, yr. IV, no. 16.

Amaral, Brás do. *Cartas de Vilhena*. Notícias Soteropolitanas e Brasílicas por Luís dos Santos Vilhena, with notes by . . . Vol. II, Bahia, 1922.

Amaral, Rubens do. 'O Chefe Político', *Política*, 2nd epoch, no. 1, p. 55 (August 1944).

Amoroso Lima, Alceu. *Indicações Políticas. Da Revolução à Constituição*. Rio, 1936.

Andrade e Silva, José Justino de. *Coleção Cronológica da Legislação Portuguêsa Compilada e Anotada*. 1640–7, 2nd series, Lisboa, 1856.

Aranha, J.M. de Camargo, 'A Primeira Campanha Eleitoral do Partido Republicano Paulista. Candidatura de América Brasíliense', *Revista do Arquivo Municipal*, May 1937.

Araúgo Castro. *Manual de Constituição Brasiliera*. Rio, 1918.

Armitage, João. *História do Brasil. Desde o Periodo da Chegada da Família de Bragança em 1808 até a Abdicação de D. Pedro I em 1831*. 3rd Brazilian ed. with notes by Eugenio Egas e Garcia Jr. Rio, 1943.

Assis Brasil, J.R. de. *Democracia Representativa. Do voto e do Modo de Votar*. Rio, 1893.

Augusto, José. Interview published in *Diário de Notícias*, 30 March 1947, under the title: 'Grave Denúncia a Nação'.

Azevedo, Filadelfo. Voto no Supremo Tribúnal Federal (11 October 1944) sôbre o fóro especial das polícias militares des Estados. *Revista de Direito Administrativo*, vol. VI, p. 31.

Azevedo Maia. See Carneiro Maia.

231 Bibliography

Barbalho U.C., João. *Constituição Federal Brasileira. Comentários.* Rio, 1902.

Barbosa, Rui. *Comentários à Constituição Federal Brasileira.* Collected and arranged by Homero Pires. Vol. V, São Paulo, 1934.

Barros Carvalho, A. de. 'Os Municípios e a Constituição', *O Jornal*, 21 March 1946.

Belisário, Francisco. See Soares de Sousa.

Belo, José Maria. *História da República. Primeiro Período, 1889–1902.* Rio, 1940.

'Eleição Livre Não É Tudo . . .', *O Jornal*, 5 March 1947.

Bilac Pinto. *Ministério Público.* Rio, 1937.

Borges, Tomás Pompeu Acióli. 'A Propriedade Rural no Brasil', *Mês Econômico e Financeiro*, yr. I, no. 2, pp. 10 ff. (December 1945).

Bouças, Valentim F. 'Os Impostos e a Constituição', *O Jornal*, 25 August 1946.

See Comissão de Estudos Financieros e Econômicos dos Estados e Municípios.

Cabral, João C. da Rocha. *Código Eleitoral da República dos Estados Unidos do Brasil.* 3rd ed., 1934.

Calmon, Pedro. *Curso de Direito Constitucional Brasileiro. Constituição de 1946.* Rio, 1947.

História do Brasil. Vol. 4. *O Império*, 1880–9. São Paulo, 1947.

História Social do Brasil. Vol. I. *Espírito da Sociedade Colonial.* 3rd ed. with additions. São Paulo. Rio, 1941.

'Organização Judiciária: (a) na Colônia; (b) no Império; (c) na República', *Livro do Centenário dos Cursos Jurídicos*, vol. I, pp. 79 ff. Rio, 1928.

Calógeras, João Pandiá. *Estudos Históricos e Políticos (Res Nostra . . .).* 2nd ed., São Paulo, 1936.

Formação Histórica do Brasil. 4th ed., São Paulo, 1945.

Campos, Francisco. *Antecipações à reforma Política.* Rio, 1940.

O Estado Nacional. Sua Estrutura. Seu Conteúdo Ideológico. 3rd ed., Rio, 1941.

Campos, Nélson. *O Município Antônomo e a Capital do Estado Federado.* Niterói, 1920.

Campos Moreira, Geraldo. 'O Municipalismo', *Revista de Administração*, yr. I, no. 1, p. 88 (March 1947).

Carneiro, J. Fernando. 'Interpretação da Política Imigratória Brasileira', II, *Digesto Econômico*, yr. IV, no. 45, p. 119 (August 1948).

Carneiro, Levi. 'O Federalismo. Suas Explosões. A Confederação do Equador', *Revista do Instituto Historico e Geographico Brasileiro.* Tomo Especial Consagrado ao Primeiro Congresso História Nacional. Part III, p. 197, Rio, 1916.

Problemas Municipais. Rio, 1931.

Carneiro Maia, João de Azevedo. *O Município. Estudos sôbre Administração Local.* Rio, 1883.

Carpenter, L.F. Sauerbronn. 'O Direito Processual', *Livro do Centenário dos Cursos Jurídicos*, vol. I, p. 187. Rio, 1928.

Carta Econômica de Teresópolis. Conferência das Classes Produtoras do Brasil. Teresópolis. E. do Rio de Janeiro. 1–6 May 1945.

Carvalho, Cromwell Barbosa de. *Município versus Estado.* Maranhão, 1921.

Carvalho, Orlando M. 'Despesas Eleitorais', *Correio de Manhã,* 3 December 1945.

Política do Município (Ensaio Histórico). Rio, 1946.

'Política Constitucional do Município', *Correio da Manhã,* 3 February 1946.

Problemas Fundamentais do Município. São Paulo, 1937.

'A Vitalidade da Tradição Municipal', *Correio da Manhã,* 20 January 1946.

'Transportes e Aquartelamento de Eleitores no Interior', *Correio da Manhã,* 24 March 1946.

Carvalho Mourão, João Martins de. 'Os Municípios. Sua Importância Política no Brasil–Colonial e no Brasil–Reino. Situação em que Ficaram no Brasil–Império pela Constituicao de 1824 e pelo Ato Adicional', *Revista do Instituto Historico e Geografico Brasileiro.* Tomo Especial. Part III, p. 299, Rio, 1916.

Castro Nunes, José de. *As Constituições Estaduais do Brasil.* Vol. I, Rio, 1922.

Do Estado Federado e Sua Organização Municipal. Rio, 1920.

Castro Rebêlo, Edgardo de. Letter to Max Fleiuss, transcribed in 2nd ed. of the latter's *História Administrativa do Brasil.*

Cavalcânti, Amaro. *Regime Federativo e a República Brasileira.* Rio, 1900.

Cavalcânti, Temístocles Brandão. Article published in *O Jornal,* 25 March 1947, under the title: 'Decretar a Inconstitucionalidade das Sobras Seria Substituir um Sistema por Outro'.

Celso, Afonso. *Oito Anos de Parlamento. Poder Pessoal de D. Pedro II. Reminiscências e Notas.* New enlarged ed. São Paulo, n.d.

Celso, Afonso (Visconde de Ouro Prêto). *Reforma Administrativa e Municipal.* Rio, 1883.

Discurso de apresentacão do Gabinete de 7 de junho. *Anais do Parlamento Brasileiro. Câmra dos Srs Deputados.* Session of 11 June 1889.

Colares Moreira. 'A Câmara e o Regime Eleitoral no Império e na República', *Livro do Centenário da Câmara dos Deputados,* vol. II, p. 13, Rio, 1926.

Comissão de Estudos Financeiros e Econômicos dos Estados e Municípios. *Finanças dos Estados do Brasil.* Report of the Secretary of Commission, Valentim F. Bouças, in the session of 6 April 1932, vol. I, Rio, 1932.

Conselho Interamericano de Comércio e Produção. *Inquerito Continental sôbre Fomento e Coordenação de Indústrias.* (Reply of the 'Departamento de Economia Industrial' of the São Paulo 'Federação das Industrias'.) Montevideo, 1946.

Cortines Laxe, João Batista. *Regimento da Câmaras Municipais ou Lei de 1º de outubro de 1828.* 2nd ed. corrected and enlarged by Antônio Joaquim de Macedo Soares. Rio, 1885.

Costa, Aguinaldo. *Apontamentos para uma Reforma Agrária.* São Paulo, 1945.

Costa Manso. Interview published in *O Jornal*, 12 December 1937, under the title: 'Uma Organização Uniforme para as Fôrças Militares dos Estados'.

Costa Pinto, L.A. *A Estrutura da Sociedade Rural Brasileira (Notas de Estudo)*. Unpublished work kindly made available by the author.

'Lutas de Famílias no Brasil (Era Colonial)', *Revista de Arquivo Municipal*. São Paulo, vol. 88, p. 7 (January–February 1943).

Delgado da Silva, Antônio. *Coleção da Legislação Portuguêsa*, 1811–20. Lisboa, 1825.

Departamento de Municipalidades (de Minas Gerais). *A Regularização das Contas Municipais*. B. Horizonte, 1947.

Duarte, José. *A Constituição Brasileira de 1946*. *Exegese dos Textos à Luz dos Trabalhos da Assembléia Constituinte*. Rio, 1947.

Duarte, Nestor. *A Ordem Privada e a Organização Política Nacional (Contribuição à Sociologia Política Brasileira)*. São Paulo, 1939.

Dutra, General Eurico Gaspar. Speech in Paraná. *O Globo*, 16 February 1948.

Mensagem presidencial de 1947.

Mensagem presidencial de 1948. *Diário do Congresso Nacional*, 16 March 1948.

Farhat, Emil. 'O Genro, o Grande Culpado', *Diário de Notícias*, 16 February 1946.

Fleiuss, Max. *História Administrativa do Brasil*. 2nd ed., n.d. (preface dated 1925).

Freire, Felisbelo. *As Constituições dos Estados e a Constituição Federal*. Rio, 1898.

Freire, Gilberto. *Casa Grande & Senzala*. *Formação da Sociedade Brasileira sob o Regime de Economia Patriarcal*. 5th ed., revised by the author and with many additional notes. Vol. I, Rio, 1946.

Sobrados e Mucambos. *Decadência de Patriarcado Rural no Brasil*. São Paulo, 1936.

Fulgêncio, Tito. *Anotações ao Código Eleitoral*. São Paulo, 1932.

Galvão, Enéias. 'Juízes e Tribunais no Período Colonial', *Revista do Instituto Historico e Geographico Brasileiro*. Tomo Especial. Part III, p. 319, Rio, 1916.

Gil, Oto. Interview published in *O Jornal*, 7 June 1946, under the title: 'Como Tudo Indica, os Municípios Acabarão por Dispender as Novas Verbas com Emprêgos Públicos'.

Gouveia, Cândido Álvaro de. 'A Reforma da Policia Civil do Distrito Federal', *Revista de Direito Administrativo*, vol. I, p. 320.

Guilherme, Olímpio. 'O Campo e a Cidade', *O Jornal*, 5 December 1944.

Handelmann, Henrique. *História do Brasil*. Brazilian translation made by the Instituto Historico e Geographico Brasileiro. Rio, 1931 (R.I.H.G.B., tomo 108, vol. 162).

Herckman, Elias. 'Descrição Geral da Capitania da Paraíba', *Revista do Instituto Arqueologico e Geographico de Pernambuco*, vol. V, no. 31, pp. 239–88.

Herrmann Jr, Frederico. *Funções Específicas dos Municípios*. São Paulo, 1945.

Higino, José. V. Pereira, José Higino Duarte. *Sinopse do Censo Agrícola. Dados Gerais.* Rio, 1948. *Análises de Resultados do Censo Demográfico*, no. 376. Instituto Brasileiro de Geografia e Estatística. *Anuário Estatístico.* Yr. VII, 1946 (Rio, 1947).

Quadro dos Municipios Brasileiros Vigorante no Quinqüênto de 1 de Janeiro de 1939 a 31 de Dezembro de 1943. Rio, 1939.

Jaguaribe, Domingos José Nogueira. *O Município e a República.* São Paulo, 1897, vol. III.

Kelly, Otávio. *Código Eleitoral Anotado.* Rio, 1932.

Kingston, Jorge. 'A Concentração Agrária em São Paulo', *Revista de Economia e Estatística*, yr. III, no. 1, p. 33 (January 1938).

Lacerda, Romão Côrtes de. Article published in *O Jornal*, 25 February 1947, under the title: 'É Constitucional a Atribuição das Sobras Eleitorais aos Partidor Majoritários'.

Láfer, Horácio. 'Relatório sôbre a proposta do orçamento da receita para 1948.' *O Jornal*, 27 September 1947.

Lessa, Pedro. *Reforma Constitucional.* Rio, 1925.

Lima, Hermes. 'O Destino de Feijó', *Notas à Vida Brasileira.* São Paulo, 1945, p. 131.

'O Povo e as Instituições Políticas', *op. cit.*, p. 5.

Preface to *Queda do Império* by Rui Barbosa ('Obras Completas', vol. XVI, 1889, tomo I, Rio, 1947), reproduced in the work cited above, p. 70.

'Que Federação é Esta?', *A Manhã*, 6 September 1935.

Limeiro Tejo. 'A Indústria Rio-Grandense em Função da Economia Nacional', *Estatística Industrial do Rio Grande do Sul. Ano de 1937.* Published by the 'Diretoria Geral de Estatística' of Rio Grande do Sul. Pórto Alegre, 1939.

Lisboa, João Francisco. *Obras.* With a biographical note by Dr Antônio Henriques Leal and a critical appreciation by Teófilo Braga. 2 vols., Rio, 1901.

Magalhães, Basílio de. 'Algumas Notas sôbre o Municipalismo Brasileiro (Carta-aberta ao Dr Victor Nunes Leal)', *O Estado de São Paulo*, 25 August 1946, p. 4.

Estudos de História do Brasil. São Paulo, 1940.

O Municipalismo em Minas Gerais. São João-del-Rei, 1924.

Magalhães, Dario de Almeida. 'O Conselheiro Afonso Pena e a Responsabilidade das Elites Dirigentes', *Digesto Econômico*, no. 38, p. 67 (January 1948).

Magalhães, Domingos José Gonçalves de. 'Memória Histórica e Documental da Revolução da Província do Maranhão desde 1839 até 1840', *Revista do Instituto Historico e Geographico Brasiliero*, vol. X, p. 263.

Magalhães, Rafael Almeida. Justificação do anteprojeto de Código do Processo Penal de Minas Gerais. *Revista Forense*, vol. 47, p. 169 (1926).

Mangabeira, João. Interview published by *Diário Carioca*, 30 March 1947, under the title: 'Inconstitucionais as Sobras, São Nulos os Mandatos de Seus Beneficiários'.

Parecer sôbre a competência da Comissão Mista de Leis Complementares. *Diário de Congresso Nacional*, 23 September 1947, p. 5993.

Marroquim, Murilo. 'A Vitoria dos Municípios', *O Jornal*, 15 August 1946.

Mata Machado Filho, Aires da. 'O Coronel e a Democracia', *Diário de Notícias*, 5 May 1946.

Maximiliano, Carlos. *Comentários à Constituição Brasileira*. 3rd ed. enlarged and brought up-to-date with the constitutional reform of 1925–6. Pôrto Alegre, 1929.

Melo Franco, Afonso Arinos. 'Democracia Eleitoral', *O Jornal*, 12 December 1946.

História e Teoria do Partido Político no Direito Constitucional Brasileiro. Rio, 1948.

Mendes de Almeida, Cândido. *Código Filipino ou Ordenações de Reino de Portugal*. N.d. (preface dated 1870).

Auxiliar Jurídico. Appendix to 14th ed. of *Código Filipino*. Rio, 1869.

Mendes de Almeida Jr, João. *O Processo Criminal Brasileiro*. Vol. I, Rio, 1901.

Direito Judiciário Brasileiro. 3rd ed., Rio, 1940.

Mendonça de Avezedo, José Afonso. *A Constituição Federal Interpretada pelo Supremo Tribunal Federal (1891–1924)*. Rio, 1925.

Meneses, Djacir. *O Outro Nordeste. Formação Social do Nordeste*. Rio, 1937.

Morais Jr, Padre Antônio d'Almeida. 'O Exodo da Populaçao Rural Brasileira', article published in *Serviço Social* and reproduced in *Revista do Trabalho*, yr. XIV, p. 389 (August 1946).

Moreira, Vivaldi W. *Anuário Comercial e Industrial de Minas Gerais (1947)*. B. Horizonte, 1947.

'Coisas & Loisas', *Folha de Minas*, 25 July 1948.

Nabuco, Joaquim. *Um Estadista do Império*. New ed., Rio, 1936.

Oliveira, Conselheiro Cândido de. 'A Justiça', *A Década Republicana* (VII), vol. III, Rio, 1900.

Oliveiro Filho, Cândido de. *A Reforma do Júri*. Rio, 1932.

Oliveiro Viana, F.J. *Evolução do Povo Brasileiro*. São Paulo, 1923.

O Idealismo da Constituição. 2nd ed., enlarged, São Paulo, 1939.

O Ocaso do Império. 2nd ed., São Paulo, 1933.

Populações Meridionais do Brasil. 4th ed., São Paulo, 1938.

Ouro Prêto, Visconde de. See Celso, Afonso.

Paranaguá, Visconde de. *Proposta e Relatório Apresentado à Assembléia Geral Legislativa na Terceira Sessão da Décima Oitava Legislatura pelo Ministro e Secretário de Estado da Fazenda*. Rio, 1833.

Paranapiacaba, Barão de. 'Eleições', *A Década Republicana* (VIII), vol. III, Rio, 1900.

Paranapiacaba (Barão de) *et al. Relatório e Projeto de Lei da Comissão Encarregada de Rever e Classificar as Rendas Gerais, Provinciais e Municipais do Império*. Rio, 1883.

Pereira, José Higino Duarte. Relatório sôbre documentos referentes ao domínio holandês no Brasil. *Revista do Instituto Arqueologico e Geographico de Pernambuco*, vol. V, no. 30 (June 1886).

Pereira da Costa, F.A. 'Govêrno holandês', *Revista do Instituto Arqueologico e Geographico de Pernambuco*, vol. IX, no. 51, p. 3.
Pereira da Silva, J.M. *História do Brasil de 1831 a 1840*. Rio, 1878.
Pereira de Sousa, Joaquim José Caetano. *Esbôço de um Dicionário Jurídico, Teórico e Pratico, Remissivo às Leis Compiladas, e Extravagantes*. Vols. I and II, Lisboa, 1825.
Pimenta Bueno, José Antônio. *Apontamentos sôbre o Processo Criminal Brasileiro*. 2nd ed. corrected and enlarged, Rio, 1857.
Pinheiro, Nuno. 'Finanças Nacionais', *A Margem da História da República (Ideais, Crenças e Afirmações)*, p. 111. Rio, 1924.
Pinto da Rocha. *O Júri e Sua Evolução*. Rio, 1919.
Pontes, Carlos. 'Um Episódio Eleitoral', *Correio da Manhã*, 3 August 1946.
Pontes de Miranda. *Comentários à Constituição da República dos E.U. do Brasil*. Vol. II, Rio, 1937.
Comentários a Constituição de 1946. Vol. I (articles 1–36), Rio, 1947.
Prado Jr, Caio. 'Distribuição da Propriedade Fundiária Rural no Estado de São Paulo, *Boletim Geográfico*, no. 29, p. 692 (August 1945). Taken from *Geografia*, yr. I, no. I, 1935.
Evolução Política do Brasil. Ensaio de Interpretação Dialética da História Brasileira. 2nd ed., São Paulo, 1947.
Formação do Brasil Contemporâneo. Colônia. 2nd ed., São Paulo, 1945.
História Economica do Brasil. São Paulo, 1945.
Prado Kelly. 'A Constituição Brasileira', *Revista Forense*, vol. 108 (1946), p. 433.
Quadros dos Impostos Provinciais Organizados no Tesouro Nacional segundo as Ultimas Leis de Orçamento Conhecidas. Rio, 1877 (the second part deals with municipal taxes).
Queirós, Raquel de. 'Recordações do Dia 19 de Janeiro', *Diário de Notícias*, 26 January 1947.
Resende, Astolfo. 'Policia Administrativa. Policia Judiciaria', *Revista do Instituto Historico e Geografico Brasileira*. Tomo Especial. Part III, p. 399. Rio, 1916.
Ribeiro, João. *História do Brasil. Curso Superior*. 13th ed., Rio, 1935.
Rio Branco, Barão do. *Efemérides Brasileiras*. Vol. VI das *Obras do Barão do Rio Branco*, edited by the Brazilian Foreign Ministry, Itamarati. Rio, 1946.
Rocha Pomba, José Francisco da. *História do Brasil*. Rio, vols. III and V.
Roure, Agenor de. *A Constituinte Republicana*. 2 vols. Rio, 1920.
Formação Constituicional do Brasil. Rio, 1914.
Sá Filho, Francisco. Acuerdo do Tribunal Superior Eleitoral (Res. 1956) sôbre o conceito de coação no processo eleitoral. *Diário da Justiça*, 23 June 1947, p. 3625.
Santos, Joaquim Felicio dos. *Memórias do Distrito Diamantino da Comarca do Sêrro Frio*. New ed. Rio, 1924.
Severo, Arquibaldo. *O Moderno Município Brasileiro*. Pôrto Alegre, 1946.
Silva, Gerson Augusto da. *Sistema Tributário Brasileiro*. 2nd ed., Rio, 1948.
Simonsen, Roberto. *A Evolução Industrial do Brasil*. São Paulo, 1939.
Soares de Sousa, Francisco Belisário. *O Sistema Eleitoral no Brasil*. Rio, 1872.

Sobral Pinto, H. 'Crônica Política'. Commentary published regularly in the review *A Ordem*. We used those referring to the following periods: 18 January 1931 to 17 February 1931; 18 September 1932 to 17 October 1932; 18 January 1933 to 12 February 1933.

Sobreira de Melo, Emílio Xavier. *Comentários à Legislação Brasileira sôbre Bens de Defuntos e Ausentes, Vagos e do Evento.* Rio, 1858.

Impostos Provinciais. Rio, 1883.

Sousa, Sebastião José de. 'Competência dos Juízes de Paz', *Revista Forense*, vol. 96, p. 751 (December 1943).

Starling, Leão Vieira. *A Nova Lei Eleitoral.* Decreto-Lei No. 7536. B. Horizonte, 1945.

Tarquínio de Sousa, Otávio. *Bernardo Pereira de Vasconcelos e Seu Tempo.* Rio, 1937.

'Vara Branca e Vara Vermelha', *Correio da Manhã*, 31 August 1947; *Revista Forense*, vol. 114, p. 245.

'Aspectos Econômicos das Lutas Políticas no Tempo do Império', *Digesto Econômico*, no. 43, p. 106 (June 1948).

Tavares Bastos, Aureliano Cândido. *A Província. Estudo sôbre a Descentralização no Brasil.* 2nd ed., São Paulo, 1937.

Tavares Bastos, José. *Organização Judiciária Federal.* Rio, 1913.

Tavares de Lira, A. *Organização Política e Administrativa do Brasil (Colônia, Império e República).* São Paulo, 1941.

'Regime Eleitoral', *Dicionário Histórico, Geográfico e Etnográfico do Brasil*, vol. 1, p. 332. Rio, 1922.

Tôrres Filho, Artur. Interview published in *O Jornal*, 24 November 1946.

Uruguai, Visconde do. *Ensaio sôbre o Direito Administrativo.* Rio, 1862.

Estudos Práticos sôbre a Administração das Províncias no Brasil. 2 vols., Rio, 1865.

Vargas, Getúlio. *A Nova Política do Brasil.* Vol. I, Rio, 1933.

Varnhagen, Francisco Adolfo de (Visconde de Pôrto Seguro). *História Geral do Brasil. Antes da Sua Separação e Independência de Portugal.* 3rd complete ed. edited by Sr Rodolfo Garcia. Vols. I, II and III.

História das Lutas com os Holandeses no Brasil. New ed., Lisboa, 1872.

Velasco, Domingos. *Direito Eleitoral. Sistema Eleitoral. Nulidades. Crítica.* Rio, 1935.

Vilhena. See Amaral, Brás do.

Willems, Emílio. *Assimilação e Populações Marginais no Brasil. Estudo Sociológico dos Imigrantes Germânicos e Seus Descentes.* São Paulo, 1940.

Burocracia e Patrimonialismo. São Paulo, 1945. Separated from *Administração Pública*, yr. 3, no. 3 (September 1945).

Xavier, Rafael. 'A Diminuição Progressiva das Rendas Municipais', *O Jornal*, 4 November 1945.

Interview published in *O Jornal*, 23 July 1946, under the title: 'Conseqüências da Política de Enfraquecimento dos Municípios'.

'A Organização Nacional e o Município', *Jornal do Comércio*, 14 April 1946.

Síntese Econômico-Financeira do Brasil. Monograph no. 2 of the collection 'Estudos Brasileiros de Economia', published by the 'Fundação Getúlio Vargas'. Rio, 1946.